Terry V. Boyce

CHEVY
SUPER SPORTS
1961-1976

MBI Publishing Company

First published in 1981 by MBI Publishing Company, PO Box 1, 729 Prospect Avenue, Osceola, WI 54020-0001 USA

MBI Publishing Company books are also available at discounts in bulk quantity for industrial or sales-promotional use. For details write to Special Sales Manager at Motorbooks International Wholesalers & Distributors, 729 Prospect Avenue, PO Box 1, Osceola, WI 54020-0001 USA

Library of Congress Cataloging-in-Publication Data

Boyce, Terry.
    Chevy super sports. 1961-1976.

    Includes index.
    1. Chevrolet automobile.   I. Title.
TL215.C5B69   629.2'222   80-22034
ISBN 0-87938-096-9

Cover photograph by Terry Boyce: 1968 Chevelle SS 396

Printed in the United States of America

To
Sally,
Gregori
and Veronica

PHOTO CREDITS

Chevrolet Division, General Motors: p. 14 (top), p. 15, p. 16 (both), p. 17 (both), p. 18 (both), p. 21, p. 22, p. 23 (both), p. 24, p. 25, p. 26 (both), p. 27, p. 30, p. 32, p. 33 (both), p. 34, p. 35, p. 36 (all), p. 37, p. 38 (both), p. 39, p. 41, p. 42 (all), p. 44 (both), p. 45, p. 46, p. 47 (both), p. 48 (both), p. 49 (both), p. 51, p. 52 (top left, bottom), p. 53 (top left, bottom), p. 54, p. 56, p. 57, p. 58, p. 59, p. 61, p. 62 (both), p. 63 (both), p. 64 (both), p. 65 (both), p. 66, p. 67, p. 70, p. 71, p. 72, p. 73, p. 74, p. 75 (both), p. 76, p. 77 (all), p. 78, p. 79, p. 80 (both), p. 81, p. 82, p. 83, p. 84, p. 86 (bottom), p. 87, p. 89 (both), p. 90, p. 91, p. 92 (both), p. 93, p. 94 (both), p. 95 (all), p. 96, p. 98 (top), p. 99, p. 100 (all), p. 101 (bottom), p. 102 (top), p. 104 (both), p. 105, p. 106 (both), p. 107 (top), p. 108 (both), p. 109 (both), p. 110 (both), p. 111 (both), p. 113, p. 114 (both), p. 118 (both), p. 119 (both), p. 120, p. 121 (both), p. 122 (both), p. 123, p. 124, p. 125, p. 126, p. 127, p. 129, p. 130, p. 131 (bottom), p. 133 (bottom), p. 136, p. 139, p. 140, p. 141, p. 143, p. 144, p. 145, p. 148, p. 149, p. 150 (both), p. 151, p. 152, p. 153 (both), p. 154 (bottom), p. 155 (both), p. 157, p. 158, p. 159 (both), p. 160, p. 161 (all), p. 162, p. 163, p. 164, p. 166, p. 167, p. 168.

Chris Daniels: p. 86 (top), p. 88 (both).

Tony Hossain: p. 131 (top).

Phil Hall: p. 174, p. 175.

National Hot Rod Association: p. 20, p. 31, p. 137, p. 154 (top), p. 156 (both).

Oldsmobile Division, General Motors: p. 8.

Paul G. Prior: p. 12, p. 13.

Perry Zavitz: p. 146 (top).

ACKNOWLEDGMENTS

My primary sources for this book were Chevrolet publications issued during the time Super Sports were in production. I used showroom *Sales Albums*, salesmen's *Finger-Tip Facts* books, shop manuals, owners manuals and a variety of promotional literature including catalogs, brochures and *Chevrolet Friends* magazine. I have used these publications' terms in much of the text (such as "bright metal" to indicate chrome, stainless, anodized aluminum, etc.) unless more explicit information was available. I have also capitalized all factory body designations (such as SS 396 Convertible) to distinguish them from common noun usage of the same words.

Every effort has been made to make this an accurate book. There may be some errors that have crept through, however. Sometimes even the factory material contradicts itself. I have tried to resolve these contradictions, and where I haven't the statements are qualified. Remember, too, that mid-year running changes were often made, many of which are recorded in this book. Finally, there was a very open attitude at Chevrolet during the late sixties to special orders. If you had connections or could get your dealer to place the order, just about anything could be built for you. This was especially true during 1966-71, so don't discount the claims of an owner of an 'odd' car from these years as to its authenticity without careful research.

Corrections verified by factory information will be welcomed by the author.

The only recorded sources for Super Sport performance and driving characteristics, when they were new cars, are articles that appeared in the numerous magazines catering to enthusiasts during the Super Sport era. Magazines like *Motor Trend, Car Life, Road Test, High Performance Cars* and others kept Chevrolet lovers up-to-date on the latest offerings. The test reports on Super Sports were a very useful secondary source of information and commentary for this book.

Then there are the surviving Super Sports. I chased down several rare examples to verify facts. Some eluded me—I never did catch the red 1964 Nova SS I've seen around town many times. If you think this sounds like it wouldn't be hard to do, start watching for a '64 Nova SS yourself and see how long it takes to spot one in any condition. Like me, you may realize how rare many of these once-common cars have become on our roads.

Production figures were supplied by Chevrolet in most instances, while total annual figures and some model figures came from Jerry Heasley's *Production Figure Book for U.S. Cars* and Tony Hossain's independent research.

Approximated option production figures and certain engine production figures were obtained from material originally supplied by the manufacturer for annual editions of *Ward's Reports.* The approximated figures were extrapolated from percentage figures. Many 1965-73 optional engine and transmission production figures have been added to this edition. They come from a recently discovered option production/sales study generously supplied by Chevrolet Motor Division.

I am especially grateful to members of Chevrolet's Public Relations staff, including Director Ralph Kramer and staff members Nancy Libby and Kay Ward. Paul G. Prior, now retired from Chevrolet Production Promotion Engineering, was very helpful in piecing together the Chevrolet performance story.

Among the many other individuals providing assistance and information were: Herman Duerr, Amber McCoy and William J. Tausch of CeCo Publishing; Helen Earley of Oldsmobile PR; Jerry Heasley; Tony Hossain; Stacey Shoffner; Jim Yesse; R. Perry Zavitz; Wally Parks and Les Lovett of NHRA; Ted Kasel; Chris Daniels; and Bruce McDonald.

INTRODUCTION

I don't know what cars mean to today's kids in terms of of status and sexuality, but I know that when I was fifteen, in 1963, they meant a heck of a lot. My friend Rex was sixteen and had a sharp Aztec bronze '57 Chevy. It was our ticket to the freedom and excitement of cruising downtown Wichita's Douglas Avenue that summer. We soon learned that having a car—even a popular '57 Chevy —wasn't always enough to attract girls. One night, coming off the Arkansas River bridge we spotted three girls coming out of a theater. I recognized one of them, which was enough to send Rex wheeling into the curb. We asked them to go riding with us and two of them were quite willing. The third, though, was not for it. "I was hoping we'd get a Super Sport," she pouted as the first girl was climbing into the '57. She backed right out, they conferred, and they agreed. They would wait for a Super Sport to pick them up.

Is it no wonder, then, that the male ego and the automobile got so tangled up in the early sixties?

Actually, the American mystique and the automobile have been intertwined since the first Model T's for the masses started their way down Ford's assembly lines. During the sixties both America and the automobile reached a peak—a peak that is still too recent to be fully understood in its meaning and implications. It was the Super Sport era, all right. Chevrolet's macho machines stand as tokens of their times. The original Super Sports were built for those who had the good life and knew how to enjoy it. The Super Sport owner almost always had more-than-adequate power at his command. By 1970, a critical year in America's self-perception, they had flowered into 454-cubic-inch excess, only to fade rapidly away in the abrasive climate of the seventies.

Today, Chevrolet Super Sports of the sixties and seventies are avidly sought-after nostalgia pieces. They are four-wheeled tokens of a recent but certainly vanished era of what seems increasingly to have been a time of undiminished freedoms. There was the freedom to run hard and fast on the open road without undue government interference; freedom to cruise the streets without worrying about energy expended; freedom to rework and modify our cars to suit personal tastes.

But it appears that the eighties aren't turning out too badly either. A surprising resurgence of performance interest generated a spate of new high-performance automobiles mid-decade. Leading the way were cars like the 1983 Monte Carlo Super Sport. No, these aren't the ground-pounding muscle-bound monsters of yore. Like the children of the sixties today, these cars are the same, yet quite different. Smoother, quieter and with better manners, the new performers utilize technology instead of cubic inches to approach performance levels no one ever thought would be available again.

The new performance cars are attractive and tempting, but there remains a great fondness for the originals, cars that pioneered traditions honored in the current American super cars. This book is written as a tribute to their remembrance and preservation. Inclusion of the 1983-87 Monte Carlo SS in this revised edition recognizes their role in keeping the Super Sport story alive.

Terry Boyce
July, 1986

The First Super Sport?

The word 'super' became a popular slang term for expressing ideal or first-rate qualities in an object during and immediately following World War I. Since one-upmanship was already prevalent in the booming automobile industry it was only a matter of time before someone represented *his* Sport model as a Super-Sport.

One of the earliest applications of the Super-Sport name to an automobile was made by Oldsmobile in 1922. That Super-Sport was a four-passenger sport touring outfitted with numerous special features. It was described as "The smartest of smart cars," as Oldsmobile modestly declared that it sparkled with originality.

Several European racing machines during the interim years between the wars were termed Super-

Sport models. The double S' was also applied to pre-war Jaguars, with a numerical suffix (such as SS-100). It was left to the Jaguar owners to decide what SS meant; the factory never explained. The SS series was terminated during World War II, as Hitler's fanatical security squads known by the same initials tainted the sound of the repeating S to Allied ears.

Chevrolet's first use of the Super Sport name (without the hyphen) came in 1957, when it was applied to a special sports/racing Fuel-Injection Corvette. Plans for a 1958 series-built production version were cancelled in the wake of the American Manufacturers' Association ban on racing activity in 1957.

There were at least two Corvair SS showcars; the 1962 'Sebring Spyder' roadster and the 1963 Monza SS XP 797 sportster.

Oldsmobile, not Chevrolet, was the first General Motors division to market a Super Sport. During 1922-23 Olds built a limited number of these special sport tourings. Cycle fenders, disc wheels, step plates and a nickel radiator shell were Roaring '20's equivalents of flared wheel wells, mag wheels and blacked-out grilles. The Olds was a V-8.

CONTENTS

CHAPTER ONE

Legendary SS & First 409
1961

*T*he National Hot Rod Association's original Winternationals drag meet at Pomona, California, in early 1961 set the tone for the coming performance decade. NHRA president Wally Parks recalled the scene in his 1966 book, *Drag Racing, Yesterday and Today*: "Probably the most popular drag racer at the 1961 Winternationals was crowd pleaser Don Nicholson from Pasadena. He received thunderous applause from the huge crowd everytime he brought his 'dyno-tuned 409' Chevy Super Sport Stocker to the line."

Nicholson piloted his Chevrolet Sport Coupe, running one of the very first 409's on the West Coast, to victory over sister GM division's red-hot Pontiacs. The Stock Eliminator trophy was Nicholson's following a 13.59-second run down Pomona's strip that resulted in a trap speed of 105.88 mph.

Chevrolet's 409 challenged drag-prepared Pontiacs, Fords and Plymouths with considerable success during the rest of the 1961 drag season, starting Nicholson and several other Chevy handlers on the road to Super Stock stardom.

Ford's response to the 409 was a new triple-carburetor setup for their hottest 390-cubic-inch V-8. Rated at 401 hp, the mid-year 390 seldom bested the 409 in drag competition, but it was a more-than-adequate competitor for the much more commonly seen 350-hp Chevrolet 348's that year.

Duels between the 409 and competitors' hot stock engines were frequent in all sorts of motoring sports during 1961. In the Pike's Peak Hill Climb held during mid-1961, the 360-hp 409 got into a fearsome joust with the Ford 390. Curtis Turner was driving the fast Ford, which was equipped with the just-released four-speed manual gearbox. Running against him was Louis Unser, using a 1961 Chevrolet Bel Air Sport Coupe carrying the potent 409. Unser made the climb in 15.6 minutes, besting Turner's Ford by a very narrow 2.4-second margin. Another 409, driven by Bob Betts, placed third in the Stock Car class at the Peak.

Racing styles, and the 409's successes, differed in the East. Pontiacs and some especially fast Fords gave the new Chevrolet 409 plenty of grief on the National Association for Stock Car Racing (NASCAR) circuit. Pontiac emerged with most of the season's trophies, but the Grand National champion for 1961 was a Chevrolet campaigner. He was Ned Jarrett from North Carolina. Jarrett won only one minor race on the difficult road to the title, but his determination and his Chevy's durability kept him consistently near the top during the entire season.

"Our Chevrolet held together real well, but its performance wasn't up to its endurance in '61," Jarrett told a *Motor Trend* correspondent after the season finished. Up in Detroit, Chevrolet engineers were working furiously to increase the 409's horsepower and reliability for 1962.

Another 1961 Impala 409 turned up in the starting field of the Silverstone International Trophy Race, running in the production sedan race during the English meet. At the wheel was Dan Gurney, more normally found at the wheel of a Porsche factory team car at that time. Gurney's blue Sport Coupe was leading the race when, during the second to the final lap, a rear wheel broke away. New, extra-heavy-duty wheels were ordered for the second race in the event, to be held May 8. These and other vital parts arrived by air freight just hours before race time. Then, to compound the frustration, race officials denied the car and Gurney permission

Chevrolet engineers compare the first 409 Impala's
performance to a 350-hp 348.

to run. The 409 had not been approved by the Federation Internationale d'Automobile (FIA) governing body. International telephone calls were made, but to no avail. The disappointed Gurney sold his blue 409 Impala to an Australian who planned to race it in his home country.

Production of the 409 V-8 had begun in January 1961. The new engine was created essentially by a rather sophisticated boring and stroking of the big-block 348 Chevrolet V-8, then in its fourth year of passenger car production. Rated at 360 hp at 5800 rpm and 409 pounds-feet of torque at 3600 rpm, the 409 had a stroke of 3.5 inches, an increase of 0.25 inch from the 348. Cylinder bores of the basic W-series block were opened up 3/16 of an inch for the 409.

Chevrolet engineers, speaking from experience, warned would-be block punchers that most 348 blocks could not take the over-bore needed to fit the 409 pistons. The 348's water jacket patterns were too touchy. Factory core modifications were made for production 409 blocks, which were easily distinguishable from the 348's by the absence of half-moon cutouts at the top of the cylinders. These indentations gave clearance for the hot 348's exhaust valves, but were automatically eliminated by the 409's enlarged bore. The lower end was milled to clear the new 409 crankshaft, with its heavier counterweights. A unique front damper pulley was used.

Main bearings and crank journals were the same size as the 348, but 409 rod bearing inserts were of the then-new Morraine 500 material.

New impact-extruded aluminum pistons were used in the 409, while cylinder heads were manufactured from the same castings used for high-performance 348's with additional machining to accommodate the 409's larger pushrods and valve springs. Valves were identical to the 350-hp 348's, however. Compression was pegged at 11.25:1, requiring super-premium fuel. The 409 used a high-lift, solid-tappet camshaft with large individual valve springs replacing the hot 348's dual units.

Production had hardly begun when 409's started appearing in every sort of organized competition. On drag strips, at Pike's Peak, in the Pure Oil Trials, even at the International races in Silverstone, England, the 409 was on the mark during 1961. Rex White introduced the 409 to NASCAR tracks with one of the 360-hp fire-breathers in his 1961 Bel Air Sport Coupe.

Topping off the Chevrolet 409 was a modified version of the 340-hp 348's aluminum four-barrel manifold. Throttle bore risers were opened up for the 409's big Carter AFB (3720S). NASCAR's outlawing of multi-carb setups negated the use of three two-barrel or dual-quad carbs in late 1961.

The new 409 was finished in Chevrolet engine red (later commonly called Chevrolet orange), with silver rocker covers. Very early 409's had red manifolds as well, but peeling was a problem, so later cars apparently had natural aluminum manifolds. The air cleaner was a large dual-snorkel assembly.

Chevrolet announced the 409 as being available with their standard three-speed transmission, but this was soon changed to four-speed only. The Chevrolet four-speed, in its third year of passenger car application, was redesigned for 1961, with a 2.54:1 low gear ratio. The only catalog rear axle ratio was 3.36:1. Positraction was a very desirable extra-cost option for the 409. The 348's 3.70 rear axle, and over-the-counter 4.10 or 4.56:1 ring and pinion sets found their way into many 409 axle housings as the cars entered drag competition.

The 409 is especially important to Super Sport history, since the original Chevrolet Super Sport was designed to showcase the new engine. The Super Sport kit became available in mid-1961, just shortly after the first 409's went into racing competition. A special brochure for the Super Sport, using modified illustrations of regular 1961 Impalas, announced the new type of car in showrooms. Most enthusiasts discovered the SS Chevrolet when their May 1961 issue of *Motor Trend* arrived. A full-page, up-front ad gave the details of the new Impala SS. The Super Sport option, the ad advised, was offered as a "complete kit only," consisting of spe-

1961 Super Sport hub cap was modified from regular Impala full wheel cover, used tri-blade fake knock-off spinner. Tires were new narrow-band whitewall for SS installation.

An authentic 1961 Super Sport, found and photographed by the author on a Minnesota back road in 1977. The owner was just completing an overhaul of its 350-hp 348. Hub caps are 1962 versions.

cial Super Sport trim for the exterior and inside, an instrument panel safety pad, full wheel covers with tri-blade spinner, power brakes and steering, heavy-duty springs and shocks, sintered Morraine metallic brake linings, 7000 rpm tachometer mounted on a steering column bracket and 8.00x14 narrow-band whitewall tires (conventional 1961 Chevrolets still had a fairly wide whitewall optional tire).

Exterior insignia for the SS (the term was widely known by drag fans, where S/S stood for the hot Super Stock classes) was created by superimposing large red-filled chrome SS badges over the Impala and crossed-flag emblems on the deck and rear fenders. Simulated knock-off tri-blade spinners with red, white and blue insert colors were added to the modified 1961 full wheel covers, which closely approximated the 1962 Super Sport wheel cover.

The interior was modified by the installation of a new Corvette-type grab bar mounted in front of the right-hand passenger. This distinctive touch would endure as a Super Sport motif during early SS model years. The shifter for four-speed cars was implanted in a small console-type plate. Hiding behind the standard, but racy, Impala steering wheel's left spoke was the 7000 rpm red-line tach, in a chrome case.

Chevrolet listed five engine/transmission combinations for the original 1961 Super Sport. The engines were all extra-cost V-8's, and all but the least powerful required the addition of an optional four-speed transmission. The smallest horsepower engine was the 305-hp 348, which could be ordered with Powerglide. Two other 348's—the 340-hp four-barrel carburetor version and the hot special-performance 350-hp job with triple two-barrel carbs—were offered. The new 409, rated at 360 hp, was at the top of the list.

Chevy Impala showster for 1961 had bucket seats, unique console, column shift for Powerglide. All production 1961 Super Sports had bench seats.

15

The Super Sport kit was offered for any of the five 1961 Impala body styles, according to sales literature (the SS brochure, in fact, shows a retouched Impala four-door hardtop Sport Sedan with SS equipment!). Most of the SS kits went onto Sport Coupes, and a few Convertibles were built as well. A very unusual car to consider would be the 1961-only Impala two-door sedan with SS equipment. If any were built, none are known to have survived.

Production of Super Sport kits for 1961 was very limited. Chevrolet indicates 453 cars left the factory with SS equipment. (Another figure quoted, of 142 cars, is apparently the number of 409-equipped 1961 Chevrolets built.) There are indications that some dealer installations of the SS trim items were made very late in the year. There is no way to identify an Impala Super Sport by the data plate. Despite the fanfare in automotive publications, it was almost completely eclipsed by its highly successful 1962 successor, and the '61 is a great, but largely forgotten, rarity today. A totally authentic 1961, especially if it has an early genuine 409, will someday be one of the most valuable cars of the sixties.

Motor Trend actually published two road tests of 1961 409 Super Sports. The first appeared in their June 1961 issue, amid the rumors and excitement of the 1962 model year's initial contractions. Road tester Bob Ames wrote of the 409 tested, ". . . without trying hard the SS will shoot away from practically anything else on the road." Ames's 409 had but four miles on the odometer when he picked it up, so a full-blown road test wasn't feasible. The car earned praise for its handling, which was aided by the Limited Production Option (LPO) 1108 heavy-duty suspension parts package included with the SS equipment. The sintered metallic brake linings,

Large shifter plate was used for four-speed control stick. No SS emblem was used here, just Impala insignia.

A 7000-rpm tachometer mounted on steering column, to the left, was obscured by steering wheel unless it was cocked as shown.

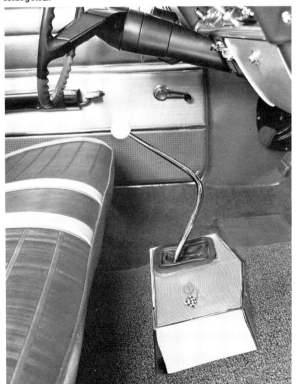

Ames reported, did an excellent job of braking the spirited Impala, while exhibiting few of the cold-weather fade characteristics attributed to such linings in earlier years. Interestingly, the LPO 1108 package, when specified for regular Chevrolets, included fifteen-inch tires and wheels, but apparently 409 Super Sports used 8.00x14-inch tires regardless.

Just as the 1962 model introduction was happening, *Motor Trend* did publish a performance road-test of the 1961 SS with a 409 engine. It appeared too late to help sell any 1961 Super Sports (the 409 may have already been temporarily withdrawn, as a slightly revised block design was prepared for 1962 production). Really wringing out the car this time, *Motor Trend*'s staff tried the 409 with its standard 3.36:1 rear axle, Positraction option and the over-the-counter 4.56 cogs.

The 4.56:1 rear end naturally gave the 409 increased acceleration capability, although it reduced the Super Sport's top end (which remained undetermined but far beyond where the 120-mph speedometer left off). This 409 stopped the clocks at 14.02 seconds for the quarter-mile run, achieving a trap speed of 98.14 mph. With the standard gear set (3.36:1) the car was 4 mph slower and lost more than a second in its elapsed time. Stop watches showed acceleration from rest to 60 mph in seven seconds with the 4.56 rear end, while the 3.36 gear set required 7.8 seconds.

The road testers complained that the SS wasn't outfitted with enough special trim for its exclusivity and worried that the car's standard instrument panel, without full instrumentation, was inadequate. A better defi-

Grab bar first appeared on 1961 SS; idea was borrowed from Corvette.

Super Sport equipment was theoretically offered for any Impala style. A few Impala convertibles were built with SS equipment; this one wasn't.

nition of the Super Sport concept would arrive in 1962, but gauges would remain the responsibility of after-market manufacturers for several more years.

Certainly the most successful and famous General Motors special model of the early 1960's, the Super Sport is often regarded as the first of its type as well. However, other GM divisions had helped lead the way. Pontiac offered bucket seats as early as 1958 for its very distinctive Bonneville models. Oldsmobile offered the Starfire, a special sports convertible with bucket seats and different trim, in 1961. Also in late 1960 Corvair's Monza coupe had unique trim, special suspension features and narrowband whitewalls (first time on a volume production car). During mid-1961 the new GM intermediates Buick Skylark, Pontiac Tempest and Oldsmobile Cutlass appeared in special sport coupe versions.

By 1962 the Super Sport had a full field of competitors including bucket-seated specials from Ford and Plymouth. But none of these cars caught the public's imagination, attention and desire as much as the Chevrolet Super Sport. As for the 409, it would be immortalized in song, becoming a true legend; an engine that few had ever actually seen, but an engine everyone had heard about.

1961 SS emblems were overlaid on Impala insignias on rear quarters and deck.

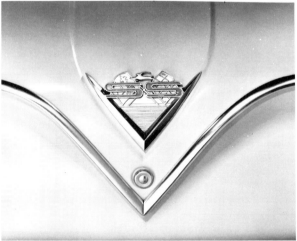

CHAPTER TWO

First Generation
Impala Super Sports
1962–1964

America entered 1962 on a wave of optimism; the clouds that would darken the decade's enthusiasm were still on the far side of the horizon. Millions of American families gathered weekly before their TV sets to watch the hit western series *Bonanza* sponsored by America's favorite car, Chevrolet, which was celebrating the fiftieth anniversary of the incorporation of the ancestral Chevrolet Motor Company by Louis Chevrolet and William C. Durant.

The 1962 model Chevrolets were cars worthy of celebration. Four lines were fielded, including a new make, the compact Chevy II. It was evident, just as it had been during the tremendous 1955 record-setting year, that Chevrolet's ideas about the cars it wanted to build meshed nicely with the ideas Americans had about the cars they wanted to buy. The 1962 sales slogan, "A New World of Worth from Chevrolet," suggested that every part of the automotive world would be well served by Chevrolet cars and trucks. By offering full-size passenger cars, the sporty and innovative Corvair, a new conventional compact Chevy II and the Corvette sports car, Chevrolet did indeed cover the market pretty thoroughly.

Regular Chevrolet passenger cars featured a highly refined style that was obviously related to the 1961 model, although in the future it would be more often associated with the 1963-64 models.

Cleaner side trim was used, but the cars kept the nose-up jet-fighter stance of 1961, accentuated by their trailing body crease line. The 1962 bodies were better protected against corrosion damage by the use of inner fender panels to seal the front wheelhouse area against moisture.

Three Chevrolet series were offered for 1962, in a full range of body styles. The middle series Bel Air featured a Sport Coupe hardtop for the last time. It continued to use the 1961 Sport Coupe's racy roof line, to the applause of drag and stock car racers who appreciated the slippery design. The rest of the world was impressed by the formal lines of the more prestigious Impala series' convertible-creased hardtop roof.

The new Impala Sport Coupe proved to be an extremely successful car, outselling the 1961 version by approximately two to one. (Combined 1961 Impala and Bel Air Sport Coupe production was 177,969, while the same figure for 1962 would total 323,427, of which just 5,950 were Bel Air hardtops.) The popular Impala convertible, in its fifth year, lost its position as the most expensive car in Chevrolet's passenger car line with the addition of the Impala station wagon (1958-61 wagons had been classified in their own series). Missing from the 1962 line was the one-year-only Impala two-door sedan of 1961 and the Bel Air Sport Sedan four-door hardtop.

Wheelbase for the 1962 Impalas remained at 119 inches. Overall length was increased only 0.3 inch to 209.6 inches, but the cars appeared longer than the 1961's by several inches due to the new styling.

Impala Sport Coupes and Convertibles could be ordered with a revised version of the rarely seen but widely publicized 1961 Super Sport equipment option. The 1962 Super Sport kit was given Regular Production Option (RPO) number 240. (RPO equipment was factory-installed at extra cost by normal ordering procedures.) Interior features for 1962 SS cars were expanded to include special all-vinyl upholstery on individual front bucket seats, with one exception: a black vinyl/cloth combination was offered for the SS Convertible.

Unlike the 1961 Super Sport, which was cataloged with special 348 or 409 engines only, the 1962 SS option could be ordered with any Impala power train, including the base 135-hp six.

The 409 and drivers such as Dave Strickler and Hayden Proffitt became drag racing legends during 1962. Many drag pros preferred the light Bel Air Sport Coupe, with its slippery, 1961-style roof line.

Impala Super Sports for 1962 featured engine-turned—or as Chevrolet called it, "swirl-pattern"—silver anodized aluminum inserts in the body side moldings; regular Impalas had contrasting painted inserts. This same material appeared in the rear deck cove (regular Impalas had a silver satin-finished cove panel). All Impalas had six taillights with backup lamps located in the center unit of each side's triple group. Super Sports had special full wheel covers, with simulated tri-bar knock-off lugs similar to those used on 1961 SS cars. Large red-filled chrome SS letters were laid over standard Impala emblems on the rear fenders, while a signature bar on the right side of the rear deck further indicated SS equipment.

Impalas equipped with the Super Sport option used anodized aluminum trim edging on their foam-cushioned bucket seats. A locking center console between the front seats could flip its lid to become a beverage tray for rear seat passengers, whose feet were illuminated by the console's lamp when doors were opened. Door reflector discs and an electric clock were standard Impala equipment.

Swirl-pattern aluminum replaced the cross-hatch brightwork of regular Impalas on the instrument panel. At the far right, in front of the passenger, was a new version of the 1961 SS grab bar, otherwise known as the passenger assist bar. Commented the *Finger Tip Facts* book for 1962, "In emergencies bar serves as grab rail for passenger, otherwise it assists him in rising from the deep-set bucket seat." Not quite so flashy, but of much more value in a real emergency, was the inclusion of underbody reinforcements for a new stronger type of optional seat belt installation.

Presumably the sort of emergencies involving the grab bar most often occurred when the driver mashed the accelerator of a 409- or 327-equipped SS to the floor.

1962 Super Sport interior. This is a 409, with 7000-rpm tachometer. All four-speed cars had big chrome shifter plate for shift lever.

Super Sports equipped with four-speed transmissions got a floor-shift trim plate, topped with an inset of swirl-pattern aluminum and the crossed-flag Impala emblem. Powerglides and three-speeds had column shifters in 1962. SS equipment added $156 to the base price of an Impala Sport Coupe or Convertible.

Impalas for 1962 were finished in Magic-Mirror acrylics in fourteen solid and ten two-tone colors. Two-tones were executed by using a different roof color, usually a lighter shade. Popular solid colors were Tuxedo black, Ermine white, Silver blue, Laurel green and Roman red. Autumn gold, often called 'anniversary gold' was seen on a number of loaded Super Sport Coupes delivered as dealers' floor cars during the golden anniversary year. Regular production 1962 Impala convertibles had white tops, but black, blue or cream could be specified on request.

Much of the Chevrolet excitement in 1962 centered on the power-team charts. Although only a few months old, the 409 was already a legend. It was continued from 1961 in two stages of tune. But, to the average Chevrolet buyer the big news was a new larger version of the famed and loved 265-283 V-8 block.

Hot rodders had been boring the 283 block to 292 and even 301 cubic inches for five years. The factory, with its unique ability to redistribute

The 380-hp 409 used single four-barrel, big dual-snorkel air cleaner. 1962 409 valve covers were painted silver.

water jacket cores for extra cylinder-wall thickness, carried out a safe 1/8-inch overbore on the 283 block for 1962. Coupled with a 1/4-inch stroke adjustment, this gave the Chevrolet small-block (a rodding term for the 265-283-327 engine family) its new displacement of 327 cubic inches.

The 327 block had other modifications, of course, but it was identical to the 283 block at casual inspection to all but the most trained eyes. Inside was a new crankshaft of forged steel with larger counterweights. Main and rod bearings were like the 283's, but inserts were Morraine premium-grade steel-backed aluminum such as had been used previously on high-performance Corvette 283 V-8's only. Cylinder heads were basically the 283 units, with the 300-hp version using larger ports and exhaust valves. Chevrolet's worshipful followers were usually adept at a curious bit of phrenology. Their educated fingers could read the bumps found on the edges of 283 and 327 heads, from which compression ratios could be determined. One bump, for instance, indicated an 8.5:1 regular head, while two bumps meant a 10.5:1 head. The bumps' shape indicated large or small ports to trained fingers feeling the front edge of the left head, which was hidden by the generator.

1962 Impala SS rear fender insignia.

1962 Chicago Auto Show display featured an Impala SS Convertible, Corvair Monza and Chevy II sedan.

23

Tuned for passenger car installation, the 327 was offered in two versions, the RPO 300, 250-hp with Rochester four-barrel and the 300-hp RPO 397. The 300-hp version used a large aluminum Carter four-barrel carburetor in addition to the dual exhausts and big heads to corral the fifty extra horses allotted to it. Both 327's used 10.5:1 heads with hydraulic camshafts (adapted from the temporarily discontinued 220-hp Super Turbo-Fire 283 and had dual exhaust systems).

Solid-lifter camshafts and valve-train gear supplied with high-performance Corvette engines were available for over-the-counter purchase, or Chevrolet owners seeking greater power could choose from the 'grinds' offered by various speed merchants.

The 327 completely supplanted the 348 V-8 in the 1962 Chevrolet line-up.

Chevrolet rated the top production 409 at 409 hp. The major addition to the RPO 587 V-8 was a second four-barrel carburetor on the aluminum manifold. Progressive mechanical linkage brought it into play during full-throttle acceleration. New heads were also used, with 2.20-inch intake valves and larger ports. Stiffer valve springs were used with the 1961-type cam at the beginning of the year.

Running modifications were made to the hot 409 during 1962 production. By spring, 409-hp engines were coming through with beefed bearings, stronger silicon steel-alloy valve springs, a single breaker distributor with vacuum advance only, lengthened exhaust pushrods and fuel delivery modifications for easier 'hot' starts. A new cam, with an increase in lift of 0.04 inch was phased in as well.

Rumors circulated that Rochester fuel injection was a possible 409 option for 1963, but it wasn't to be. Rochester engineers did apparently build an experimental fuelie 409 that gave 440 hp on the dynamometer at 6000 rpm.

Roger Huntington, who tested a late 1962 SS 409 Sport Coupe for *Motor Trend*, felt that the 409's rated horsepower was conservative for the late production engine. In fact, the little-changed 1963 version would be rated at 425 hp.

One of the very first 1962 model 409 Super Sports
at rest after a test session.

Huntington pushed his 409 test car to 60 mph in just 6.3 seconds. The quarter was run in 14.9 seconds at 98 mph. These figures came from a car equipped with a 4.11 rear end and the 2.20:1 close-ratio four-speed. Huntington had tested a 1961 model 409 with 3.36 gears and 2.54:1 low transmission a year before. It had turned the quarter mile in 15.6 seconds at 92 mph. (However, *Motor Trend*'s second 409 road test in 1961, using a car pulling 4.56:1 cogs, came up with figures very nearly matching the 1962 car's performance.) Just to remind his readers that drivers and tuning do make a difference, Huntington pointed out that Don Nicholson had pushed *his* NHRA stock-legal 409 Chevrolet to mid-twelve-second runs at speeds of 112 mph on the quarter-mile acceleration strip.

The 'other' 409 for 1962 was the single four-barrel-carbed 380-hp RPO 580. It shared the dual-quad's 11.0:1 compression heads. *Car Life* tested a 380-hp SS 409 Impala for its March 1962 issue. Using a 2.20:1 low four-speed and 3.70 Positraction axle, they managed 0-60 mph in 7.3 seconds and turned the quarter mile in 14.9 seconds at 94 mph.

Both of these 409's featured silver valve covers with decals indicating the engine was a Turbo-Fire 409 of the designated horsepower. Manifolds were natural aluminum, while air cleaners were big black dual-snorkel jobs. The 409's shared the fuel-injected Corvette's 35-ampere generator (other Chevrolets used a 30-amp unit), with the new Delcotron alternator available optionally for all V-8's. Chevrolet installed 15,019 409 V-8's in 1962 passenger cars.

Thousands of Chevrolet buyers opted for the new 327 small-block V-8 in 1962. The 327 would become as famous as its parent, the 283.

Regular Chevrolet passenger cars continued to use the 283-cubic-inch V-8 as the base V-8 model engine. For 1962 a 170-hp two-barrel version was the only 283 offered. New heads, allowing coolant circulation around the spark plugs were used. Six-cylinder models used the 135-hp 235, modified by the use of a newly designed water pump to give a lower silhouette for hood clearance.

Standard V-8 models, with the 170-hp 283, were priced a bit higher than standard six-cylinder models. During 1962 the model 1867 Impala Convertible with the 283 V-8 of the 1800 series was delivered for $109 more than model 1767, the Impala six-cylinder Convertible in the 1700 series. (Chevrolet had adopted separate model designations for six-cylinder and V-8 cars in 1958. V-8 series models were numbered one hundred higher than comparable six-cylinder models.)

Chevrolet's expanded power train availability for 1962 included a choice of ratios for some V-8 cars equipped with four-speeds. RPO 685A, with 2.54:1 low, was offered for all 327 and 409 V-8's; but the 2.20:1 low four-speed was reserved for the big V-8's only (as RPO 685B). All used aluminum cases this year. Chevrolet's conventional three-speed manual gearbox was standard in all V-8's; it differed from the six-cylinder unit only through the use of a stiffer clutch gear-shift and strengthened bearings. Overdrive could be specified for installation with the three-speed on six-cylinder and base V-8 cars. Manual transmissions were mated to Corvette-type aluminum clutch housings on 300-hp 327 cars.

Optional rear axle gear sets for 327 and 409 V-8's included 3.36 or 3.08:1 ratios. The big 409's, if equipped with 2.20:1 low four-speed, could be factory-fitted with 4.11 or 4.56 cogs. Positraction was offered with all axles. Additional ratios could be obtained from Chevrolet parts departments for dealer or owner installation.

Powerglide, Chevrolet's proven two-speed automatic, was continued without change for six-cylinder and standard V-8 cars. An improved version, using a cast-aluminum case and extension (the whole unit weighed just 146 pounds installed), was reserved for 327 V-8's in 1962. The new Powerglide used a disc-type reverse clutch with drum instead of the 'iron case' band. There were many other improvements as well. A lesser version of the new transmission was used for the new Chevy II, while the big Chevrolet type was used in Corvette, although it was liquid-cooled for passenger

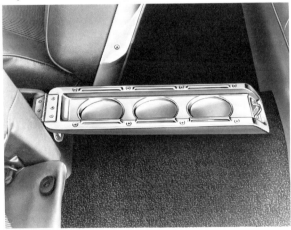

Lid on 1962 console flipped over to create beverage tray for rear seat occupants.

Corvair SS was 1962 show car; SS meant Super Spyder in this case.

car installation and air-cooled for the sports car. All 1962 409's had manual transmissions, but Powerglide would meet the big V-8 in 1963.

A number of fourteen-inch and fifteen-inch tires were optional for 1962 Impalas. RPO 1814 Highway Nylon blackwall tires in 8.00x14 size were "recommended with 409 V-8 engines," or were required additional extra-cost equipment, depending on which 1962 Chevrolet literature you look at. Other Super Sports came with the standard Impala tire sizes of 7.00x14 for the Sport Coupe and 7.50x14 for the Convertible unless optional tires were specified.

Popular performance and heavy-duty options ordered by most 409 and many 327 buyers included Positraction rear axles, heavy-duty front and rear springs, heavy-duty shocks, sintered metallic brake linings, a 70-amp battery and an electric tachometer (mandatory with four-speed-equipped 300-hp 327's and both 409's) mounted on the steering column.

The appearance of a 409 continued to create a sensation at any of the nation's rapidly multiplying drag strips during 1962. Recalling the scene at the second Winternationals held at Pomona, California, that year Wally Parks wrote, "In the stock-car action, defending champion Don Nicholson rolled up to the line to do battle against a strong challenger from York, Pennsylvania, Dave Strickler, driving the Bill Jenkins-tuned, Ammon R. Smith '409' Chevrolet. Nicholson was also driving a '62 Chevrolet . . . he emerged the winner with marks of 12.84 seconds and 109.22 mph . . . his victory also gave additional proof of the appeal of this fast-moving segment of drag racing when he received a standing ovation from the capacity crowd upon his return from the top end shutdown areas for the trophy presentation."

During the 1962 NHRA Nationals in Indianapolis, another battle of the 409's took place. This time it was Dave Strickler hashing it out on the strip with the West Coast's Hayden Proffitt. When the smoke cleared Proffitt had won the Mr. Stock Eliminator title with a scorching 12.83-second run, clocking in at 113.92 mph.

To deal with the on-rushing deluge of factory speed equipment being released by the major manufacturers during 1962 the NHRA instituted new Factory Experimental (FX) classes mid-year. They were for cars using factory-available and engineered parts not necessarily for assembly-line production. Late 1962 409's with revised cams and heads ran in FX classes. Very late in the year a few B/FX 409's, with aluminum front fenders, bumpers and hoods were showing up on the strips.

The excitement of the 409 carried over into pop culture that summer as the surf-rock music group, the Beach Boys, released their very successful hit single, "409." It was about a young man who was going to save his pennies and his dimes to buy a new Chevrolet 409.

1962 Super Sport wheel covers used tri-blade spinner with modified Impala cover.

Over on NASCAR's circuit the 409 had a rough year, as it had in 1961. Chevrolet hadn't been really competitive since 1957. (There had been just two Chevrolet victories on major tracks during the past four bleak years; when Junior Johnson won at Daytona in 1960 with his 1959 Chevrolet and in June of the same year when Joe Lee Johnson took the gold at the Charlotte World 600.) Then, in the last race of the 1962 NASCAR season Rex White's 380-hp 409 Bel Air Sport Coupe made it to the big-time winner's circle at Atlanta Raceway, coming in just ahead of Joe Weatherly in one of the frequently victorious 421 Pontiacs.

Stock car and drag racers may have preferred the Bel Air, but on the street the Impala Super Sport was one of the year's hottest cars. A whole generation lusted after the new Chevys, waiting impatiently for the latest issue of *Motor Trend*, *Car Life* or *Hot Rod* to hit the newsstand with the latest news about the 409 Chevrolet's feats. Caught up in an almost fanatical fervor, these teenagers would be the young men and women who purchased subsequent Super Sports by the hundreds of thousands. (In the meantime, many thousands of teenage youths occupied themselves by building scale plastic models of the Chevrolet Super Sport and other great cars of the time. Model cars became popular during the early sixties.)

Like the model kits, the real car was available with an amazing array of options. Chevrolet emphasized the choices in their 1962 promotional material, saying, "Chevrolet adds a new dimension to its value tradition—made to measure motoring . . . personal fun cars." By carefully combing the option list, 1962 Super Sport buyers could end up with vastly differing personal interpretations of the SS theme. An SS equipped with the 409-hp 409, heavy-duty suspension, blackwall tires, after-market headers with 'dumps' just under the front fender's lower edge, and a slight frontal rake had little in common with the middle-aged uncle's 'anniversary gold' Impala SS Coupe running a 250/327 with Powerglide, narrow-band whitewalls, dual rear fender aerials (for the all-transistor AM Deluxe pushbutton radio). All-Weather air conditioning, Flexomatic six-way power driver's seat, power windows and the RPO FOA 140 Body Equipment Group A with its outside rearview mirror, non-glare inside mirror, grille and bumper guards.

Chevrolet sold at least 99,311 Impalas with the Super Sport option in 1962. All-out performance and all-out luxury versions were scarce, but the rarest were the few cars built with both high-performance chassis and luxury comfort and convenience features. Rival Ford had offered a competitor to the Super Sport in 1962 with its Galaxie XL, which sold less than half as many units as did the SS Chevrolet. Ford and Chevrolet's other competitors were planning strategy for the immediate future, however. Fastback roof lines, wild engines bumping right against the 427-cubic-inch NASCAR limit announced late in 1962, and hot factory S/S and FX cars for NHRA drag competition were all in the works.

Chevrolet engineers were preparing their defenses with a dual effort. A new, 427-cubic-inch version of the 409 was being readied for drag racing, while a totally new and very potent 427 was being prepared for NASCAR stock car activities. Sadly, the powerful new big-block would prove to be only a flash in the pan, and the new Z-11 drag engine, while successful, would likewise lead nowhere. To the chagrin of Chevrolet's competitors, who were funneling millions of dollars into their racing efforts, it wouldn't really make much difference in that most important of all competitive events, the sales race.

Chevrolet's 1963 models were offered with a number of special performance engines and drive train components as the year opened with the promise of being a crucial one in the performance wars. Competitive response to the 409's publicity coup of 1962 rolled in with the 1963 models. Ford's 406 was a fire-breather that would grow to a truly strong 427 by mid-year, while Chrysler's big 426's were being stuffed into the lightest MoPars to make them formidable drag cars in pro-stock and factory-sponsored team efforts (Chevrolet's famed V-8's still maintained a strong domination of the lower stock and modified classes, however).

The NHRA's new Factory Experimental classes, created for wild factory-built hybrids using available over-the-counter special performance parts, was successfully campaigned by Chevrolet, which had announced late in 1962 that its future drag racing efforts would be channeled in this direction rather than into overt sponsorship of factory racing teams.

Chevrolet built its 1963 FX drag engines around the old 409 'W' block, but for the NASCAR stock car effort in 1963, it used a completely new design. Unveiled at the beginning of the year, this new Mark II V-8 displaced NASCAR's maximum number of cubic inches—427. It was a sensational engine. Unofficial reports from GM's Phoenix testing ground said the 427 registered 573 hp at 6000 rpm on the dynamometer. A full-size Chevy running the Mark II 427 was allegedly clocked in excess of 180 mph at the Arizona facility, acceleration from 90 to 150 mph in eighteen seconds.

Under its wide, flat-faced rocker covers the new 427 carried some strange-appearing valve gear. Rocker arms and pushrods were scattered apparently at random down the head, giving rise to the 'porcupine' head's nickname.

Chevrolet was prepared to unleash the 427 on nervous competitors at Daytona, but sudden confusion erupted just before the race. Chevrolet and Pontiac announced they were backing off from promotionally-related race activities. Translated, it meant the 427 Mark II was dead. Its production had already stopped.

Late 1962 Impala 409 SS Sport Coupe ran **B/FX** because of factory-revised valve gear kit and other modifications. Driver Dick Harrell became a top Chevy drag racer in the sixties, then lost his life in a 1972 funny car crash.

Five Mark II 427 Chevrolet race cars were prepared for Daytona, however, and they were allowed to run. Junior Johnson's white Mark II, prepared by Smokey Yunick, had clocked more than 165 mph in qualifications and promised to sweep the field. The new engine's components hadn't been fully developed, however, and a water pump failure blew the race for the recently disowned Chevrolet and its driver. Johnny Rutherford was the only driver to bring a Mark II 427 into the top ten, placing ninth.

Undaunted, Junior Johnson continued on the 1963 NASCAR circuit, using spare parts stashed before the Detroit tap had been turned off; when those ran out, he used parts made by his crew. Through the summer, Johnson rode on with all the aplomb of such famous fellow southerners as General George Pickett at Gettysburg. But, trouble dogged him constantly, to the relief of competitors. At the Charlotte World 600, Johnson blew a tire just two laps from the flag. Finally, in what was sort of a Chevrolet tradition by then, victory came in the last major NASCAR race of the year. It was the National 400 that brought the hard-earned victory, a fitting finish to Johnson's dramatic season.

Junior Johnson knew when enough was enough; just a few days before the National 400, his race mechanic, Ray Fox, had leaked the news: Junior would drive a Mercury for 1964. The Chevrolet Mark II 427 was still one of the most potent engines around, but spare parts fabrication was nearly impossible. Besides, it had been pretty gracious of NASCAR's officials to allow the Mark II 427 to remain in competition for even the rest of the 1963 season. Though no specific quota had yet been set, stock car engines were supposed to be production-line engines, readily available to the public in their basic form. Only the five Daytona Mark II 427's were ever delivered to anyone, as near as can be determined.

Chevrolet enthusiasts were left confused and hurt by the Mark II 427 affair. The engine became a legend. To this day it is reverently referred to as the "Daytona Mystery Engine," even though it did provide the basic design

1963 Super Sport Convertible. Amber turn-signal lenses were used on all 1963 cars.

for the 1965 Mark IV big-block V-8's. (The Mystery Engine and Junior Johnson's efforts to keep it going were part of Tom Wolfe's best-selling 1965 book, *The Kandy-Kolored Tangerine-Flake Streamline Baby*, which added greatly to the fame of both.)

Why *did* Chevrolet do a number on the 427 Mark II? It may have been the result of thinking like this: Chevrolet (and Pontiac) wanted out of NASCAR's over-heated competition. But once the 427 Mark II was thoroughly de-bugged by Smokey Yunick (who quit Johnson shortly after the 427 ban), it was sure to win most NASCAR races. This would create untold and unwanted race-bred publicity directly contradicting the corporation's new policies. So, all support to the racers was cut off in February 1963. The afterglow didn't fade completely until the end of the season as we've seen.

Between the NASCAR confusion and Chevrolet's policy of providing special performance drag-racing parts, the *other* 1963 model 427 was almost lost in the shuffle. This was the enlarged 409 specifically designed for drag racing. Technically, it was available as RPO Z11 for installation in any full-size Chevrolet, although the order form stated, "Buyers require approval from the Central Sales Office before the order can be filled." In reality, of course, only a few got into the hands of professional drag racers.

Chevrolet's Paul G. Prior explains how the engine was created: "The Z-11 was a further extension of the 'W' engine—348-409—excepting it had different heads and manifolding. The ports were bigger with a higher roof in them, and that required an intake manifold with a higher entry angle such that it became, if not necessary, then certainly convenient to separate the intake manifold from the valley cover."

Using a valley cover was almost unique to the Z-11, but there was a precedent according to Prior. "There was some number of that equipment in a single four-barrel arrangement—the same heads, though—with a separate manifold and valley cover produced for NASCAR use late in 1962 for the 409." The 1963 advent of the Mystery 427 totally eclipsed this development. A few of these strange, very late 1962 409's found their way into FX drag cars as well.

One of the handful of 427-cubic-inch Z-11 Impalas built in 1963 lifts its nose coming off the line. Bill Thomas was prime West Coast Chev builder, with close factory connections.

The 1963 Z-11 used new high-top pistons with a 12.5:1 compression ratio. The displacement increase came via the boring of the 409 block to 4.406 inches. Stroke was unchanged.

Bill 'Grumpy' Jenkins campaigned a Z-11 with great success during the 1963 drag season. It was supplied by Ammon R. Smith, the Pennsylvania Chevrolet dealer who sponsored several of the decade's great drag racers. Jenkins's car carried a window sticker which indicated that an extra charge of $1,237.40 was added for RPO Z11. Included was the 427-cubic-inch, 430-hp V-8, four-speed transmission, metallic brake linings, 4.11 Positraction rear axle, heavy-duty springs and shocks, tachometer, 6.70x15 tires on fifteen-inch rims and aluminum components including hood, front fender inner and outer panels, under hood panels, both bumpers and their brackets and even the battery tray. The total weight savings was about 140 pounds, and the delivered price of an Impala Sport Coupe so equipped was $4,073.65. Completely stripped of extra weight to the NHRA limit, a Z-11 might stop short of 3,400 pounds. Quarter-mile speeds of 115 mph in the twelve-second range were possible, as tuned horsepower approached 500.

Most Chevrolet buyers in 1963 never heard of the Z-11, and had only Sunday sports page acquaintance with the Mystery Engine. For them the biggest Chevrolet V-8 was the 425-hp 409, as shown in the sales catalog. Slightly improved from 1962, this top 409 used the revised heads, valves and headers found on late 1962 production engines. The RPO L80 409 was once again fed by two big aluminum-bodied four-barrel carburetors atop an aluminum manifold, A twin-snorkel dry-element air cleaner announced the engine's potency to gas station attendants and others invited to peer beneath the hood. The big 409's 11.0:1 compression ratio required frequent visits to Super-Premium gas pumps. Mileage might exceed 10 mpg if the right foot wasn't too vigorously applied.

A step down was the single four-barrel 400-hp 409 (RPO L31) sharing the dual-quad version's mechanical lifters, cam and compression ratio. It red-lined at 5800 rpm instead of 6000. The 400-hp engine's dual-snorkel

1963 Impala SS console and shifter plate were nearly integrated. Powerglide and four-speed SS cars had floor controls this year. SS emblem was mounted ahead of shifter.

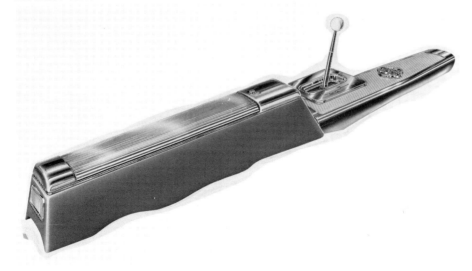

air cleaner used an oil-wetted element, and, like all 409's, had dual exhausts with 2½-inch tailpipes.

New for 1963 was a 340-hp 409 (RPO L33),often called the 'police option' 409. It shared the more powerful versions' garnishes, including chrome (single snorkel) air cleaner, valve covers, oil filler cap, dipstick, fuel lines, fuel filter top and automatic choke tube. It was really a different breed of cat, though, with a mild hydraulic lifter camshaft for street flexibility. Weight was increased by the use of a cast-iron alloy conventional manifold for the four-barrel carburetor. Pistons were alloy aluminum. Heads contained smaller valves and compression was pegged at 10.0:1.

Rated horsepower for the 340-409 was shy compared to the all-out jobs, but its torque chart indicated a strong 420 pounds-feet generated at 3200 rpm, very close to the output of the stronger engines. Chevrolet owners who got their kicks whomping it around slow-moving vehicles weren't likely to soon forget the punch packed by any 409. *Car Life* tested a 340-hp 409 in March of that year, using a car equipped with Powerglide and 3.36:1 rear axle. Sixty miles per hour came in just 6.6 seconds, and 100 mph was reached in less than twenty seconds. The car would burn rubber at 40 mph and hit 124 mph at the top of its range. Fuel consumption was 12 mpg.

The 409's carried no decals on their valve covers this year. Instead, 425-hp engines had die-cast crossed flags and 409 numerals atop their air-cleaner cover near the front, while 400- and 340-hp units had a similar emblem bonded to the front vertical face of the air-cleaner body.

Mechanical-lifter 409's continued to come with three- or four-speed manual gearboxes. A choice of 2.20:1 close ratio or 2.54:1 low gears were offered to 409 buyers who specified four-speeds. Only the 340-hp unit could be had with Powerglide.

Buyers who specified the 327 V-8's, basically unaltered from 1962, could order the 2.54:1 (RPO M20) four-speed for their engines. Horsepower remained at 250 for the RPO L30 327, and 300 for the RPO L74 version. All manual-transmission 327's had aluminum bell housings for 1963. Cooling capacity was improved, also, by the use of redesigned radiators.

Rear axle ratios included 4.11 and 4.56:1 gear sets for 409 buyers who ordered the 2.20:1 low four-speed. A special Performance Cruise 3.08:1 axle was offered in conjunction with the 2.54:1 low four-speed and 409. Positraction was optional with any standard catalog axle ratio.

Vinyl-covered top was a big fad in 1963. Factory photo is 1962 prototype, part of 1962 side trim has been air-brushed out.

Steel cables were used to keep 1963 convertible top edges snugly against top frame, helped prevent drawing up of material from shrinkage.

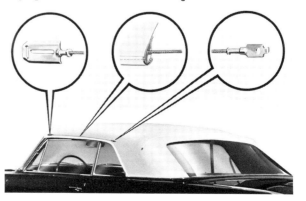

Self-adjusting brakes were added to 1963 Chevrolet passenger cars. Optional sintered metallic brake linings were improved for extra-duty service.

Standard engines for 1963 regular Chevrolet passenger cars were the old reliable 283 V-8 and a new six. The 283 was now rated at 195 hp, courtesy of the installation of the 250-hp 327's cam and heads (with 9.25:1 compression ratio). The new six was a 230-cubic-inch unit rated at 140 hp, the first deviation in Chevrolet six displacement since 1950. The new engine used seven main bearings for "exceptional sturdiness." Thin-wall block-casting techniques were applied to the six for the first time. Like all 1963 Chevrolet engines, the six featured positive crankcase ventilation.

Both standard engines were available with three-speed overdrive manual or Powerglide automatic transmissions. All 1963 Powerglides were of the aluminum-case design.

Impala's five 1963 styles featured a major styling facelift with the body side trailing lines of 1961-62 giving way to a blunter, chiseled look. Chevrolet said the car had "crisp formal lines in good taste for any occasion." Joining other auto manufacturers, Chevrolet adopted amber parking light lenses. This move brought on a stampede to paint lenses and bulbs of 1962 and earlier cars amber, much to the delight of bulb and bulb paint kit manufacturers.

A new feature of the 1963 Chevrolet's Fisher-built Unisteel body was 'air washed' rocker panels. Air and water were ducted from the cowl air intake to rocker panels, then back to an exit just ahead of the rear wheels. Dirt was flushed out this way, and drying was enhanced to prevent corrosion.

Impala Sport Coupe and Convertible models were offered with RPO Z03 Super Sport equipment, in combination with any power-team offered. All Super Sports did have heavy-duty coil springs this year. There were no 1963 Bel Air two-door hardtops, to the dismay of drag racers.

Swirl-pattern anodized aluminum trim panels within body side moldings and on the rear body cove panel continued to distinguish Su-

Impala Super Sports were frequently seen in a new 1963 color, Cordovan brown, as shown in *Showroom Album*.

per Sports. Red-filled, encircled SS letters were used with the Impala insignia on rear fenders, while the word Impala was spelled out within the trim strip below. 1963 Super Sports did not have the rear deck SS bar. New fourteen-inch full wheel covers were included in the $161 Super Sport equipment option. These were somewhat similar to the popular Olds Fiesta tri-blade caps of the 1950's. Plastic SS emblems filled the depressed center area.

All-vinyl upholstery featuring individual front bucket seats continued to be the SS interior's most obvious special feature. Seven combinations were offered for interior trim, including all-black (offered for Impala Sport Sedans with bench seats as well). Saddle-colored leather-grained vinyl was a new listing for 1963.

Super Sports with four-speed or Powerglide transmissions used a new, much longer console decorated with an SS emblem and a swirl-pattern insert. This year's locking console featured color-keyed carpeting inside, with an interior lamp in addition to the rear floor light unit.

Super Sport owners were reminded of their status by a special SS steering wheel emblem and the swirl-pattern insert on the instrument panel in front of them. The panel itself was totally new, with deeply recessed instruments and a glovebox twice as large as previous models. The grab bar was gone, but full instrumentation was still in the future. A new housing for the electric tachometer (extra cost with optional V-8's; standard with the M20 four-speed option on 409's) was mounted in the center of the panel top.

Although they looked heavier, 1963 Impala Super Sports were marginally lighter than their 1962 counterparts. SS buyers were increasingly tempted by luxury and comfort options this year, so there were a lot of 'loaded' 1963 Super Sports. Popular options were: Powerglide, power

New instrument panel design was used for 1963; grab bar was no longer available.

steering and brakes, the latest version of All-Weather air conditioning (except 400- and 425-hp 409's), power windows, power seats, dual rear antenna (one was a dummy), bumper guards and vinyl top covering—the accessory coup of the year! An AM-FM radio became available on January 21, 1963.

The instantly popular vinyl tops were first seen on a few luxury cars, such as Cadillac's Eldorado, in the mid-1950's. Buick put a white vinyl top on its mid-1962 Wildcat Sport Coupe. But it was the adaptation of the synthetic top to Chevrolet's Impala that really started the fad. Chevrolet offered vinyl roof covering only on the Impala Sport Coupe in 1963, in white or black with any of the twelve solid exterior colors. Two-tone combinations, with the top carrying the second color, were still available as well, in more than a dozen choices.

The rather heavy-looking and garish wire wheel cover used in thirteen- and fourteen-inch size on 1962 Corvairs and Novas was made available for full-size installation in 1963. It replaced the SS wheel cover on numerous Super Sports. Almost never seen, on the other hand, was the RPO PO5 factory chrome-plated wheel, which came with the small standard Chevrolet hub cap mounted. The author has never seen a 1963 Chevy with factory chrome wheels, but the 1963 small hub cap was very popular with owners of 1955-57 and 1961-62 Chevrolet models during the 1963 through 1965 period, at least in Kansas. They were used with black rims and narrow whitewalls, and were very definitely a fad for awhile.

Station wagon and 409-equipped Chevrolets had 8.00x14 Highway Rayon tires for 1963. SS Convertibles came standard with 7.50x14 tires, while Sport Coupes had 7.00x14 tires. Numerous fourteen- and fifteen-inch tires were optional. Wheels included 14x6JK rims for heavy-duty use.

Heavy-duty options listed for 1963 but not yet mentioned included special shock absorbers and a 70 amp-hour battery.

Chevrolet offered the Sport Coupe only in the Impala line for 1963, but production jumped anyway to 399,224 units, an increase of more than 75,000 from the combined 1962 Impala and Bel Air Sport Coupe production figure. Convertible production also increased, but not so dramatically, going from 1962's 75,719 cars to 82,659 for 1963. Super Sport equipment was installed on 153,271 Impala Sport Coupes and Convertibles during 1963 production. Converted to percentages, this represents an increase of seven percent, to a total of thirty-one percent of Impala production for the year.

1963 engine identification insignia found on front fenders. Emblems for 1962 are identical except 409 numerals are below crossed flags and vee. 1964 rear quarter SS emblem (bottom, right) did not have Impala symbol as had 1962 and 1963.

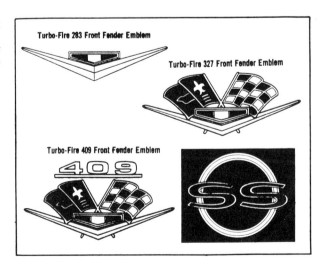

Though it was of little consequence to most buyers, Chevrolet made a major change in Chevrolet Super Sport merchandising for 1964. For the first time Impala Super Sports were actually classed as distinct models by the manufacturer. Since Chevrolet continued to list six-cylinder and V-8 models separately, there were four 1964 Impala Super Sport models: the six cylinder Sport Coupe model 1347, six-cylinder Convertible model 1367, V-8 Sport Coupe model 1447 and V-8 Convertible model 1467. Super Sport models listed for $161 more than comparable regular Impalas, an amount identical to the figure charged for the 1963 SS option.

Rumors that Chevrolet would introduce a 1964 SS four-door hardtop model proved unfounded (although Buick, Chrysler and Ford expanded their special models into full series during this same period).

Fisher's original 1961 Unisteel body was in its final revision this year. The restyle for 1964 was an excellent example of Chevrolet designers' ability to create a fresh new look within an established theme. The 1964 Super Sport's boxy, formal lines belied their smaller dimensions (they were two inches narrower and 0.6 inch shorter than their 1963 counterparts).

Fifteen solid Magic-Mirror acrylic colors and eleven two-tone combinations were offered to the 1964 Super Sport buyer. Goldenwood yellow, a very warm color, was offered for two-door models only in the Chevrolet line and required the black interior. Vinyl tops were offered in black or white again, while convertible tops were white unless black or beige was ordered (at no extra charge).

Pushing accouterments, Chevrolet said the 1964 Super Sports were "identified outside as SS bucket-seat Sportsters by distinctive emblems, trim and special wheel covers." For the first time, the Impala SS cars used totally different body side moldings. Impalas had narrow bright-metal moldings outlining the concave side sculpture, while Super Sports had

Chevrolet show car for 1964 World's Fair was Toronado convertible. It was more a customized 1964 Super Sport than an 'idea car.'

Console for 1964 Impala was designed as one unit, housing storage bins and transmission controls. This is a Powerglide version.

Impala SS Convertible looked sleeker but heavier for 1964. Lithe ready-to-race styling was gone.

single wide moldings running the length of the body along the sculpture's upper ridge. The now-familiar swirl-pattern anodized aluminum inserts began mid-way on the door and continued to the rear within the moldings. Traditional red-filled encircled SS emblems (without the Impala symbol this year) appeared within the sculpture toward the rear, with Impala spelled out in block letters just ahead. An additional swirl-pattern insert filled the cove area, which was painted body color on regular Impalas. The SS signature returned to the right side of the deck lid for 1964.

New, flat disc Super Sport wheel covers with elongated tri-blade spinners were part of the package, although many buyers opted for a newly designed simulated wire wheel cover (RPO PO2) instead.

Super Sport interiors were the plushest yet. Fully carpeted, all-vinyl-upholstered interiors continued to feature front bucket seats. Eight interior combinations were offered, including RPO 845a, white with aqua instrument panel, steering wheel and carpet; and RPO 845b, white with red instrument panel, wheel and carpet.

A revised full console for cars with Powerglide or four-speed now had the SS emblem on the console lid, with swirl-patterning around the shifter gate.

On the instrument panel, swirl-pattern inserts on the left side continued to distinguish Super Sports, although the 1964 steering wheel merely said "Impala," as did a new bright-strip crossing the right side of the instrument panel and glovebox door. Round SS emblems were mounted in brushed panels on the doors.

1964 Impala SS Sport Coupe interior used SS emblems on door panels, console.

Full-size Super Sport buyers still could not order engine vital-sign gauges for 1964. The electric tachometer, contained in a streamlined case for mounting atop the dash, was included with 300-hp 327 and all 409 installations and was optional with other V-8's.

There was little mechanical news for 1964 SS buyers. The standard engine in six-cylinder models continued to be the 140-hp Turbo-Thrift 230. The virtually unchanged 195-hp Turbo-Fire 283 V-8 was the standard engine for V-8 models. Optional V-8's were also nominally unchanged from 1963, including the 250-hp 327 (RPO L30), 300-hp 327 (RPO L74,) 340-hp 409 (RPO L33), 400-hp 409 (RPO L31) and 425-hp 409 (RPO L80).

Although the sort of drag-strip performance needed to stomp a mean 427 Ford or nasty 426 MoPar wasn't in the 409's realm anymore, Chevrolet did offer a little news in the gearbox charts. Two four-speeds were offered for 1964. The familiar M20 option now brought a redesigned box with 2.56:1 low gear and numerically lower ratios in second and third as well. The close-ratio 2.20:1 low box was now designated as RPO M21, and was offered for mechanical-lifter (400- and 425-hp) 409's. By ordering the M-21 box, the buyer could further choose 4.11 or 4.56:1 High Performance rear axle ratios, with Positraction. The 425-hp 409 came with 3.08 Performance Cruise gears in its rear axle as standard.

The extensive torque of the 409 was murder on standard three-speed manual transmissions; so for 1964 one of the two available four-speeds was a required option for the 400- and 425-hp engines. These were the only alternatives to Powerglide for the 340-hp 409 as well. The three-speed was retained as the standard box for the six, 283 and 327. Overdrive was available with either standard engine, and for the first time in quite awhile the 283 could be ordered with the 2.56:1 low four-speed. Powerglide automatic transmission was offered for all engines except the 400- and 425-hp 409's.

Many buyers selected Positraction for their rear axles this year. The anti-spin device gave increased traction by applying power to the wheel with the greatest traction automatically. Chevrolet literature recommended it for farmers, rural mail carriers, doctors, salesmen, hunters and boaters. Somehow they forgot drag racers, who were some of the prime customers for Positraction.

SS Coupes still came with 7.00x14 tires, while the 7.50x14 size continued to be standard on Convertibles. All 409's though, had 8.00x14 tires. Rarely seen, the RPO PO5 chromed wheels were still listed, along with a new chromed 14x6JK wheel option (RPO N98).

Full-size Chevrolets were notably absent from organized competition's victory circles during 1964, although impromptu street racers still had a healthy respect for any Chevrolet with the little chrome 409 numerals above its crossed flags on the front fenders. Ford was seizing the opportunity to grab the youth market with an ambitious program offering engine dress-up accessories kits, called Cobra Kits, for its small-block V-8's. Their "performance advisor," Ak Miller, ran a paid advertising column called "Ak's Flak" in enthusiast magazines, offering friendly technical advice for the 427 big-block boys concurrently. The mid-year Mustang (introduced in April 1964 as a 1965 model) from Ford and mid-year sensations such as the GTO from within General Motors further eroded Chevrolet performance prestige.

On the nation's top drag strips, MoPars were cleaning up the top stock classes. New quarter-mile heroes included the Dodge Ramchargers team, with Jim Thornton the top driver, and Roger Lindamood in his "Color Me Gone" Dodge. By the time the 1965 NHRA Winternationals rolled around, it had gotten so bad that Top Stock Eliminator went to famed Chevrolet handler Bill Jenkins, from York, Pennsylvania, driving a *Plymouth*.

The mighty 409, now one of the smallest top-displacement V-8's offered as full-size-automobile optional-performance equipment, did rack up one triumph in 1964. Chevrolet made what was very close to a clean sweep of the 1964 Pure Oil Performance Trials, placing its cars first in five of the six engine displacement categories. The 409 won in Class I, 401 to 440 cubic inches, by out-braking and out-distancing competitors on a gallon of gas. Although its combined points gave it the award, the 409 was drubbed in the acceleration contest by 421 Pontiacs, 427 Fords, 426 Dodges and even the 425 Buicks present. Two cars participated as a team in each class. For the Class I events, Chevrolet used a pair of 340-hp 409's, one with Powerglide and one with four-speed.

In the nation's automobile dealerships, the Chevrolet Super Sport won hands down, however. Of the 442,292 regular Chevrolet Sport Coupes and 81,897 Convertibles built in 1964, 185,325 (or about thirty-five percent) were Super Sport models. By comparison, Ford's comparable XL models accounted for 73,475 sales and Plymouth's Sport Fury production was miniscule.

Chevrolet was obviously reaching in the right direction with the Super Sport, and it was away from the acceleration and stock car market. "As you can see," said the 1964 *Sales Album*, "Chevrolet has gone all-out for owner prestige, comfort and room in '64 Impala Super Sports." Note that performance was not mentioned.

A fine array of new options helped the SS owner obtain the aforementioned comfort, prestige and room. Popular new options for 1964

Golden Gate Bridge provides back-drop for 1964 Impala SS Sport Coupe. Wheel covers were among the 1964 SS detail changes.

included AM-FM radios (for regular Chevrolets and Corvettes only, actually introduced in mid-1963); the Comfort-Tilt steering column (RPO N33) offering seven wheel positions; and a rarely seen Sports-styled dual-spoke, walnut-grained-rim steering wheel similar to the special Corvette wheel.

Comfort and appearance options once again outsold heavy-duty and performance options by a wide margin. A new performance option, a full-transistor ignition system (RPO K66), was made available for 409's in 1964. The Super Sport concept was turning away from performance so much that even the name was becoming something of a misnomer. Beginning with a new model in mid-1965, however, Chevrolet would eventually relieve the SS of its luxury pretensions and point it back toward the performance buyers who by that time would be greatly dissipated in the large-car market.

1964 engine insignia (l. to r.) for 283, 327, 409 V-8's.

CHAPTER THREE

Pocket Edition Super Sports by Chevy II 1962–1965

*F*our distinct and individual makes were marketed under the Chevrolet bow-tie emblem in 1962. These were the regular Chevrolet passenger car, the Corvair rear-engined compact, the Corvette two-passenger sports car and the new 'senior compact,' Chevy II.

The Chevy II, built on a 110-inch wheelbase, was in many ways the junior Chevrolet that the always 'different' Corvair could never hope to be. Subject of much speculation about its final form, rumors of the H-35 (Chevy II's pre-production code name) were widespread during 1961. When it made its debut as a 1962 car model, it offered the first four-cylinder Chevrolet engine since 1928, in addition to an optional 194-cubic-inch six. The 153-cubic-inch four was a lively engine that found little immediate acceptance, although it did spawn a small industry providing speed parts for its adaptation to lightweight circle-track burners. (The 153 would later provide a base for developing GM's 1977 four-cylinder sub-compact engines.)

Three Chevy II series were offered for 1962, with the top models in the Nova 400 line, consisting of a Sport Coupe (hardtop), Convertible and Station Wagon. The 153-four wasn't offered in this line. Nova 400's were nicely trimmed with their version of Chevrolet's ribbed rocker panel moldings and other bright trim. All 1962 Novas used thirteen-inch wheels. Sport Coupes and Convertibles used 6.50x13 tires; no other size was offered optionally.

Technically, Chevy II's major claim to fame was its then-unique single-leaf rear springs. The *Finger-Tip Facts* book for 1962 tersely explained: "Rear Hotchkiss-type rear suspension with Mono-Plate single-leaf rear springs. Single-leaf design eliminates inherent harshness found in multi-leaf springs, and contributes to a smoother, quieter, more cushioned ride."

Chevy II used a fully unitized Fisher body with bolt-on front fender skins for easy replacement.

No Super Sport equipment option was offered for the 1962 Chevy II, but the customer could order front bucket seats on Nova 400 two-door models. Heavy-duty springs, shocks and sintered metallic brake linings were offered also. These, along with the 3.36:1 rear axle with Positraction that could be specified for three-speed-equipped cars, could approximate

H-35 Convertible as it was proposed on December 1, 1960. Production Chevy II Nova convertible was nearly identical.

Chevy II was a fairly conventional car, its main innovative claim was Monoplate rear springs. Front suspension used independent high-mounted coil spring spherical joint design.

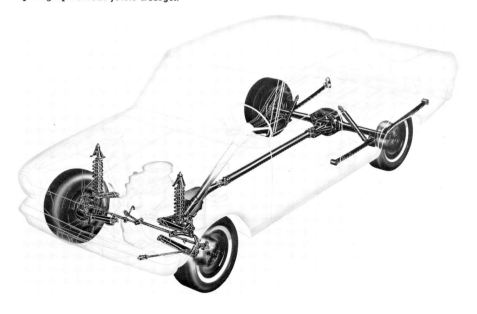

the larger Super Sports' handling in some respects, but brute acceleration was certainly lacking.

Hot-rodding, hobby of thousands of ingenious Americans, was an especially growing sport in the early 1960's. Chevrolet's light and high-revving V-8's became the heart of many hot rod specials. The new Chevy II was quickly spotted as a lightweight berth for the Chevy small-block V-8's. Chevrolet had been thinking along the same lines.

An engineer from Chevrolet Product Promotion Engineering told the author that the Chevy II was ". . . originally released on paper with a V-8. All the engineering work was done and the design existed. There was some corporate marketing decision that said 'thou shalt not build them in production with eights in '62.' I can only guess at the reason for that—probably because the BOP's [Buick-Olds-Pontiac] with their versions of the same car, had that 215 aluminum V-8 and the smallest V-8 we had was the 283, which although it was iron would run the ass off a 215."

Chevrolet's parts department quietly made the parts needed for conversion of the Chevy II to V-8 power available during mid-1962. Later in the year, part numbers appeared for 283 and 327 blocks specifically machined for Chevy II installation. These special blocks had modified oil filter housings (two inches higher) for a one-inch-shorter throw-away filter cartridge to give extra room for linkage on the left side of the V-8. Special exhaust manifolds, with outlet flanges turned thirty degrees to the rear, were also fitted. Other part numbers were listed for Chevy II V-8 oil pans, air cleaners, fuel pumps and lines; all designed to help shoehorn the small-block V-8 into the Chevy II's engine compartment. By the end of the year, special suspension parts, spindles and linkages were listed, too. The tiny 6.50x13 tires on 5½-inch rims continued to be the only available rolling stock for Chevy II's, however, by the parts book.

All 1962 Chevy II V-8's, then, were field conversions by dealers or individuals. The cost of having, say, a 300-hp 327 conversion executed could run as high as seventy-five percent of the list price of the whole $2,264 base-priced Nova 400 Sport Coupe. Few conversions were made at that rate.

Ray Brock wrote an article in *Hot Rod* illustrating the Chevy II's potential with small-block V-8 power. His test car was a Nova two-door carrying a 360-hp fuel-injected Corvette 327 which had been installed by Bill Thomas, who was just then developing his reputation for such

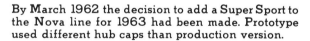

By March 1962 the decision to add a Super Sport to the Nova line for 1963 had been made. Prototype used different hub caps than production version.

handiwork by doing special high-performance work for Los Angeles-area Chevrolet dealers.

Using many of the available conversion parts, plus some of his own fabrications, Thomas dropped the Corvette engine into the Nova, backing it with a 2.20:1 low four-speed and 3.08 Positraction rear axle. This, Brock discovered, created a real screamer. The Nova shot to 60 mph, from rest, in 5.2 seconds; more than two seconds faster than a similarly equipped Corvette. The tiny thirteen-inch tires and Nova's single-leaf springs made for some touchy clutch work in bringing the car off the line without useless wheel hop and spin.

Following a run through nearby canyons, Brock commented, "With some chassis preparations and a good driver behind the wheel, the V8-Two could be quite the Grand Touring sedan." (Brock's prophecy would be born out by a Chevy II V-8 victory in Canada's 1964 Shell 4000 Rally.)

Chevrolet did authorize dealers to install the 360-hp fuel-injected Corvette engine in 1962 Novas for FX drag racing purposes. Don Nicholson campaigned one at the 1962 Winternationals.

Chevrolet enthusiasts were alerted to watch for assembly-line production of Novas with V-8's in 1963, but it was not to happen, just yet.

Novas for 1963 were very slightly restyled, with a bolder grille making the major appearance change. The big news for the year was the addition of Super Sport equipment (RPO Z03) to the Nova's option list. It was an instant success. By the end of the year 42,432 Super Sport kits had been installed on Nova Sport Coupes (out of the 87,415 total production) and Convertibles (which numbered 24,823 in Nova and Nova SS versions for the year). This represented more than thirty-seven percent of total production for the two body styles. Sport Coupe production increased by an incredible sixty-

1963 was only year for Chevy II Nova SS Convertible.

seven percent for the year compared to 1962, while Convertibles were built in only a marginally larger number, about 1,000 units more.

Super Sport equipment for the Nova 400 cost the same as for the larger Impala: $161. The package itself had some variations, of course. Most notably, the Nova SS carried a four-gauge (oil-amp-temp-fuel) instrument cluster in place of warning lights in the right opening of the instrument housing. Additional instrument panel features were a bright peak-molding

Bucket seats were standard on 1963 Nova SS. Since four-speed wasn't offered, only Powerglides had floor shift plate. Standard three-speeds had column shifts.

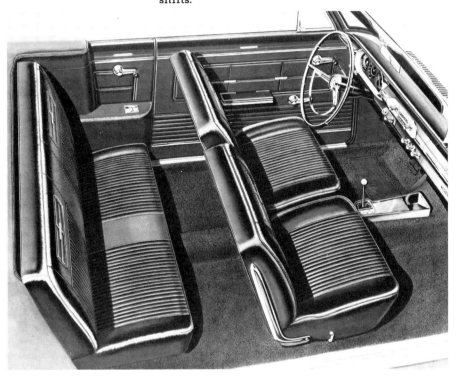

Nova SS Sport Coupe for 1963 shared Impala SS wheel covers. Six-cylinder was only power plant choice.

47

crossing the panel horizontally, with a Nova SS emblem on the lower right. An electric clock was standard. A Deluxe steering wheel, with an SS center cap, was also part of the deal. It was color-keyed to the car's all-vinyl interior, except on cars with black, red or saddle interiors. Black vinyl was reserved for SS use only. Individual front bucket seats and bright metal outside hinge moldings were included with SS equipment.

Nova Super Sports equipped with Powerglide used a "decorative floor-mounted range selector trim plate," to house the transmission shifter. A light at the rear of the semi-console provided rear-compartment floor lighting when doors were opened.

1965 Nova SS interior was nicely appointed.

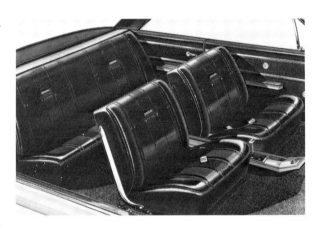

Top production engine for 1965 Chevy II was 300-hp 327. Special headers, block and other parts were used for Chevy II installation.

Exterior Super Sport identification was achieved by filling the Nova 400's full-length side trim strip with silver from mid-door to the rear. Special body peak moldings capped fenders and doors. The rear cove was painted silver, and a Nova SS badge bar was mounted therein. Nova SS emblems were placed on each rear fender as well. Wheel covers were borrowed from the 1963 Impala SS and were fitted to wheels with the "required additional equipment" 6.50x14 tires.

Most of the big Impala's appearance and comfort options were echoed on the Nova 400's option list. Nova also shared the new self-adjusting brake system with the larger Chevrolet. Many lubrication points on the Chevy II required attention only every 6,000 miles this year, due to the use of Teflon bushings and other advances that would soon be adopted industry-wide.

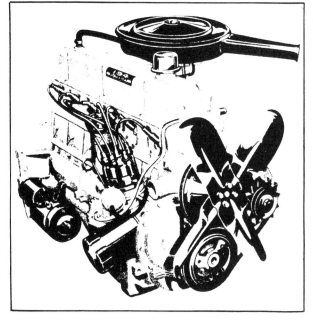

194-cubic-inch six was standard 1964 Nova engine.

Super Nova was shown at April 1964 New York Auto Show. Styling suggested 1966-67 Nova, but car was used to develop Camaro as well.

A 283-CU.-IN. V8 NEVER FOUND A HAPPIER HOME — We slung a big 195-hp 283-cubic-inch V8* into the Chevy II Nova Sport Coupe and now you'd think it was born that way.

This is the same Chevy II that spent a couple of happy years building up a following as one of the most wholesome things since brown bread. The one down-to-earth American car you wouldn't mind bringing home to mother or showing off to your friends. And the last car in the world you'd ever accuse of being pretentious. In short, a regular darb.

Now, with that V8 up front, Chevy II spends most of its time doing impressions of performance types. Give it a 4-speed all-synchro shift* and it's very close to being just that. After all, it started out with certain advantages: taut suspension, trim size, no-nonsense construction.

Is this any way for a nice, quiet, sturdy, sensible, unpretentious car like Chevy II to behave? Strangely enough, yes. Despite its new vigor, it's still a nice, quiet, sturdy, sensible, unpretentious car. With sharper teeth. Grrr. **CHEVY II NOVA** *CHEVROLET*

Chevrolet Division of General Motors, Detroit, Michigan   *Optional at extra cost

50

Although it was a pretty attractive package, the Nova Super Sport was still lacking in the power ratings. All 1963 factory-built Nova Super Sports had the same 120-hp 194-cubic-inch six introduced for 1962. This year, however, positive crankcase ventilation was added. There were plenty of heavy-duty options otherwise, including Positraction, front and rear springs, shock absorbers, clutches and sintered metallic brake linings of a new type.

A four-speed gearbox was not offered, though. Nova customers had to choose between the standard 'three-on-the-tree' manual or Powerglide. Both used a 3.08:1 axle as standard, with 3.36:1 cogs being listed for optional installation with the three-speed manual.

A few knowledgeable Chevrolet enthusiasts, equipped with large bank accounts, continued to build Chevy II 283 and 327 V-8's using parts purchased over-the-counter at their Chevrolet dealers. The total cost of a conversion, including kit and labor, could be $1,500 or more. It was prohibitive, to say the least. Most of the conversions that were done were for FX drag racing purposes. Finally, in 1964, the V-8 would become readily available in Chevy II's. But, there would still be perplexing news for Nova enthusiasts as the year opened.

Pity the poor Nova customer at the time of the 1964 model's introduction. He'd been waiting two years for V-8 power and it was finally available to all who chose to check the space on the order blank for RPO L32, the 195-hp 283 Turbo-Fire V-8. Best of all, it only cost him $108. But, there was astonishing bad news, too. The Nova Sport Coupe and Convertible and their Super Sport kits had been dropped from production!

Chevrolet management must have seen too many Chevy II sedans on the streets of Detroit in the hands of spinster-school-teacher types to understand that the car did have a performance-orientated, youthful following. But, happily, they heard the howls of protests from customers and dealers; by mid-year the Nova Super Sport Coupe (Model 0437), returned, along with a new Nova Super Sport Coupe (Model 0447). The convertible was gone forever, though, even as convertible production in some compact lines neared record highs (compact convertibles would account for nearly fifty percent of all soft top production for 1963).

External identification of a 1964 Nova SS was created by stripping off the regular Nova's body-side belt moldings and adding thin body peak moldings similar to the new Chevelle's along the upper edges. This produced a fresh, clean new look on the three-year-old body. At the rear, the cove area was painted silver. A Nova SS badge bar was affixed to the upper right corner of the cove. Bold Nova SS emblems went onto front fenders just ahead of the door for 1964. Wheel covers were of the 1963 Nova/Impala SS design, making an encore, and 6.50x14 tires were a required added-cost option again.

Nova could be ordered with a four-speed for first time in 1964. Backing the new 283 V-8, it was the M20 box with 2.56:1 low gear.

All Chevy II buyers benefited by the addition of the V-8, as larger brakes and stronger suspension components were fitted to all. Nova models were not sold with the tiny 153-cubic-inch four used for lesser Chevy II models. The standard Nova engine was once again the 194-cubic-inch 120-hp six. The 155-hp 230 six was a seldom chosen option. As in Chevelle installations, the 230 had chrome garnishes.

Inside, Nova Super Sports featured what had become traditional Super Sport appointments: individual front bucket seats, floor console for Powerglide or four-speed (offered with the 283 V-8 this year) transmissions, and all-vinyl upholstering. Gauges were included on SS cars.

Chevrolet cataloged fourteen solid colors for the Nova SS, along with eleven two-tone combinations. These were the same as larger Chevrolets, with the exception of Goldenwood yellow which was not listed at the beginning of the year. This color was reserved for hardtops in the larger lines; possibly it was extended to the Nova Super Sport as well when it made its debut mid-year, although no confirmation of this has been made.

A Canadian Chevrolet dealer, Maurice 'Moe' Carter, used a Nova V-8 two-door sedan to show that Ray Brock's 1962 prediction that a V-8 Chevy

Nova SS had cleaner version of Impala SS hub cap (right). Accessory wire wheel covers could be ordered at extra cost (left). Early cars may have used left-over 1964 Impala SS covers, as shown on car below.

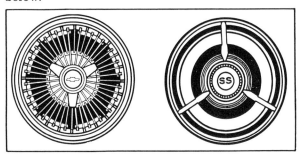

1965 Nova SS engine identification (l. to r.), 230 six-cylinder, 283 and 327 V-8's.

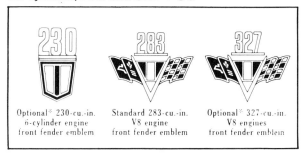

Optional* 230-cu.-in. 6-cylinder engine front fender emblem

Standard 283-cu.-in. V8 engine front fender emblem

Optional* 327-cu.-in. V8 engines front fender emblem

Nova SS for 1965 used full wheel covers, on standard 14-inch rims. 1965 had cleanest styling yet on original H-35 body.

II could be a GT-class performer was right on. Carter and Ian Worth, working as a driver/navigator team, pushed their Nova V-8 4,044 miles in six days to win their class in the really rough 1964 Shell 4000 Rally. They also placed second over-all in the event, which crossed Canada from west to east that April. Class 4, which found the Carter/Worth team victorious, was for cars of 244.16 cubic inches and larger. The Nova team bested eleven finishing cars, leaving nine DNF's in their wake.

The Shell Rally Nova was equipped with most factory heavy-duty parts, including four-speed, heavy-duty clutch, 3.36:1 Positraction rear axle and 7.00x14 tires on six-inch rims. Other modifications were minor, except for the addition of armor plate protection for the oil pan and gas tank with its reserve backup tank used for '400 miles to the fill-up' cruising. Although the rally was mostly run by time and distance regulations, there were five 'speed' sections included where the cars could cut loose and cover ground as rapidly as conditions permitted.

Chevrolet announced the Nova victory with a screened black-on-orange matte-paper folder telling of the Shell 4000 and Nova's success there. On the last fold a small photo of the 1964 Nova Super Sport Coupe was included, making this one of the very few items of 1964 Chevrolet literature to include the Nova SS Coupe.

The late introduction of the Nova Sport Coupe models cut deeply into sales, as did the hot-selling new Chevelle Super Sports. Still, 30,827 1964 Nova two-door hardtops were built of which 10,576, or thirty-five percent, were Nova Super Sports.

Nova Super Sport Coupes were offered right from the beginning of 1965, but sales remained sluggish as the slightly higher priced Chevelle SS (about $100 separated list prices of V-8 Chevelle and Nova Sport Coupe models) grabbed the attention of American car buyers. By the end of 1965's model run, 28,380 Nova Sport Coupes would be built, including 9,100 Nova Super Sports representing thirty-two percent of 1965 Sport Coupe production.

Chevrolet listed two Super Sport models for the 1965 Nova, the six-cylinder Sport Coupe, model 11737, and its V-8 equivalent, model 11837. They were mildly facelifted with new color-accented, bright lower-body moldings in conjunction with wheelhouse and rear fender lower moldings.

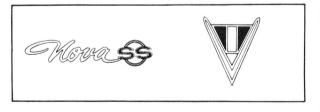

1965 Nova SS rear quarter emblem (left). 1964 engine insignia for 283 V-8 (right).

Showroom Album's silhouette of the 1965 Nova SS illustrates clean design. Rear cove was refreshingly new, too.

The Nova SS emblem moved to the rear fenders this year, and the previous rear SS badge bar was moved up out of the cove area on the right. Body crown moldings were abbreviated for 1965, beginning at the door opening and extending to the rear where they turned down. The chrome hood windsplit running down the hood center, used on 1964 Novas and Nova Super Sports, continued only on the SS for 1965 as standard equipment. The cove area was redesigned at the rear to use a ribbed filler containing taillights and the Chevrolet emblem, with silver paint filling the balance of the area below.

Unique SS full wheel covers apparently reached production sometime after the beginning of 1965 assemblies; some early Super Sports may have used the flat-faced 1964 Impala SS fourteen-inch covers. Tires were 6.95x14 on five-inch rims on Nova SS cars with V-8 power.

Under the hood the big news was the availability of the 327-cubic-inch Chevrolet V-8 for Chevy II. It was offered in the familiar 250- and 300-hp (RPO L30 and L74 production was just 324 and 319 respectively) tunes. The standard V-8 continued as the 195-hp 283, while the four-barrel, dual-exhaust 220-hp version of this famed Chevrolet engine was added to the Nova option list mid-year. The 140-hp 230 six-cylinder continued as an option for six-cylinder models (without its chrome dress-up kit, however), with the 194-cubic-inch 120-hp six remaining the standard Nova and Nova SS engine. (The 153-cubic-inch four remained in production for Chevy II 100-series sedans; reportedly only 367 were built with the tiny power plant in 1965.)

Three-speed manual gearboxes with 3.08 axles were standard in six-cylinder and base V-8 Novas, with 3.36:1 gears optional. The 327 V-8's used a stronger standard three-speed, with 3.07 gears (unless the optional 3.31 "special purpose or mountain" gear set was specified). All V-8's could be ordered with a new 4.56:1 low M-20 type four-speed and 2,014 were. Powerglide automatic transmission was offered with any engine choice, and Positraction was available for any rear axle specified.

At mid-year Chevrolet discontinued the 3.31:1 option for the 327 and made a 2.73:1 gear set standard with 250-hp 327's. At the same time, the new fully synchronized optional M13 three-speed manual gearbox was extended to Chevy II buyers ordering the 327 V-8. Then, shortly after the February 1965 revisions, yet another transmission choice, RPO M15, was announced. This was the M13 box with a different, 2.84:1 low gear, set of internal ratios.

Heavy-duty 1965 Nova SS options not already mentioned included dual exhausts for the 250-hp 327 V-8, sintered metallic brake linings, special front and rear suspension components and a tachometer for V-8 models.

All 1965 Chevy II's were distinguished by a new, cleaner front end ensemble with bumper-mounted parking/turn-signal lamps.

The first-series Nova Super Sports are rather rare today, with the V-8 models being especially sought-after by today's collectors, along with the one-year (1963) six-cylinder Nova Super Sport Convertible.

Nova SS script moved back to rear quarter panel on the 1965 Nova SS, after spending 1964 on the front fenders.

CHAPTER FOUR

Chevelle, Instant SS Success
1964–1965

*T*here was no lack of confidence in Chevelle's potential. A 1964 catalog announced the premier models of the new Chevrolet line with this statement: "First year out and Malibu Super Sport has everything going for it."

Chevelle was the third new line of automobiles introduced by Chevrolet in four years. Corvair had made its debut as a 1960 model and Chevy II had arrived in 1962. By far the most conventional of the trio, Chevelle signaled an end to General Motors' technically innovative interlude of the early sixties. It had been an exciting time; with the release of the rear-engined Corvair, turbo charged Oldsmobile Cutlass Jetfire (and Corvair Spyder), slant-four-with-transaxle Tempest, V-6 Buick Skylark and the aluminum V-8 shared by the compact GM cars.

Everything about the Chevelle was tried and true. Chevrolet said, "It's freshly created, yet includes all of Chevrolet's traditional value and reliability." Perhaps that was the secret of its success. Chevelle outsold its lower-priced first cousins in almost every instance during 1964. Only the Corvair convertible and Chevy II two-door sedan out-paced comparable Chevelle models that year.

Chevelle's Super Sport was a perfect entry into a market rapidly expanding into younger age brackets. At the beginning of the year, anyway, Chevelle was an ideal package for the youth market. (Some clouds would appear on the horizon midway through the year, as will be seen shortly, as the thunderheads of a performance storm swelled above Pontiac and Lansing.)

The only introductory base V-8 offered for eight-cylinder Chevelles was Chevrolet's 283. It had become something of a national institution by 1964. The Chevrolet small-block V-8 was favored by hot rodders and street-performance enthusiasts. Among young Americans, these engines were the hearts of their favorite cars—Chevrolets of the 1955-57 era. Thousands of youthful drivers cherished their peppy, taut 'little' Chevies. In many cases, these same young people were just reaching the new-car market's entry levels of income.

For them, the Chevelle was a natural. It seemed as though Chevrolet's engineers had gathered around a table and hammered out a new car based on the question: What would we get if we built a new version of the '55-'57 Bel Air for today's youth market? The new car would incorporate the 1955-57's comparatively compact dimensions; but would also include the latest performance-type options, such as four-speed manual transmissions, engine gauges and bucket seats, which were being installed as after-market items on thousands of earlier Chevrolets. Under the hood would be young America's most acclaimed engine, the Chevrolet Turbo-Fire 283 V-8. Just for old time's sake, the optional four-barrel dual-exhaust version would be rated at 220 hp—exactly the rating known to one and all as the figure quoted for 1957's famous 'Power-Pak' 283.

Even the styling would be reminiscent of the 1955 Chevy—crisp and rectangular and clean. The Chevelle was a fine heir to the 'classic' 1955-57 Chevrolets.

Chevelles were built in four series for 1964, with a total offering of thirteen models. The new body was based on the Fisher 'A' substructure shared with Oldsmobile's F-85, Pontiac's Tempest and Buick's Skylark. All used curved side-window glass and a number of minor innovations such as adhesive-compound window-glass seals in place of rubber channels. Chevelle's chassis used coil springs on all four corners. Frames were of the perimeter type (coming for big Chevrolets in 1965). Four variations of the basic frame were used on the different Chevelle models. A front stabilizer bar was standard with the modified long-and-short-arm suspension. Rear axles were positioned by four links, and the axle assemblies were of the Salisbury type.

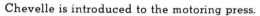

Chevelle is introduced to the motoring press.

Top models of the Chevelle line were the Malibu Super Sports: Sport Coupe models 5737 (six-cylinder) and 5837 (V-8), and Convertible models 5767 (six-cylinder) and 5867 (V-8). The regular body styles included the Sport Coupe and Convertible, plus a sedan and two four-door station wagons. Baseline Chevelles were in the 300 series, which included two models not found elsewhere: the rather racy-looking two-door station wagon (which had a Nomad-like door post) and a two-door sedan.

The two-door wagon could have served as a basis for revival of a fancy Nomad-type wagon (the 1955-57 Nomads were already on their way to cult-car status by 1964) if Super Sport equipment had been offered for it. But, buried in the 300 line, the two-door wagon was almost unknown. Just 2,710 units were built for 1964.

The 300 series Chevelle two-door sedan was also something of an enigma. It had a different roof line from the other A-body GM intermediates (which used doors with window frames and a divider post but carried the basic roof line of hardtop styles). During mid-1964 and later, Pontiac, Buick and Olds sports-equipped intermediates could be ordered in two-door sedan styles; but not Chevelle. The Chevelle two-door sedan was restricted to the lowest line and somehow never caught on with the speed set.

Chevelle's fourth series was like another dream come true for American youth. Chevrolet's stylish 1959-60 El Camino passenger car-pickups were hot items on used car lots in the early 1960's, and their demise was frequently lamented. Then came the new Chevelle, with a reborn El Camino, offered in basic or Custom variations. It was an immediate success. Right from the start, El Caminos could be ordered with all of the Super Sport model's special items. Custom El Caminos even used the SS car's wheelhouse, rocker molding and rear fender molding.

Chevelle Super Sport equipment on the real SS models included most of the features found on Impala Super Sports. All-vinyl interior upholstery, with front bucket seats, was standard. A floor console came with four-speed- or Powerglide-equipped Super Sports. Complete Malibu SS emblems were found on the glovebox and just the double S on door panels.

Chevelle Super Sports were embraced immediately by young Americans. Sport Coupe version was most popular.

Seven Chevelle interiors were offered; two of these were only for Super Sports—black vinyl (RPO 714) and white vinyl with red instrument panel, steering wheel and carpeting (RPO 729).

To many buyers, a meaningful mark of the Super Sport's status was the replacement of the standard Malibu warning-light cluster, with a four-gauge unit (temperature, ammeter, oil pressure and fuel). An optional tachometer could be ordered to replace the clock in the smaller center circle of the instrument cluster housing. When such an installation was made, the clock was replaced with a universal-mount pod-type timepiece mounted on top of the dash pad at the center (it was the same clock offered as a dealer-installed accessory on Chevelle's lower lines).

Exterior identification was made by the use of Malibu SS emblems on rear quarter panels and by a small SS insignia on the deck lid lip, to the right. Chevelle Super Sports did not use a silver-painted cove area at the rear, although big '64 Chevrolet and Nova SS cars did.

Malibu Super Sports had cleaner bright-metal highlights than did conventional Malibus in 1964. There was as much, if not more, shiny trim, though, if you looked for it. Super Sports had bright rocker moldings, wheelhouse moldings and an extension along the lower rear fender edge creating an unbroken trim line from front to rear. Another thin bright-trim strip capped the Super Sport's upper body edge. Regular Malibu used the rocker panel chrome, and had an additional full-length beltline trim strip. The Super Sports looked cleaner, but suffered from the lack of this strip. Door dents were the bane of Chevy Super Sport owners (as well as owners of other GM cars) during the era of clean, flaring body side panels.

Chevelle Super Sports were available in fifteen solid colors, including the SS-only Goldenwood yellow. Eleven two-tone combinations were offered for the Sport Coupe. Convertibles came with white tops; black or tan could be specified at no extra cost.

The Chevelle SS shared the larger Impala Super Sport's full, flat-faced fourteen-inch wheel covers. Tires were 6.50x14's. SS equipment

Malibu SS Convertibles featured clean-side styling; beautiful to look at but sadly prone to damage.

added $162 to the bottom line of a Chevelle sales contract when compared to a Malibu with the same body style.

Standard engine in six-cylinder Chevelle models was the 120-hp Hi-Thrift 194, borrowed from Chevy II. Positive crankcase ventilation (PCV) was standard on all Chevelle engines. An optional six was also cataloged as the 155-hp Turbo-Thrift 230 (RPO L61). The Chevelle 230 was based on the full-size Chevrolet's base power plant, but was rated at fifteen more horse-power. The extra ponies were corralled by the use of a "general performance" camshaft in place of the 'economy grind' camshaft found in sixes destined for the bigger Chevrolets.

There had been a lot of interest in six-cylinder intermediates in the first few years of the sixties. Pontiac was working on developing its overhead-cam six about the time Chevelle came out, while Chrysler's slant-six and some Ford sixes had been issued with factory hop-up kits. Chevrolet evidently envisioned the 230 as the sports engine for six-cylinder Chevelle buyers. Extra detailing was lavished on the optional engine. Chrome was applied to the valve cover, oil breather cap, dipstick, fuel and vacuum lines, and the air-cleaner top plate. (Collectors sometimes get pretty excited at finding one of these 'chrome' engines under the hood of a well-used Chevelle. Rumors have been circulated that these were introductory or show car engines, but it just isn't so.)

Early 1964 sales literature and the 1964 *Finger-Tip Facts* book indicated that a six-cylinder emblem identical to that used on contemporary Novas would evidence six-cylinder power plants in Chevelles. Production cars seem to have been issued with no engine insignia at all if the 194-cubic-inch six was installed, while 230-equipped cars had rectangular emblems with a checkerboard design and engine displacement numerals.

Interior of **Malibu SS** followed the theme set by larger models. Shifter had reverse lock-out.

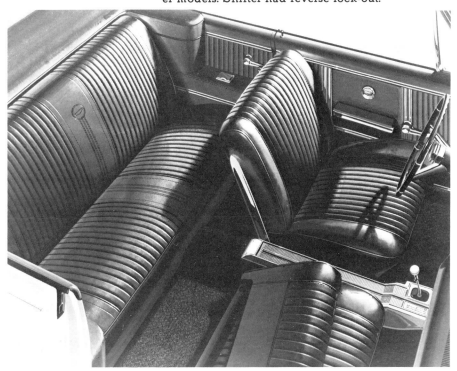

The base V-8, as mentioned previously, was the 195-hp version of Chevrolet's well-known 283. The four-barrel dual-exhaust 283 was available as option RPO L77. Both versions used 9.25:1 compression. Gross horsepower ratings were shown on decals affixed to air-cleaner covers on all 1964 Chevrolet products. Few modifications were necessary to adapt the 283 to Chevelle's chassis. Exhaust headers were revised, though, with exit openings at the rear instead of the center as had been traditional Chevrolet V-8 practice.

A new M20 four-speed, with 2.56:1 low, was optional with V-8 power in Chevelles. Rear axle gearings with a 3.08:1 ratio was specified for all four-speed installations and all other engine/transmission combinations as well. Optional ratios included 3.36:1 for the 155-hp six, Powerglide or three-speed manual. Overdrive was optional with any engine, using a 3.70:1 general performance axle. Powerglide could also be specified with any engine.

Motor Trend road tested one of the first Malibu Super Sports delivered to the Los Angeles area. That Sport Coupe was ideally equipped, in the eyes of many young Chevrolet enthusiasts, with the 220-hp 283, four-speed and AM radio. Not-so-common options on the test Chevelle were power steering, brakes and windows; and the new woodgrain steering wheel. The options, which also included whitewalls, heater, seat belts and a few minor items brought the *Motor Trend* test car's list price to $3,462.35. This was more than $800 over the Malibu Super Sport Coupe base price—and the *Motor Trend* test car didn't even have the new optional Comfort-Tilt steering column (AM-FM wasn't extended to Chevelle buyers this year).

The test drivers found the Chevelle offered medium-high performance, with 60 mph from a dead stop in 9.7 seconds. Quarter-mile times were around 17.5 seconds at 80 mph or better. This wasn't screamer performance in 1964, but it was good enough for many buyers desiring a sporty and fairly quick car that didn't compromise fuel consumption or comfort.

Rating their Chevelle as very good in almost every category, the *Motor Trend* crew admitted they weren't very excited by the new car, although they did report it caused a lot of comment and interest during the test. The Chevelle was, in fact, exactly what Chevrolet tradition dictated a car should be. It offered an excellent compromise of performance, handling, ride and comfort characteristics at a very reasonable price.

Sales got off to a good start and continued at a brisk pace throughout the model year. Super Sport production accounted for an astonishing 48.7 percent of Chevelle Convertible and Sport Coupe production in 1964. The combined total of Super Sports in both styles was 76,860. During the year,

Finger-Tip Facts illustration of '64 Malibu SS demonstrated clean side panels.

production lines building Chevelles intermixed with other GM intermediate and full-size cars devoted as much as fifteen percent of their production to the new Chevrolet line in an effort to meet demand.

There were some bad moments for Chevelle's engineers during 1964, even as their new car found its niche in the market with great success. Chevrolet's sister GM Division, Pontiac, had finally given in to a natural desire to stuff the big 389-cubic-inch V-8 under the hood of its intermediate Tempest; thus creating the first of the legendary GTO Pontiacs. Oldsmobile quickly fired a return salute with the 442 Cutlass, using a hop-up kit for the 330-cubic-inch V-8 (during 1964, 4-4-2 stood for four-speed, four-barrel and dual exhausts). Buick was a little slower on the draw, but would soon unveil a 401-cubic-inch Skylark Gran Sport (as a 1965 model).

The 326-cubic-inch Tempest V-8 had been stiff competition for the 1964 Chevelle right from the beginning; fitted with the 389, the Tempest GTO outshone any Chevrolet passenger car in performance.

Chevrolet engineers chafed at GTO's success. They hadn't even been able to install the 327 Chevrolet V-8 in their Chevelle, since the corporation's antiracing policy prohibited engines in excess of 326 cubic inches for intermediates (Pontiac's 326 was really around 336 cubic inches, interestingly enough). But, in the face of the challenge by the maverick Pontiac Division, pressure was brought to bear and the 327 was OK'd for Chevelle installation in mid-1964. Original press reports indicated that all carbureted 327-cubic-inch RPO engines would be offered in Chevelle, right up to the Corvette's 365-hp version. This proved to be wishful thinking, at least for the time being. Factory experimental 365-hp 327 Chevelles were apparently tested, since a rumor was circulated that a Chevelle so equipped had shown itself capable of 0-60 mph times of less than six seconds. A few F/X 365-hp dragsters were built.

The 327 V-8's that *were* offered in mid-1964 for Chevelle were the 250- and 300-hp versions. These made fairly impressive street performers, readily capable of dicing with Ford's sensational new Mustang, at least. To really get into the big leagues, though, Chevelle needed big-block power. Rumors of a hopeful nature accompanied the Chevelle's birth. They said that a new big-block based on the fabulous 1963 Daytona Mystery Engine 427 would power the Chevelle by mid-1964. Actually, more than a year would pass before any big-block Chevelles were built, and it would be the 1966 model year before they went into volume production.

Chevelle achieved a lower and longer appearance for 1965 by a careful facelift of the 1964's A-body design. Actual length increase was 2.7

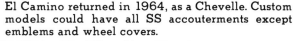

El Camino returned in 1964, as a Chevelle. Custom models could have all SS accouterments except emblems and wheel covers.

inches, due to the new vee'd grille and front bumper used in 1965. The extended hood line gave Chevelle "a forward rake at the vehicle centerline," the 1965 *Engineering Features* book explained. Softer springs resulted in a decreased overall height of 1.3 inches on most models.

Underbody and chassis refinements were minor on 1965 Chevelles. New rubber mounts for the radiator support and increased insulation were featured. Thick jute matting and asphalt mastic sheeting over the passenger floor area (applied to Chevelles since mid-1964) effectively dampened road noises. Rear cove trim was redesigned for 1965, and backup lamp units moved down to the bumper bar.

Malibu SS exterior trim for Malibu Sport Coupes (models 13737, six-cylinder, and 13827, V-8) and Convertibles (models 13767, six-cylinder, and 13867, V-8) was revised. Rocker moldings were different, and although wheelhouse moldings were continued, the lower rear fender bright trim

Prototype 1965 Malibu SS Sport Coupe, with simulated rear brake cooling ducts, which were deleted for production. This is a study shot for the 1965 showroom poster.

1965 Malibu SS Convertible leads the way for Chevrolet's 1965 stars. Corvair and Impala SS follow, while Corvette joins parade from its own path.

strip from 1964 was deleted this year. Regular Malibus had standard bright wheelhouse moldings, too, for 1965.

Malibu SS insignia appeared on rear fenders again, but engine identification for the 230 six and V-8's moved ahead of the wheelhouse on front fenders. A new badge emblem was used for the 230.

Super Sport recognition was added to the frontal view by the simple addition of flat black paint to background portions of the anodized aluminum Chevelle grille. (Like so many Chevrolet styling touches, the blacked-out Chevelle Super Sport grille started a fad, with imitations and variations appearing on thousands of owner-modified older Chevrolets and, eventually, on competitors' grilles.)

At the rear, the cove panel was redesigned with a new SS emblem at the right. Satin black paint was used here to form a distinctive band around the cove area (except on black cars, which had silver accent bands). Twelve exterior color choices were offered, including the new and rather strange Evening Orchid metallic. A new and rarely seen option was RPO CO8 black vinyl roof covering for Sport Coupes. Chrome divider strips at the base of the rear roof pillars were used on two-tone and vinyl-topped Sport Coupes.

A fresh look in wheel covers was created for the 1965 Chevelle SS by adding a very stylized tri-bar overlay, with red-filled troughs, to the deluxe Chevelle wheel cover. At the center was a large textured-black circle with SS lettering. All Super Sports had 6.95x14 tires as standard equipment.

Early 1965 Chevelle sales material showed Super Sports with a pair of stacked "rear fender accent moldings" just ahead of the rear wheelhouse. They were suggestive of cooling vent ports for the rear brakes. Apparently they were dropped before production began, since there have been no reports of any 1965 Chevelles with the moldings in place.

Chevelle enthusiasts found a very slightly revised instrument panel inside the 1965 SS cars. It was a subtle two-tone design; the darker upper color was for reduction of glare. Instrument-cluster styling featured a new

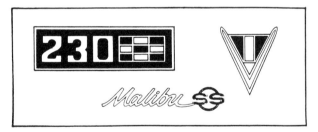

1964 Chevelle engine insignia, (l. to r.) 230 optional six-cylinder, 283 V-8. Rear quarter emblem for 1965 Malibu SS is below.

Chicago Auto Show car was 1965 El Camino Surfer I roadster pickup. It was displayed with a Chevy-powered drag boat. This was first and only 1965 El Camino to have 396 Mark IV engine.

trim plate with a bright center line carrying some of the switch and accessory lettering. As in 1964, the trim plate was made of plastic, plated with anodized aluminum powder. Instruments were recessed deeper into the 1965 panel to further reduce glare problems. Super Sport Malibus continued to feature a full complement of real gauges in the right-hand instrument panel bezel. As in 1964, the addition of a tachometer displaced the clock centered in front of the driver, necessitating the use of the Custom Feature style pod-clock on top of the panel pad. Glovebox trim was revised slightly, but continued to feature the SS logo. Door panels carried stylized die-cast Chevrolet bow-tie emblems this year in place of SS discs.

Super Sports standard front bucket seats were upholstered in a corduroy-patterned vinyl early in the year. A textured vinyl soon replaced it. Cushion and backrest panels were darker in tone than seat bolsters and

El Camino Custom for 1965 used SS body trim, even had SS-style hub caps with different centers. Inside, buckets were optional.

1965 Malibu SS was even more devoid of chrome than 1964 version. Black accent band on rear panel signaled SS equipment from a distance.

facings, except on black and white combination interiors. Seat inserts were of a new broad-pleat stitching pattern.

Powerglide and four-speed cars continued to feature a floor console with Super Sport equipment. Eight interior colors were cataloged for 1965.

Despite Chevrolet's avowed policy of confining high-performance equipment to over-the-counter parts sales for racers serious enough about performance to build their own engines, Chevelle did have a hot new engine for 1965. It was RPO L79, a 350-hp Turbo-Fire 327 V-8. The 1965 *Engineering Features* book described it thusly: ". . . this new engine will have the same components as the 365-hp, 327-cubic-inch V-8 offered for Corvette in 1964, except for a new high-lift camshaft with hydraulic lifters, chrome-plated rocker covers, chrome plated air cleaner with dual air horns, four quart oil pan, and exhaust manifolds with rear outlet."

The 350-hp 327, as delivered in a Malibu SS (or a straight Malibu, ordered by really serious street racers who begrudged the SS car's extra fifty pounds of weight) was one of the really hot street setups in 1965. Although it was described and pictured in the Chevelle section of the 1965 *Engineering Features* book, the 350-hp 327 wasn't listed in Chevelle sales literature or specification charts until mid-year. Production was strongly influenced by ads which appeared in February 1965 issues of several enthusiast publications announcing the engine, and 6,021 350-hp 1965 Chevelles were built.

More commonly found optional 327 V-8's were the 250-hp (RPO L30) with 36,261 built, and the 300-hp (RPO L74) that was installed in 13,593 1965 Chevelles. Basically unchanged, the 327 featured new oil-wetted air cleaners and more durable dipsticks among their minor modifications. The standard engine in Chevelle's V-8 models was the 195-hp 283. The 283 op-

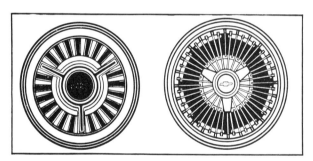

1965 Malibu Super Sports came with full wheel cover at left, wire wheel caps (right) were popular extra-cost option.

Malibu SS Convertible for 1965 was lower than 1964 version.

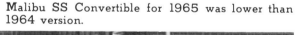

tional V-8 (RPO L77), rated at 220-hp, was missing at the beginning of the 1965 model year, but it would return with the February 15, 1965, engine application revisions for Chevelle, Nova and the big Chevv

Chevelle's standard six for 1965 remained the 120-hp 194. The optional six (RPO L26) was down-rated to 140 hp from 1964's 155-hp rating. The 1965 version carried the economy grind camshaft. Heads were revised to provide better cooling at the center exhaust ports, and improved cylinder head gaskets made a better seal. The chrome garnishes of 1964 were gone this year.

Transmission choices for 1965 were the standard three-speeds, overdrive for sixes and 195-hp V-8's, Powerglide with any engine except the 350-hp 327, and the M20 four-speed (39,092 produced) with any available V-8. Fully synchronized three-speeds became optionally available in mid-February, with the M15 box using a 2.85:1 low for the 283 and the M13 heavy-duty transmission with a 2.41:1 low for 327's.

Rear axle ratios ranged from 2.73:1 cogs for the 250-hp 327 with Powerglide, to 3.36:1 gears for 283's with manual boxes. The mid-year 350-hp 327 came with a 3.31:1 rear axle. Positraction was offered for any axle, as usual.

During 1965 Chevelles started appearing with the hot 350-hp 327, which used 365-hp Corvette parts in conjunction with a wild hydraulic cam to make Chevelle a street-screamer.

Chevelle continued to share most of the big Chevrolet's comfort, appearance, safety and heavy-duty options. A mid-year adapter kit was released to install the new AM-FM Multiplex stereo system in Malibu and Malibu SS Convertibles.

The 1965 Super Sport Chevelles were every bit as successful as their 1964 counterparts, accounting for 81,812 of the 152,650 production 1965 Chevelle Sport Coupes and 19,765 Convertibles built. Super Sports again amounted to nearly fifty percent of total Malibu series production.

Although not counted as a true Super Sport, the popular Custom El Camino continued to feature many of the Malibu Super Sport's distinctive touches. The SS body moldings were used, and even SS wheel covers with different centers were part of the Custom trim group. Bucket seat interiors and the full range of Chevelle accessories were offered for El Camino installation. The unique Chevelle two-door wagon continued in production for 1965 as well, but was still confined to the lower ranks and not offered with many of the Super Sport goodies.

There was one more 1965 Chevelle model that came out mid-year. Carrying an earth-shaking 375-hp 396 from the new Turbo-Jet Chevrolet engine family, this Chevelle was limited to 201 units for 1965. Most people never knew it existed. Except for sheet metal, it was closely related to later Chevelles.

1965 engine insignia, (l. to r.) 230 optional six-cylinder, 283 and 327 V-8's.

Optional 230-cu.-in. 6-cylinder engine front fender emblem

Standard 283-cu.-in. V8 engine front fender emblem

Optional* 327-cu.-in. V8 engines front fender emblem

Protect-O-Plate

Beginning in 1965, Chevrolet furnished each new-car owner with a 'Protect-O-Plate' card which was imprinted at the factory with his name and address, his car's vehicle identification number, engine number, production information and coded RPO equipment data. The Protect-O-Plate can be a valuable authentication guide to the SS restorer, since it documents year, model, engine displacement and most of the RPO options delivered on the car from the factory.

Single-letter codes were used for most RPO options. The decoding lists may be found in Chevrolet parts books. The SS owner possessing an original Protect-O-Plate for his car should consult his local Chevrolet dealer's parts department for assistance in decoding the RPO data. The plates duplicated and supplemented information found on firewall data plates of 1965-72 Chevrolets. The firewall plate usually carried body style and paint code information but did not list RPO codes.

The vehicle identification number may be broken down to authenticate the car's series, model designation and body style and, in later years, the base engine. Part of this number is the sequential number of the car at the assembly plant where it was built. During years when Super Sports were designated models, the identification number (VIN) can verify that the car was actually a Super Sport. Cars carrying SS option packages will carry the basic series identification number for that model, however.

Chevrolet used several revised versions of the Protect-O-Plate through 1972. Subsequent cars have most of the information, including RPO codes, on their firewall data plates.

First Protect-O-Plate, for 1965, looked like this.

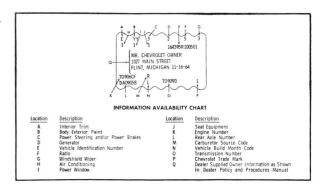

1966-68 Protect-O-Plates used this layout.

CHAPTER FIVE

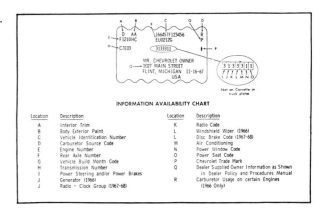

Impala Super Sports at the Peak 1965–1966

Chevrolet's full-size offerings were almost the freshest cars from that GM division in a decade. As in the great year of 1955, the body design was dramatically new. For 1965, Chevrolets appeared heavier and larger. A semi-fastback roof line on the Sport Coupe was a radical change from prior years. Higher rear fender kick-ups over the rear wheelhouses gave the cars a more substantial appearance. A high, thin bumper was used at the front, with a valance panel (formed from bumper-grade steel) finished in galvanized silver enclosing the lower grille, below the bumper.

Six taillight assemblies were located high on the 1965 Chevrolet's deck lid and fender wraparounds, above a sturdy three-piece bumper. The outboard light units, on the body structure, were visible even with the deck lid raised.

A new Girder Guard perimeter frame was used with a semi-unit body assembly for 1965. The front tread was widened two inches, while rear tread was expanded a full three inches. Chevrolet called it Wide-Stance design; somehow it didn't catch the imagination as well as Pontiac's Wide-Track of 1959.

The full-size 1965's were dimensionally larger in almost all measurements, although wheelbase remained at 119.0 inches. Overall length, at 213

69

inches, was up three inches, while the new bodies were 2.6 inches wider than the 1964 version.

Curved side-window glass was new for the year. Numerous advances aimed at a quieter, smoother ride were incorporated. The frame was now attached at twelve points on coupes and fourteen points on convertibles. A new front-end assembly 'floated' on rubber biscuits, rather than using metal shims as in the past.

But, the new engines developed for this new Chevrolet body and frame missed the introductory parties in September 1964 and there was little news on the power-train charts. The sophisticated new power-teams would finally show up in February 1965, however.

Two-door hardtop and convertible bodies were again reserved exclusively for Impala and Impala Super Sport models in 1965. Four SS models were offered: the Super Sport Coupe, models 16537 (six-cylinder) and 16637 (V-8); and the Super Sport Convertible, models 16567 (six-cylinder) and 16667 (V-8). Super Sport models listed for $158 more than comparable Impala models this year. Like all full-size Chevrolets, they featured flush-and-dry rocker panels again. (The rocker structure was designed to allow water to flow through, followed by ducted air to dry remaining moisture to prevent rust formation.)

Visually, 1965 Super Sports were tamer than previous SS models. Side panels were almost completely clean, with bright metal trim used only around wheelhouses (and window openings on the Sport Coupe). Minimal use of chromium enhanced the lines of the sleek semi-fastback Sport Coupe body (used with distinguishing outer sheet metal on some Pontiacs, Oldsmobiles and Buicks as well). Lesser Impalas actually had more bright trim than Super Sports, coming with rocker panel and lower rear fender moldings in addition to wheelhouse outlines.

Chevrolet's buy-word for 1965 was "luxury," so the Super Sport's character was softened by not-very-bold Super Sport script nameplates on front fenders, without Impala or Chevrolet trademarks. Impala SS badge appeared on the left of the grille. At the rear the insignia was at the right, within the black-insert (silver on black cars) trim band running the width of the car above the rear bumper panel. Newly designed tri-blade Super Sport full wheel covers, destined for lasting popularity, were standard.

1965 Impala Super Sport Convertible shared new body and frame with all full-size Chevrolets.

Fifteen Magic-Mirror acrylic lacquers were offered for exterior finishes. One, a metallic called Evening Orchid, was something of a sensation, but suffered from a lack of durability. Convertible tops, using bonded-insert tempered-glass rear windows for the first time, came in white, black or tan. The vinyl roof option (RPO CO8) for Sport Coupes was cataloged in black only, but may have included white later in the year (several vinyl roof colors were offered for the mid-1965 Caprice Custom Sedan).

All-vinyl upholstery, in eight combinations, was part of Super Sport equipment again. Front bucket seats with bright aluminum seatback outline moldings, key-noted a Super Sport's special interior trim. All seats were done in 'ultra-soft' expanded vinyl. All Super Sports had a newly designed console, with an SS emblem and rally-type clock sharing deck area with the shifter gate. A rear compartment lamp was built into the console's foot. SS emblems were mounted on door panels for further recognition.

Totally new for 1965, the instrument panel featured a broad horizontal speedometer housing with round bezels at each end. For the first time, full-size Super Sports came with engine-vital-sign instrumentation, and the gauges weren't even optional. They were located in the left-hand bezel on the instrument panel. The right-hand bezel contained a vacuum gauge, unless the tachometer offered with optional V-8's had been specified in its place. Super Sport instrument-panel detailing included a brushed-aluminum lower panel facing (in place of Impala's wood-grained appliqué).

The major disruption in power train availability occurred during the middle of Chevrolet's 1965 production run. In effect, this created two mechanically distinct lines of cars during the model year. To avoid undue confusion here, the announced 1965 power-teams will be examined before the mid-year engines and transmissions are described.

The 1965 Chevrolets provided more individual adjustments for driver and passenger comfort than ever before. Comfort-Tilt steering column was popular option.

BACKREST ANGLE

10 DEGREES

2.7 INCHES

TELESCOPIC TRAVEL

TILT TRAVEL

HEADREST TRAVEL

30 DEGREES

6 POSITIONS

3.1 INCHES

CHAIR HEIGHT

1.2 INCHES

SEAT TRAVEL   4.75 INCHES

The base engine for 1965 Chevrolets was the 140-hp Turbo-Thrift 230 six, continued basically unchanged from 1964. The standard engine in V-8 models was the also relatively unaltered 195-hp 283. Optional small-block V-8's were the 327-cubic-inchers: RPO L30 with 250-hp (and new design heads); and RPO L74, the 300-hp dual-exhaust and premium-fuel version. Closed positive-type crankcase ventilation systems were optional on all engines except the big 409's where PCV was standard.

The 409, to the surprise and, it must be confessed, disappointment of Chevy fans, remained the car's big V-8 option. *Hot Rod* commented, "A lot of Chevrolet fans have anxiously awaited the '65 models to learn if they will be back in the swing of things with some blazing performance . . . sorry fellows but you still won't be able to choose off the MoPars and Fo-MoCos at the drag strip."

To make matters worse, the 409 had been humbled by Chevrolet. Lopped off the option list was the strongest 425-hp 409, leaving the chrome-laden 340-hp (RPO L33) ox and the truly strong but rarely seen 400-hp (RPO L31) 409's to succor the big-block buyers.

The 409, great engine that it was, had already passed into performance history before the beginning of its 1965 finale. It was anachronistic to

Concours show car for 1965 suggested 1967-68 styling, used 396 V-8.

S. E. Knudsen stands beside an early Caprice with the new 396 Turbo-Jet V-8, at Mesa, Arizona. Caprice was offered in hardtop sedan form only for 1965. Within a few months Knudsen would be replaced as Chevrolet's chief.

place the legendary 409 numerals above the crossed flags on the fenders of a swoopy new 1965 Impala. Even in 1965, spottings were rare; 2,086 340-hp and just 742 400-hp 409's were built in 1965.

Very late in the 409's life several ads promoting it appeared in enthusiast magazines. Apparently Chevrolet was trying to create a little demand to clear out its warehouses. No hint of the engine's coming disappearance from the available power-team chart was given.

Car and Driver, perhaps unknowingly, paid a farewell tribute to the legendary 409 with a road test of a white SS Sport Coupe in its December 1964 issue. The *Car and Driver* Impala carried a 340-hp 409 and weighed in at 4,200 pounds. Respectable performance was still evident, as the car hit 91 mph in 16.4 seconds on the quarter-mile strip. Zero-to-60 mph came in just eight seconds flat, and with the car's 3.31:1 rear axle the testers estimated top speed at 130 mph.

The *Car and Driver* test car was equipped with the Powerglide, but the M-20 four-speed was offered with all optional Chevrolet V-8's and 60,941 were installed (the M21 close-ratio box could also be ordered and 1,550 were sold). Powerglide was offered only for the 340-hp 409. No three-speed unit was available for the big engines. Cars with smaller engines came with a standard three-speed manual, with overdrive optional for base engines, and Powerglide available for drivers desiring an automatic transmission.

Positraction was offered for all available gear ratios. Most V-8's came with 3.36 or 3.31:1 rear axle gearing. In a futile attempt (that was contrary to the elimination of the 425-hp 409) to add a little more performance competitiveness to the 400-hp 409, special gear sets of 4.10, 4.56 and 4.88:1 ratio were cataloged for installation in combination with the M21 four-speed.

Sport Coupes with standard engines used 7.35x14 tires, while Convertibles and all Super Sports with 327 V-8's used the 7.75x14 size. The 409's standard 8.25x14 tires were optional on other Chevrolets, as well as numerous other fourteen- and fifteen-inch tires.

Early 1965 was indeed a tough time for big-Chevy performance enthusiasts. They left the 409 mostly to middle-aged traveling salesmen who liked to cruise fast, and the occasional resorter looking for something capable of hauling a big boat at 70 mph all day. Just 2,828 of the 409's were installed in 1965 Chevrolets before production ended early in the model year. There were brighter times ahead, however, as long-standing rumors came true.

Junior Johnson's legendary 1963 Daytona Mystery Engine 427 Chevy stock car had hardly cooled down from its last race before overly enthusiastic Chevrolet followers started relaying tales of a new version of the Mystery Engine developed for installation in regular production pas-

Vinyl roof coverings continued to be a popular option in 1965, although the new semi-fastback roof didn't carry them as well as the formal-type 1963-64 designs.

senger cars. These stories persisted through 1964, heating up at 1965 introduction time, but they remained in the rumor category until the middle of
the model year when they were finally proven to be true.

Chevrolet claimed the mid-year 396-cubic-inch V-8 was an all-new
design, but thousands of racing fans weren't fooled. The new engine was a
direct descendant of the 1963 Mystery Engine, which had first carried the
new engine's most sensational feature, the so-called porcupine heads (the
bristling rocker studs, sticking out at all angles, gave the engine its animal
nickname). Arrival of the 396 caused tumult in the 1965 specification manuals; new charts were issued in January, just prior to the February 15 official
kick-off for the new V-8, and again in May.

Final 1965 specifications listed two 396 variants: RPO L35 rated at
325 hp and RPO L78 rated at 425 hp. The 325-hp version was restricted to
Impala, Impala SS and the new Caprice Custom models; while the very
potent 425-hp engine was offered for any full-size Chevrolet (and Corvette,
of course). The moment the 396 was officially offered, the old 409 was axed
for good. 'Limited availability' was anticipated for 250-hp and 300-hp 327
V-8's, as well; the 325-hp 396 was expected to supplant these power plants,
and did sell rather well, with production at 55,454 by the end of the model
year.

The 396 was the first of a new generation of production passenger
car V-8's given the family name 'Turbo-Jet' by Chevrolet. The 396 block
had potential for boring and stroking to nearly 500 cubic inches. Why was it
pegged at 396 cubes initially? Probably because it was originally intended
to be (and eventually was) the 'big' engine for the intermediate Chevelle,
which was subject, at least for the time, to GM's internal edict of having not
more than 400 cubic inches in an intermediate body. Then too, NASCAR
was again rumored (as in late 1963) to be looking at a 6.5-liter limit for the
1966 stock car season.

Both 396 V-8's came with a new, fully synchronized heavy-duty
three-speed manual gearbox unless an optional transmission was speci-

Show model of the 325-hp 396 Mark IV V-8, with
new Turbo Hydra-matic transmission, as phased into
1965 production during January of that year.

fied. Just in case someone wanted to order a Biscayne two-door sedan with the 425-hp 396, Chevrolet offered the new truly rugged M22 'rock crusher' (it was noisy, too) four-speed with a 2.20:1 close-ratio low; and rear axle ratios as low as 4.88:1, for super drag-strip performance. The normal heavy-duty four-speed was also offered.

Powerglide was often matched to the new 396 in 325-hp trim. A bit of good news for enthusiasts who preferred automatic transmissions was the addition of the Turbo Hydra-matic to the option list. This three-speed automatic, introduced in 1964 by Cadillac and Buick (as Super Turbine Drive), then extended to Olds and Pontiac at the beginning of 1965, was an ultra-modern, very durable and very capable transmission.

There was even news for the six-cylinder buyer when the mid-year revisions came around. A new 150-hp 250-cubic-inch six was offered as RPO L22. Similar to the old 230 in some respects, the new engine did feature a twelve-counterweight (as opposed to a more usual four- or six-counter-weight) crankshaft for "smoother, quieter operation and long engine life."

Just for added good measure, the venerable 220-hp 283 V-8, with four-barrel carburetor and dual exhausts, was hauled out of mothballs and reinstated on the option list when the mid-year revisions were made.

The new 396 Turbo-Jet V-8 was identified by a large vee insignia on the front fender, ahead of the wheels. The emblem appeared most often on new Caprices, Chevrolet's mid-year present to its luxury-minded customers. The Caprice Custom Sedan was actually an Impala Sport Sedan with

Console for 1965 Super Sport with automatic transmission carried clock in nacelle ahead of shifter plate.

Super Sport interior continued to feature buckets, vinyl upholstery in 1965. Impala Super Sports with four-speeds used a different console than those with automatic transmissions, with clock aft of shifter gate. New instrument panel featured housing for vacuum gauge or tachometer to the right of radio.

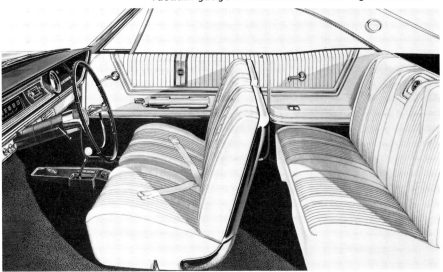

RPO Z18 Caprice trim and appointments. Available only with V-8 power, many Caprices were loaded with power accessories that almost demanded the 325-hp 396. Many had Turbo Hydra-matic, AM-FM Multiplex stereo, wire wheel covers (in place of the standard full Caprice covers, which were the Super Sport caps with different centers) and various other comfort and convenience items. New optional tires, 7.75 or 8.25x14 Special Nylon type, were recommended for the Caprice to provide ". . . the ultimate in a luxurious ride." Dual exhausts for the 325-hp 396 were apparently an option restricted to Caprice in 1965.

Actually, the Caprice was considerably modified when compared to an Impala of the same year, much more so in fact than the Super Sport. Differences were more than skin deep here. Even the frame was heavier, as were the rockers and body crossbar under the front seat. Special body mounts, softer rubber bushings in some suspension components and re-calibrated shocks helped make the Caprice ride more like a 'little Cadillac' than any previous Chevy. Additional noise-suppression features included a denser rubber covering on the front dash mat and special seals between the cowl and front fenders.

Exterior special parts for the Caprice included the Super Sport's black-accented front grille, color-accented rear trim panel with Caprice identification, special body-sill moldings and Caprice emblems on all sides. The triple *fleur-de-lis* emblems on rear quarters of the Caprice roof would become a popular style in the late 1960's. Caprices were almost always delivered with vinyl tops, in black, blue or beige.

Caprice was distinctive and luxurious inside, with contour-padded molded seats covered with a combination of fabric and expanded vinyl upholstery. Door panels and steering wheels had special simulated walnut-grain appliqués. Caprice emblems abounded.

Current Chevrolet chief Robert Lund told a reporter in 1979 that he inspired the Caprice. "Back in the early 1960's 'Bunkie' Knudsen was general manager of Chevrolet and I was general sales manager," Lund said. "Con-

Turbo Hydra-matic came to Chevrolet in mid-1965, with the 396. This is a cutaway of 1966 version.

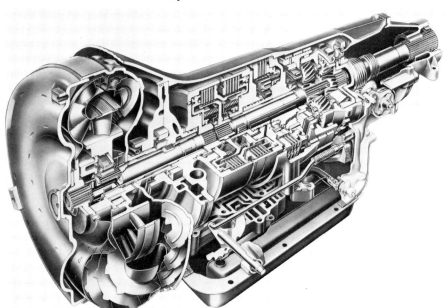

sumers were buying up right through Chevrolet into other full-size cars at other GM Divisions. We had only the full-size Impala. I proposed a deluxe Impala and Knudsen agreed. It was the Caprice, which came out in '65."

During 1965 the Caprice Custom Sedan complemented the Super Sport's models. In many ways it was sort of a four-door hardtop SS. The Super Sports had a tremendous year, with production reaching a record level for any Chevrolet Super Sport model, as 243,114 cars bearing the SS script were sold (27,842 of these were SS Convertibles). This represented 38.5 percent of Chevrolet's total full-size production for 1965 of an incredible 558,459 Sport Coupes and 72,760 Convertibles.

For performance lovers, though, 1965 will always be the year the Mark IV big-block was born. The heavy-duty V-8 would, in much modified form, power virtually every sort of racing car and hundreds of drag and special water craft as well during the following fifteen years.

Like its ensuing descendants, the 1965 production 425-hp special performance V-8 used a four-bolt main bearing cap for great strength. Bearing surfaces were actually slightly larger than the 1963 Mark II Mystery Engine, for increased durability as the engine's displacement was expanded. The 396 weighed slightly more than the 409, no doubt due to its heavy head castings, which actually contained the combustion chambers.

The famed porcupine heads, a direct translation of the 1963 Mark II's engineering, used Chevrolet's stud-mounted ball-joint rocker arms. The neat new trick was the tilting of the valves in all sorts of directions both across and the length of the heads. Large valves were used; 425-hp versions had 1.72-inch exhausts and 2.19-inch intakes (identical to the 1963 Mark II). Even the 325-hp version had valves as large as the 409's.

Phased into production on early 325-hp 396 Turbo-Jets was Rochester Product's new Quadri-Jet carburetor that featured a giant, venturi-

All 1965 engine insignias except 396 used the same badge, with displacement numerals above.

1965 Impala SS full wheel cover (left) was one of the most popular hub caps of all time, did encores on 1966 Impala SS and 1967 Nova SS. 1965 and 1966 Super Sports used this front fender script (right).

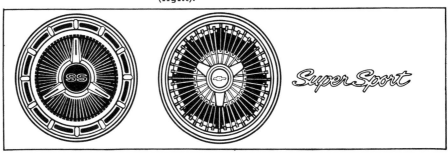

less secondary barrel system that dumped tremendous amounts of fuel into the intake manifold when it was cut in. Primary barrels were smaller than previous four-barrel carburetors had used, however.

Chevrolet's announced over-the-counter speed parts program really began with the 396. During the coming decade following its 1965 debut, a long line of special heads (some of aluminum), manifolds, cams, pistons and other strengthened, lightened or otherwise special-duty parts would quietly waft their way into Chevrolet's special parts catalogs. Even aluminum *blocks* would be cataloged.

Many of the 396 four-bolt main blocks were bored to 427 cubic inches and immediately installed in stock cars. Out on the West Coast, top engine builder Bill Thomas unveiled a 427 Chevy-powered Impala Sport Coupe, built for Tom Friedkin, San Diego race driver. Friedkin entered his hot new Chevrolet in the Charlotte NASCAR race, where it created a sensation. Thomas insisted he'd built the engine from a 396, but rumors were widespread that the whole assembly had arrived, ready to go, in a crate from Michigan with instructions to bolt it in and go.

Whether they were trickling out the back door at Detroit or being built in garages, the 427 Turbo-Jets proliferated during the 1965 NASCAR season. Among the starters at the Dixie 400 in 1965 were no less than eleven Chevrolets, most of them running Mark IV 427's. Buck Baker reportedly barely finished the engine switch from the 409 (which had become a first-rate boat anchor overnight) to the 427 in time to repaint the cubic-inch displacement figures on his hood before race time.

But the 427's, set to avenge the Chevrolet defeats of the previous seasons, sadly suffered teething problems. Blown rods and, more frequently, clutch problems brought early retirements in many races. However, the appearance of the 427 did excite Chevrolet fans, who had been bored to tears by the "which Ford'll win today" races of 1964.

Chevrolet hadn't turned out a memorable stock drag since the 1963 Z-11 427. Yet in 1965, Chevrolet dominated the sport as its V-8's powered innumerable dragsters, modifieds, street machines and lower stock class machines to strip trophies nationally. Although the showy top stock classes were largely dominated by MoPars, Chevrolet-powered racers held twenty-seven of the NHRA's record slots at the time the 396 was introduced.

The fact that the 425-hp 396 was the one designated for installation in any big Chevy body (while the 325-hp version was restricted to Impala and Caprice) indicates someone at Chevrolet was watching the NHRA specifications. Almost instantly demand for the cheap, light Biscayne two-door sedan increased as orders for the lightweight coupes with the new 425-hp screamer rolled in from drag racers who had been itching for a new Chevrolet kick, although their numbers were relatively few—1,838 total units—among the 59,650 buyers who opted for 396 power in 1965.

Super Sport wheel cover and accessory wires were unchanged for 1966, accessory simulated mag wheel cap was introduced in February 1965.

The obviously NASCAR-inspired cubic-inch displacement of the 396, its easy conversion to the current (1965) 427-cubic-inch limit and availability concessions were all moves indicating that someone in Mr. Knudsen's domain was quietly, but rapidly, moving toward a real incursion into those territories marked off-limits since the corporate anti-performance ban of January 21, 1963.

The pools of racing enthusiasts throughout the giant Chevrolet organization must have empathized with Charlie Brown as 1966 neared. Just as Lucy persistently yanks the ball away as Charlie starts his annual football kick-off in the comic strip, GM management once again cut Chevrolet short. Several incidents apparently contributed to the sudden fade-out of Chevrolet's widely heralded (but never officially announced) "return to racing."

The turn-about began when 'Bunkie' Knudsen was transferred, to be replaced by E. M. 'Pete' Estes in July 1965 (the GM management structure was shaken to the very top that summer as James M. Roche replaced John F. Gordon as president). Concurrently, Robert F. Kennedy, then serving as U.S. senator, started making corporate brass nervous by assailing the giant's efforts, or lack of same, to promote automotive safety. An all-out highly visible Chevrolet racing program just at this time didn't seem to be the sort of red flag to wave at the federal government. Retrenchment was the only solution. By the end of the year the excitement was ebbing.

Mid-year engine changes, management restructuring and the tentative swipes at racing activity had little impact on a nation swept along on a Chevrolet-buying frenzy. Yet another record was posted for 1965, with 2,587,487 Chevrolet automobiles built. Counting trucks, too, more than 3.2 million vehicles bearing the bow-tie trademark were assembled as 1965 models.

Industry commentators said some of the spectacular sales resulted from pent-up demand for cars after the late-1964 UAW strikes at GM plants. To ease demands on their labor force, Chevrolet rushed completion of their new 1,725,000-square-foot Lordstown, Ohio, assembly plant. Despite their efforts, production wouldn't begin there until October 1966, when an already expanded plant was finally dedicated.

Show car for 1966 circuit was Caribe four-door convertible. It was strictly a one-off.

Throughout the industry the trend was to larger V-8's in 1965. One out of every ten new American cars carried an engine displacing more than 401 cubic inches in 1965. Most of these were installed in top-line models, where the emphasis was on cruise performance and not acceleration capability. Moreover, increased cubes gave more horses to run the ever-growing host of power-robbing accessories. Further evidence of this trend was found in the number of four-speeds installed in 1965 Chevrolets. About 62,000 cars were so equipped, but speaking in percentages their popularity continued to decline.

Following the tremendous success of the almost all-new 1965 Chevrolet, it was no surprise that 1966 would be sort of an add-on year. Full-size Chevrolet passenger cars were mildly restyled versions of the previous year's offerings for the most part. Sales softened during 1966, but there was one bright spot in the Chevrolet line. The Caprice, now a four-model series, found increasing acceptance with Chevrolet buyers.

A new Caprice Custom Coupe, with a distinct formal roof line all its own, joined the Caprice sedan this year. The Custom Coupe's roof line and general luxury theme would set the standard for Chevrolet's top models through the early 1970's. Viewed from this angle, the Caprice coupe is undoubtedly a historic Chevrolet milestone. Two station wagon models were also added to the Caprice line, both featured simulated exterior wood pan-

Two cars that set the pace for Chevrolet's future in 1966. The Caprice Custom Coupe would prove a serious challenger to Super Sport popularity, while the SS 396 Malibu in the background was indicative of a new policy of building performance packages around an engine option.

Super Sports were losing their identity in 1966; Super Sport script and wheel covers were main distinguishing characteristics.

eling. The total number of 1966 Chevrolet passenger car offerings was forty-three, an increase of six from 1965.

This year, the Caprice eroded the Super Sport's prestige as Chevrolet's flagship line. Super Sport sales plummeted, dropping from 1965's record by more than fifty percent. Just 119,314 of the 1966 Super Sports were built (the lowest total since 1962). Super Sport Convertibles accounted for 15,872 sales, also a sharp decline from 1965. Perhaps the rapidly increasing military build-up, as the Vietnam War deepened in late 1965, had an effect on Super Sport sales as well. Thousands of prospective SS buyers were donning olive drab and shipping out for the Far East during this period. They were out of the market for two to four years, if not forever.

Impala Super Sports for 1966 were the Sport Coupe models 16737 (six-cylinder) and 16837 (V-8); and the Convertible models 16767 (six-cylinder) and 16867 (V-8). They shared the facelift given the rest of the Chevrolet full-size models. To give the little-changed rear end sheet metal new distinction, stylists abandoned the six round taillight units that had been Impala trademarks since 1958 (except for 1959). The new lamps were large rectangular units divided into three segments. Frontal styling was made cleaner and more massive in appearance. Super Sport emblems on the grille and above the right taillight provided identity. For the first time since 1961 Super Sports shared side trim common to regular Impalas, although Super Sport script replaced the Impala medallions on front fenders. The 1966 cars had a full-length molding along the body side crease line, serving as protection against door dents (a real problem on the clean-sided '65 models). Wheel covers, carried over from 1965, were the ever-popular full cover with stylized tri-bar spinner.

Hottest stock engine for 1966 Impala SS was the rarely seen 425-hp 427 Mark IV.

Engine insignia continued to be found ahead of the front wheelhouse on the fender.

1966 Impala models were 0.1 inch longer than their 1965 predecessors. All had heavier frames than 1965 cars had used (frame rails were increased in gauge by thirty-three percent). More durable brake lines and shock absorbers were additional improvements.

Strato-bucket front seats, upholstered in vinyl, were part of the 1966 Super Sport equipment. The console for the package was redesigned, and the heater ducts now directed warm air alongside the console to rear seat passengers. A Super Sport emblem adorned the glovebox door. Otherwise, 1966 SS interior appointments were very similar to standard Impalas, further signifying the decline of Super Sport prestige.

Options included a tachometer and a new gauge cluster (included with Strato-buckets on Caprice coupes). 1965's standard instrument panel-mounted gauges had vanished. New comfort options were the Tilt-Telescope adjustable steering column, power adjustment for the driver's bucket seat and front seat headrests. The tilt wheel was offered only on cars equipped with four-speed or floor automatic transmissions. Comfortron, GM's fully automatic interior temperature control, was extended to Chevrolet for 1966. It was fully integrated with the heating system and kept temperatures between sixty-five and eighty-five degrees, year around, depending on the owner's whim.

Eight 1966 Super Sport interior color codes were listed including (RPO 844) bright blue and (RPO 885) white and black. Exterior colors numbered fifteen solids and eight two-tone combinations (for Sport Coupes). Super Sport Convertibles could be ordered with black, beige or white tops. Vinyl tops, riding a popularity surge, were now offered in black or beige. (In June 1966, Chevrolet announced a spray-on vinyl top kit for used-car/aftermarket installation by dealers. The kits included glue-on welt strips. All factory installations were real vinyl material, however.)

Handsome new gauge cluster bridged gap between console and instrument panel on 1966 Chevrolets. It was optional on SS cars, came with bucket-seat option on Caprice (as shown here).

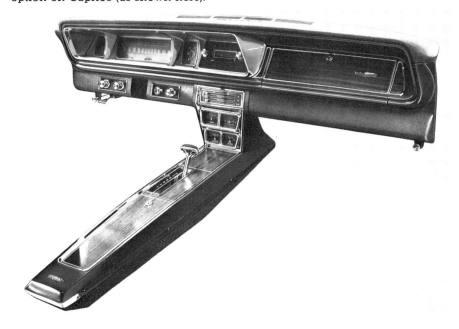

The vinyl top fad was a bitter pill for some GM stylists. Their efforts to blend the roof line into the deck area were moving toward an ultimate statement for 1967.

1966 Super Sports came with a variety of optional tires and wheels. The new 7.75 or 8.25x14 NF Nylon tires were a popular choice. All optional whitewalls had 'thin line' styling, with a 0.6-inch white band.

Only 912 1966 Super Sports were built in the standard six-cylinder models. The mid-1965 optional 250-cubic-inch six was used as the base power plant in 1966. Powerglide, overdrive or standard manual gearboxes were offered to the six-cylinder purchaser.

The base V-8 remained the 195-hp 283, with the resurrected 220-hp 283 (with dual exhausts and four-barrel carburetor) being the first step up. Both 283's came with the new light-duty, full-synchro three-speed as standard. A new four-speed (RPO M20) was offered for 283 and 327 V-8's. It had a 3.11 low for 283 application and 2.54:1 low for 327's. Overdrive was offered for the 283, and Powerglide was available with all small-block V-8's. The 327 was offered in just one state of tune for 1966, rated at 275 hp. It was created by placing a larger four-barrel carburetor on the (1965) 250-hp 327 with reworked spark advance.

Turbo-Jet 396, in 325-hp form, was virtually unchanged from its mid-1965 introduction. A new triangular-shaped generator brace was one of the few visible 1966 differences. Top engine options were new 427-cubic-inch versions of the Mark IV block. The street-intended 427 was rated at 390 hp, while the 'special performance' job was pegged at 425 hp with its solid-lifters, four-barrel with aluminum manifold and heavy-duty four-bolt main block.

The 396 and both 427 V-8's came with the M13 three-speed heavy-duty manual gearbox as standard (it had made its debut in mid-1965). The RPO M20 four-speeds were stronger than the boxes listed under the same RPO number for smaller eights. Additional optional four-speeds were the M21 close-ratio box and the new M22 rock crusher. Transmission installations were 30,467 of the M20's, 1,595 M21's and just two M22 heavy-duty

Wraparound taillamps, blunted front fenders gave 1966 Impala SS new look. Popular 1965 wheel covers were retained.

boxes! This special-performance transmission had extra-rugged—and noisy—gears. The RPO M21 and M22 transmission options were for the 425-hp 427 only. Powerglide was offered for the 325-hp 396, and Turbo Hydra-matic could be ordered with either 427, as well as the 396.

Chevrolets equipped with Turbo-Jet V-8's could be ordered with a new heavy-duty suspension kit that included a stronger front stabilizer, higher-rate springs, stiffer shocks, 14x6 wide-rim wheels and a newly designed rear stabilizer attached to each lower control arm.

The 427 was a strong performer (a 427 Biscayne took Junior Stock Eliminator at the 1966 NHRA Winternationals), but it was obvious that Chevrolet's heart wasn't in the racing effort. Although owner-modified Chevys continued to clean up in all sorts of racing activities, for the most part Chevrolet passenger cars were not among the top stock performance cars in the nation. (Activities in the Corvette camp were quite another story, however.) Chevrolet's hot street models were found in the small Chevelle and Nova lines during 1966, and even there they were few in number and hard to get.

More power to haul around more luxury continued to attract buyers in 1966. More than half of all 1966 cars had engines with displacement in excess of 300 cubic inches. Chrysler and Lincoln opened up new vistas of power, expanding their blocks to 440 and 462 cubic inches respectively. For full-size Chevrolets, the 396 accounted for 105,844 sales.

Traditional performance options geared to street acceleration continued to decline in 1966 sales figures. Dual exhausts also suffered a loss in sales percentages. Limited-slip Positraction rear axles were more popular in 1966, however. The Super Sport concept, which had ridden a narrow fence between luxury and performance, was knocked out of the luxury market by the Caprice during 1966. The performance market went into a decline simultaneously, and although it would come back in a few years, the Impala SS wouldn't be there.

1966 engine identification insignia. The 396 badge was unchanged from its debut in mid-1965. There were no numerals for 283 this year.

283-CU.-IN. V8 ENGINE

327-CU.-IN. V8 ENGINE

396-CU.-IN. V8 ENGINE

427-CU.-IN. V8 ENGINE

CHAPTER SIX

Big-Block Power Strikes Chevelle 1965–1967

*C*hevrolet engineers watched with envy during late 1964 and most of 1965 as the Pontiac GTO, produced and marketed by Jim Wangers, John DeLorean and company, swept the nation. Pontiac's intermediate-size hot rod was establishing that Division as the performance headquarters of GM, a post Chevrolet had held without challenge for nearly a decade. Pontiac achieved this by flying in the face of GM corporate policy forbidding cars such as the GTO.

At the beginning of 1964 an official 326-cubic-inch limit on intermediate engine displacements was in effect, resulting in a ban on the 327 Chevrolet V-8 for the new Chevelle (Pontiac put its '326' into the A-body Tempest, although it actually displaced around 336 cubic inches). Chevrolet pressure to use the 327 was finally successful in mid-1964, but by that time Pontiac had jumped ahead again, offering the GTO with the 389 Trophy V-8. Buick and Oldsmobile quickly followed suit, and both fielded 400-cubic-inch V-8's for their intermediates by the beginning of the 1965 model year. Very shortly after the 1965 introduction, a really strong 350-hp 327, RPO L79, became available in Chevelle. But, there was still a prevalent feeling at Chevrolet that the Chevelle needed big-block power, and needed it quickly, to be competitive with the GTO, Buick Gran Sport and Oldsmobile 442.

Perhaps as a face-saving gesture, at the beginning of 1965, GM corporate policy was revised to allow V-8's a maximum displacement of 400 cubic inches for the A-body intermediates. Chevelle was still stuck with the 327, since the only big-block Chevrolet V-8 in production at the beginning of the model year was the 409, a muscular but aging and heavy engine. By mid-year, though, a revived and revised version of the famous 1963 Mark II Daytona Mystery Engine was scheduled for introduction in big Chevrolet and Corvette models. Displacing 396 cubic inches, the Mark IV, as it would be known, would be the ideal power plant for a big-block Chevelle.

The new 396 V-8 was getting into production too late in the year for widespread use in the 1965 Chevelle, so it was decided to build a very limited number of the intermediates with the engine, in strong tune, as teasers for the 1966 models when 396 availability would be limited only by sales acceptance. A special styling and chassis package was prepared for the limited run of 1965 SS 396 Chevelles, creating a tantalizing, very rare automobile that would be almost impossible to obtain. Chevrolet announced at the outset that just two hundred would be built. Despite strong demand, they kept their word—201 were assembled.

Those lucky buyers who did obtain an SS 396 Chevelle in 1965 did so by having their order for a car equipped with RPO Z16, SS 396 equip-

Most 1965 SS 396 Chevelles came with vinyl top and bumper guards. Chris Daniels's car is original except for the wheels and frontal rake.

Z-16 Chevelles had clean rear quarter panels and a distinctive rear deck cove treatment. This car appears to have clear taillamp lenses, possibly because lamps are on. 1965 SS 396 was one of the rarest and most exciting performance cars of that year.

ment, accepted. The prototype had been seen at GM's Mesa, Arizona, proving ground in January 1965 (the brand new 396-equipped Caprice Custom Sedan was also shown to GM officials at the same time). Assembly of SS 396 Chevelles began at Kansas City in a matter of days. All were finished in one of three colors: red, yellow or black. Most had black vinyl tops, but there were exceptions.

The SS 396 was released in the midst of the fanfare surrounding its new engine (the first new Chevrolet production V-8 engine type since 1958) on February 15, 1965.

Most SS 396 Chevelles were destined for duty as demonstrators and dealer floor cars. They were usually loaded with options, many of which were included in the RPO Z16 package to begin with. The Z16 equipment added an astounding $1,501 to the $2,431 base price of a stripped Malibu SS, but numerous appearance, performance and luxury items were included.

To the eye, SS 396 cars were simply but distinctively different from regular Malibu Super Sports. Malibu SS emblems moved from rear quarter panels to front fenders, just behind the wheelhouse openings, on the SS 396. The rear deck cove was given a cleaner, special look by the use of standard Chevelle taillight lenses and a unique black-filled panel that covered the lower half of the cove area. A rectangular SS 396 deck emblem, high on the right, attested to the special Chevelle's potent engine.

All Z-16 Chevelles came with the newly introduced simulated mag wheels. *Motor Trend* called them ". . . the most handsome and authentic looking simulated custom wheels we've seen," while *Car Life* thought the same covers were ". . . the homeliest phony 'mag wheel' hubcaps imaginable." These controversial wheel covers hid wide fourteen-inch wheels mounting 7.75x14 Firestone gold-stripe tires.

To the informed eye, the most striking addition made to the Chevelle's exterior with Z16 equipment was the large 396 V-shaped emblems

This SS 396 Chevelle was used in tests at Mesa, Arizona, in February 1965. Only 201 units were built during that model year. All used the truly muscular 375-hp 396 Mark IV V-8. The cars served as teasers for the 1966 SS 396, which was produced in volume. Simulated mag wheel covers, Firestone gold-stripe tires, AM-FM Multiplex unit under dash were among the goodies thrown in with the Z-16 396 package.

on the front fenders. These emblems weren't referring to just any 396, either, but to a very hot 375-hp special version. Chevelle's 375-hp 396 was virtually identical to the 396 V-8 rated at 425 hp when assembled for Corvette installation. Or was it? The SS 396's tested by car magazines in late 1965 were almost certainly equipped with hot hydraulic camshafts, instead of the solid lifters used in 425/396 Corvettes. But, 1966 'L78' 396 Chevelles, offering what was allegedly the same 375-hp engine, had the higher revving solid-lifter valve trains, as did, possibly, some of the 1965 SS 396 V-8's. For our purposes, then, the 1965 SS 396 Chevelle will be considered as originally depicted: with hot hydraulic cam allowing 6000 or more rpm. Keeping the required quantities of fuel flowing through the fast-moving and large valves was the responsibility of a new Holley 4150 four-barrel. Cast exhaust headers emptied waste gases into a low-restriction exhaust system terminating in a pair of 2.25-inch-diameter tailpipes. A strong, four-bolt main-bearing-cap special 396 block was used in Chevelle and Corvette assembly.

The Z16 was more than a trim kit and a big V-8. Chassis components were greatly refined, even the frame was a beefed convertible-type unit. Front suspension was strengthened with cast-steel wheel hubs and shot-peened ball studs. Antiroll bars were used front and rear. Big-Chevy eleven-inch-diameter brakes, with standard vacuum assist, replaced normal Chevelle binders. Steering was speeded up with a 15:1 power-assisted gear (in place of 17.5:1 steering on other Chevelles). Chevrolet's large rear axle was installed, coming with 3.31 gears and *no* Positraction in standard form.

Taking the torque loads of the virile 396 was a considerable chore for Chevrolet's heavy-duty eleven-inch clutch (the clutch would prove to be one of the 396's weak points that year). All SS 396 Chevelles carried Muncie four-speeds with 2.56:1 low gears in 1965.

Chevrolet apparently never issued any sales literature for the 1965 SS 396, nor was the car featured in any advertising. But Chevrolet did make an effort to place the cars in the hands of motoring journalists, resulting in at least five published drive reports describing the new model. (SS 396 drive tests appeared in *Car Life*, September 1965; *Motor Trend*, July 1965; *Popular Hot Rodding*, month unknown; *Motorcade*, September 1965; and in an eastern hot rodding magazine, name unknown.)

Heart of RPO Z16 package was 375-hp 396, nearly obscured by huge, chromed air cleaner. The 396 emblem here was used only on 1965 SS 396.

Z16 package featured 160-mph speedometer, 6000 rpm tachometer. 'Pod-type' clock was mounted atop dash. AM-FM Multiplex stereo (included with RPO Z16) had tuning controls centered beneath dash.

The test drivers agreed: The Chevelle SS 396 had more-than-adequate acceleration capabilities. Featuring a power-to-weight ratio of just one pony for each ten pounds of car weight, the SS 396 could scoot down the quarter-mile in under fifteen seconds, accelerating from a dead stop to right around 100 mph in the same distance. Top speed was estimated at 130-135 mph. Substitution of available Chevrolet gear sets, which were offered as low as 4.56:1, would have pushed the Chevelle into easy 100-mph-plus drag runs; whereas a higher ratio, such as 3.08 rear axle gears might provide, could have allowed the car, as *Motor Trend* suggested, to come close to wiping the face of its special 160-mph speedometer.

Most of the testers described the SS 396's handling in non-specific terms, but *Car Life* pointedly found fault here, noting that the fifty-eight-percent frontal weight bias of the SS 396 created excessive understeer and other ride disturbances on rougher roads.

In addition to a 160-mph speed indicator and a tachometer red-lining at 6000 rpm, all SS 396 Chevelles had the newly introduced AM-FM Multiplex stereo radio system, thrown in as part of RPO Z16. That was nice, but it did little to east the pain of the car's prohibitively high price (which, as we've established, was intentional). A well-equipped 1965 GTO listed for about $1,000 less than the $4,500-range SS 396. The SS 396 had but one mission in life: to form an association between the new 396 V-8 and Chevelle. The special little Super Sport accomplished this mission with verve.

Incidentally, the Z-16 Chevelle was the first Chevrolet to become widely known by its RPO option designation (the 1963 Z-11 drag car isn't counted, since its fame was mostly confined to quarter-mile enthusiasts). But, did *Car Life* really suggest it first? Consider this quote from its SS 396 road test: "Perhaps Chevrolet could rename its package-equipped cars, such as Pontiac *et al* have done. Since 'Super Sport' has been usurped, Chevrolet nomenclature experts might simply resort to the option code of 'Z-16.' " The idea wasn't really successful; it was only in retrospect that the 1965 SS 396 became known widely as the Z-16 Chevelle. However, when the same tactic was applied to the 302-cubic-inch "Z-28" Camaro in 1967, it was a sensation and caused imitations worldwide.

396 Turbo-Jet badge (right) appeared on front fenders of 1965-67 SS 396.

Full production of SS 396 Chevelles started with the 1966 model introduction. SS 396 Coupe used 325-hp 396 as base engine.

About twenty Z-16 Chevelles are known to belong to enthusiasts as this book is written. They are increasingly sought, but seldom found, especially in original condition. Like the 1961 Super Sports, they make fascinating collector cars because they were ahead of their time.

The planned limited availability of 1965 SS 396 Chevelles seems to indicate its purpose was to promote future SS 396 cars, but evidence also suggests there was confusion about 1966 Chevelle models right up to introduction time. When the dust settled, all 1966 Chevelle Super Sports carried a 396-cubic-inch Turbo-Jet V-8 and, with one exception, the big V-8 was banned from other Chevelles. The exception was the El Camino Custom, which continued to offer all the options, now even the engine, needed to make a Super Sport 'sedan pickup' minus only the SS emblems. Some early 1966 press photos showed SS cars with 283 V-8 insignia, while the 1966 *Sales Album* illustrates a straight Malibu hardtop and convertible with 396 insignia. No cars were actually released in either configuration, however.

All 1966 Chevelles featured new styling, giving them a larger appearance even though they were dimensionally just 0.4 inch wider and longer. They continued to use Chevelle's original 115-inch wheelbase and, in fact, the original chassis was little changed. To handle the 1966 396 V-8 recalibrated shock absorbers, it was necessary to add stronger springs, special ball joints and a larger-diameter front stabilizer to SS 396 chassis. Frame reinforcing for the large V-8 was done between upper and lower control-arm pivots.

The new Chevelle SS 396 Sport Coupe and Convertible shared their bodies with Malibu counterparts. Sport Coupes featured new roof lines, with a 'tunneled' rear window inset between the sailing roof side panels.

Priced at $2,776, the SS 396 Coupe listed for $292 more than Malibu's Sport Coupe. This was quite an increase over the surcharge for Super Sport trappings from 1965. However, the 1966 SS equipment included the new 396 Turbo-Jet V-8 in 325-hp tune. It was the first Chevrolet SS in volume

An SS 396 Malibu with bucket seats, four-speed, console and tachometer mounted to the right of steering wheel. Instrument panel was all-new for 1966.

production to use an engine as the core of its package. Even with the higher cost, several items long-associated with SS equipment were now optional on Chevelle's SS 396. Bucket seats and special wheel covers were extra-cost options this year. Special styling features included were twin simulated hood air intakes, special color-accented body sills and rear fender moldings, a black-filled rear cove panel with special Chevelle nameplate and SS 396 emblem, and a black-accented grille with series identification. Super Sport lettering was found on each rear fender in large, block-like script.

Red stripe 7.75x14 NF Nylon tires, on wide six-inch rims came with SS 396 cars during 1966. Wheels were painted the body color and, unless optional covers had been specified, wore small, plain hub caps.

Interiors were all-vinyl, in seven color combinations. Strato-buckets, available optionally, could not be ordered in turquoise, however. For the first time, the Chevelle owner could enjoy power adjustment of the front bucket seats. Headrests also joined the option list this year. Cars equipped with manual gearboxes had floor shifts, as did automatics when the console with bucket seats was installed. A gauge package consisting of a tachometer, parking-brake warning lamp and temp-oil-amp gauges replaced the standard warning lights if the owner desired this option.

Exterior colors numbered fifteen solid and seven two-tones (for coupes only, of course). Two-tone Super Sports were quite rare, although quite a few sported black or beige vinyl tops. Convertibles could be ordered with black, white or beige tops this year.

The 1966 SS 396 came standard with the 325-hp 396 (offered as RPO L35 in El Camino, where it accounted for 1,865 sales), or optionally with RPO L34, a 360-hp version of the 396. The L34 had the stronger four-bolt main block and gathered its extra horses by use of a larger four-barrel carburetor and wilder camshaft. Closed positive crankcase ventilation was standard on the 396 L34.

Engine dress-up items for the SS 396 included chrome valve covers, crankcase breather head and oil filler cap. The 360-hp engine had a Cor-

1966 Super Sport rear quarter script (left); 1967 was similar, but words were stacked.

SS 396 for 1966 came with standard hub caps and bench seat unless optional items were specified. Tires were red-stripe type.

vette-type air cleaner with 'full circle breathing.' The air cleaner top plate was chromed on both engines.

Both engines came standard with the mid-1965-style heavy-duty, fully-synchronized three-speed manual transmission. A newly revised M20 four-speed, with 2.52:1 low, was offered optionally (close-ratio gears, with 2.20:1 low, were offered for the 360-hp V-8 as well). Powerglide, which had received liquid cooling in mid-1965, was offered for both 396 engines.

There was a third 396 available, RPO L78, the 375-hp 396, now very definitely a solid-lifter terror. Only 3,099 1966 Chevelles were built with the engine, a duplicate in almost all respects to the 1965 Corvette's 425-hp 396. The 360-hp 396 scored 24,811 sales.

By March 1966, it must have become apparent that not all Super Sport types were enamored of big-block power. The small-block Chevy was, and would continue to be, a revered engine. To placate the small-block enthusiast, Chevrolet made a mid-year addition to the engine option list for regular Malibus. It was the 350-hp 327. Bucket seats, all-vinyl uphol-

1966 Chevelle standard hub caps and optional covers, shared with SS 396.

Chrome garnishes adorned the SS 396 standard 325-hp 396. A 360-hp optional version was cataloged, and a few 375-hp versions were built on special order.

stery and other goodies were offered on straight Malibus as well as SS 396 cars; so it was possible to approximate an SS-style car with the 350-hp 327, or any V-8 for that matter, in a Malibu. There is no way to determine how many of these RPO L79's were built; they are not listed in the 1966 option production book.

A 1966 Malibu SS 396 in standard catalog trim was quite a plain car, especially with those red-line tires and small hub caps. This seemed to be the sort of car for those who were serious about performance. The hip image in 1966 was a no-frills, all-business drag machine on the street. Chevelle still did not offer the stripped two-door sedan body with Super Sport equipment. Nevertheless, they were leading the way, with the plain-Jane SS 396, to the new generation of muscle cars in unadorned wrappers (a concept rightfully attributed to the 1968 Plymouth Road Runner, since it was the first car to be *specially* designed as a cheap, plain runner).

Chevelle production increased during 1966, although Super Sport sales declined slightly, falling to 72,272 Sport Coupes and Convertibles. Four-speed installations were 73,022 M20's, 5,012 M21's and twelve M22 "rock crushers."

Chevrolet continued to officially ignore racing as the 1967 model year approached, although orders for 375-hp RPO L78 Chevelles for drag racing purposes continued to be filled. Then, on the NASCAR circuit, Curtis Turner popped up with a very slippery Malibu coupe prepared by legendary car and engine builder Smokey Yunick. Turner's Chevelle sported all sorts of air-flow tricks, and ran a bored-out 396, displacing 418 cubic inches. Unfortunately, it was destroyed in a spectacular crash during practice for the 1967 Atlanta 500 when it became airborne at more than 150 mph, then flipped and rolled repeatedly. Turner was not seriously injured, although he was no doubt deeply disappointed to have lost his ride, which was generally acknowledged to have been one of the fastest independent cars to have run for quite awhile.

Reportedly, Yunick built a duplicate Chevelle stocker, but never ran it due to continued NASCAR official harassment over many of the car's details.

A mild facelift gave the 1967 Chevelle Super Sport a heavier look. Frontal appearance was cleaned-up by the use of a simple horizontal-bar grille; while at the rear, taillights pushed out into fender caps giving additional side visibility not apparent with 1966's recessed units.

El Camino continued to list almost all of the SS 396's options; it was the only Chevelle not a Super Sport to offer the Mark IV V-8. Fender emblems indicate this is a 396.

Super Sport models listed for $285 more than comparable Malibu Sport Coupes and Convertibles for 1967, representing a seven-dollar decrease in price for the option compared to 1966. The 1967 Super Sports had more distinction, however. Only SS cars had bright metal wheelhouse moldings as standard in 1967 (1966 Malibus had the moldings, too). Gray-accented body sill moldings spanned the area between wheelhouses at the bottom of the body, while color-keyed body stripes ran along the sides farther up (where Malibu models had a bright strip). A special black-ac-

Horizontal lines defined the 1967 rear on this proposal for the SS 396.

A fairly rare option on 1967 Chevelle SS 396's was the power front disc brake package, which included special slotted wheels with center caps and trim rings. This SS 396 Convertible is so equipped.

94

cented grille mounted an SS 396 emblem in the center, which was repeated at the rear in the center of the Super Sport's black cove panel. Large Super Sport wording on rear fenders was split and stacked for 1967. Raised simulated hood air intakes continued to distinguish SS cars in 1967.

New nylon wide-profile tires, designated F70x14 in size, appeared on 1967 Super Sports with red or white accent stripes. Rims were 14x6, with standard small Chevelle hub caps fitted unless optional covers or wheels were specified. Special Super Sport wheel covers, using SS center plastics with the conventional deluxe Chevelle cover, were on order. Cars with the new optional power front disc brakes came with four handsome Rally-style fourteen-inch slotted rims which had bright trim rings and center caps.

Chevelle SS 396 interiors continued basically unchanged from 1966. An all-vinyl, bench-seat interior was standard; Strato-buckets were optional. The instrument panel had black accents and an SS medallion. An SS horn button was found at the center of the steering wheel. Gauges and a tachometer were again tied together in an optional gauge pack. Interior and exterior color choices were unaltered, for the most part.

Government's continuing interest in vehicle safety, and what the car manufacturers were doing about it, had flowered during 1966. As a result, 1967 Chevelles, along with other Chevrolet passenger cars, included numerous new safety items such as: dual master cylinder brake systems, energy-absorbing steering columns, padded instrument panels, smooth-contour knobs and levers, front and rear seat belts, padded sun

Standard small hub caps came on 1967 SS 396, any available full cover could be ordered optionally.   New for 1967 were Rally-type wheels, included with power front disc brake option.

SS 396 Coupe was mildly facelifted for 1967. Standard small hub caps continued to come on cars unless optional covers were ordered. Tires were red-stripe 14-inchers.

visors, four-way hazard flashers, standard windshield washers, reduced-glare windshield-wiper arms and more.

The SS 396 continued to feature the 325-hp 396 as part of the equipment package. The L34 optional version was now rated at 350 hp, a rating loss of ten from 1966. The 375-hp L78 Turbo-Jet, though not listed on option lists, was delivered in 612 1967 Chevelle Super Sports (and 17,176 more had the 350-hp L34).

Standard, fully-synchronized heavy-duty three-speed gearboxes, with floor-mounted shift levers, were installed in cars without optional gears. Optional transmissions continued as in 1966, with an M20 wide-ratio four-speed for either 396, and an M21 close-ratio unit on order for the 350-hp engine. The M20 numbered 48,354 1967 installations and the M21 accounted for 12,886 units. Powerglide was now one of two optional automatic transmissions, as Turbo Hydra-matic also was offered for 396-powered 1967 Chevelles. Automatic shifters were on the column, unless bucket seats were ordered; then they were moved to the console.

Small-block Chevy enthusiasts could still outfit a 1967 regular Malibu with most of the Super Sport goodies. RPO L79, the 327 V-8 with hot hydraulic cam, was still offered, but it lost twenty-five horsepower from 1966, now being rated at 325 hp. It was still enough, though, to give 325-hp 396 Chevelles fits on the street. There were 4,048 sold. Both of the SS 396 V-8's were offered in the El Camino once again, although the sedan pickup was still not officially a Super Sport when so equipped.

Chevrolet's overall sales declined to a six-year low during 1967's calendar year. Chevelle sales alone were down 43,436 units from 1966. The 1967 Chevelle production total of 369,144 included 63,006 Sport Coupes and Convertibles wearing SS emblems. The new disc brake option found favor with 5,153 1967 Chevelle buyers.

The vinyl upholstery pattern was changed on 1967
SS 396 interiors. Optional Strato-bucket seats were
ordered by many buyers.

CHAPTER SEVEN

A Super Nova
1966–1967

*F*ollowing the introduction of new body shells for big Chevrolet and Corvair passenger cars in 1965, GM's star division turned its efforts to creating totally new Chevelle and Chevy II lines for 1966.

A redesigned Chevy II replaced the original 1962 H-35 style, which had served in good stead without any major facelifting for four model years (a long time in that style-conscious decade). The new Chevy II line was led by the Nova Super Sport series: six- and eight-cylinder models using the Nova's new two-door hardtop body.

Newly styled, the 1966 body was just 0.1 inch shorter than the 1965 model had been, but its overall width expanded 1.4 inches due to revised bumpers. Tread and wheelbase were unchanged from 1962-65 dimensions.

Under its sheet-metal skin, the 1966 Nova used many of the previous years' structural panels from the cowl back. But, visually, it was a clean break with past Chevy II's. Large single-unit headlamps were now mounted in fender ends that were somewhat reminiscent of Buick's 1965 Riviera with its lamps exposed. Body sides were high and relatively flat; rear-end styling was angular. The whole car gave a rather boxy appearance, modified only slightly by the semi-fastback taper of the roof line. It was a design that grew increasingly attractive to many Chevy enthusiasts who might have been initially unsure of their reaction to the new Nova.

Nova Super Sports accounted for 21,000 of the 1966 Chevy II's 172,485 sales.

Super Sport equipment for the 1966 Nova featured bright metal trim running along the lower edge of the car from front bumper to rear, hopping over the wheelhouse openings en route.

Super Sport identification was found on the grille, which was newly designed and made of extruded aluminum. Another SS emblem was found on the right side at the rear, within the special ribbed panel created for SS cars. Super Sport script appeared on rear fender panels. Chevelle's 1965 Super Sport wheel covers made an encore appearance on the 1966 Nova SS as part of the RPO package.

Nova SS was freshly styled for 1966, could be ordered with strong 350-hp 327 to make hot street setup.

A formidable automobile was the 1966 Nova SS equipped with 350-hp 327. Hot hydraulic lifter cam and big four-barrel gave excellent acceleration. Air cleaner had opposing dual snorkels, was fully chromed.

A rather nicely appointed all-vinyl interior with Strato-bucket front seats was included in the $159 charged for Super Sport equipment on a 1966 Nova. A console, with shift lever for optional four-speed or Powerglide transmissions, was also included. SS identification for the interior was found on the console and in script above the glovebox door.

A new full-width instrument panel contained few gauges for the Nova driver. A tachometer was optionally available, but there was no optional gauge cluster. The Nova SS owner was left to after-market sources if he wanted more than warning lights.

Performance options did include Positraction rear axle, sintered metallic brake linings, heavy-duty clutch and full transistor ignition.

Chevrolet kept many of its host of ever-increasing options from the Nova. Power windows and seats were not offered. Radios were all AM units, with front or rear antenna (a power antenna was also offered). The instant-repeat SS wheel covers (from the '65 Chevelle SS) were popular; so not many buyers ordered extra-cost simulated wire wheel covers, and (judging from observation) even fewer opted for the fake mag full covers. Tire size was 6.95x14 on five-inch rims.

Bucking the trend within Chevrolet to tie Super Sport packages to specific high-performance engines, Nova SS was offered with any Chevy II power train except those using the tiny and nearly extinct 153-cubic-inch four.

The six-cylinder Super Sport model used the 120-hp 194-cubic-inch engine as a standard power plant and the 140-hp 230 as an option.

Base V-8 for the 1966 Nova was the tried and true 283 which would power so many Chevrolet passenger cars and trucks that year that it would account for more than twenty-three percent of engine production in all *General Motors* cars built that year. The ever-popular optional version

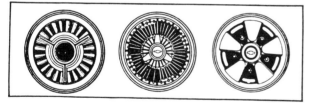

1966 Nova SS wheel cover was same as 1965 Malibu SS. Wires and mag-style cover were seldom-seen options.

1966 Nova SS interior with standard Strato-bucket seats, console for four-speed control lever. Upholstery was all vinyl.

of the 283, with four-barrel carburetor and dual exhausts, continued to rate at 220 hp and was little changed; although for the first time it was listed as a regular-fuel engine in owners manuals.

Replacing the 250- and 300-hp 327 V-8's offered in 1965 was a new 275-hp version using a combination of 250-hp components and a new four-barrel carburetor of larger capacity along with a revised spark advance curve to achieve the extra twenty-five horses. Of extra special interest to Chevy power fans was the inclusion of the potent L-79 version of the 350-hp 327 on Nova's option list. Chevrolet's mid-1965 fully synchronized heavy-duty three-speed was standard with the L79 option, and optional with other V-8's. A newly revised RPO M20 four-speed could be had with any V-8, while L79 buyers could specify the M21 close-ratio box, now offered for the first time in Chevy II's. (Powerglide was optional with all but the L79 engine.)

The 350-hp 327, first found in 1965 Chevelles, was one of the hotter street engines of the country during 1966. For out-of-the-showroom green-light derbies it was just about the king. Stuffed into a Nova SS which barely topped 3,000 pounds ready to run, the 'special performance' high-compression, hydraulic cam 350/327 cruised with an authority unlikely to be disturbed. *Car Life* tested one of these hot small-blocks in May 1966. Their car, using the standard 3.31 rear axle, took 7.2 seconds to reach 60 mph, but just 18.2 to top 100 on the test speedometer. Without opening the hood, it ran the quarter in 15.1 seconds at 93 mph. Just the smallest bit of tuning could dramatically increase the L79's performance. The fast set reacted with 5,481 orders.

Under the hood a big chromed air cleaner with opposing dual snorkels announced a 350-hp 327. Valve covers, oil filler and its cap were also chromed. The silver aluminum manifold contrasted nicely with the 'engine orange' (Chevrolet called it red) of the block and heads.

Super Sport script used on rear quarters of 1966 and 1967 Nova SS. Nova engine insignia for 1966 was found on front fenders. Cars with standard 194-cubic-inch six used no emblem.

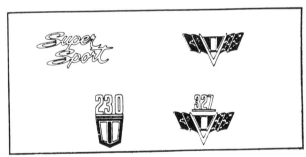

Nova Super Sports were always borrowing hub caps from another Chevrolet product. 1966 version used the 1965 Malibu Super Sport full wheel disc. Sport Coupe was only SS body style.

Even with a 275-hp 327, a 1966 Nova SS could be a good performer. Quarter-mile times near the lower reaches of the sixteen-second bracket could be expected. *Motor Trend* tested a 275-hp Super Sport for its July 1966 issue, in which author Steve Kelly admitted he liked the car after he got acquainted with it. He was especially impressed with its gas mileage, which was as high as 19.2 mpg in average traffic. This now much more important aspect of the Nova's performance was attributed to the car's excellent 11.4-pounds-to-the-horsepower power-to-weight ratio. Kelly summed up the Nova SS as being ". . . practical and safe enough for a family car, sporty and peppy enough for any young man on date night, and economical enough for about everybody's budget."

In many respects, the 1966 Nova SS was worthy of wearing the 1965 Malibu Super Sport hub caps. It was seen as a logical successor to the 1964-65 Malibu by some Chevelle owners who disdained the new SS 396 and chose a Nova SS instead. Nova Super Sports of 1966-67 held their value well as used cars, and are valued collectors' cars today, whether they house a hot 327 or not.

Nova Super Sports were very slightly restyled for 1967. A horizontal-bar-type grille, with black accents and Nova SS signature on the lower left distinguished the front. The rear's ribbed panel was altered a bit, but still carried the SS emblem. Cursive script Super Sport nameplates continued on rear fender panels. A ribbed bright metal strip tied wheelhouse moldings together and extended forward and rearward to the bumpers. Body panels below this line were now painted black, a styling touch reducing the body's bulk by stretching it out visually. Body-side accent stripes were laid on the stamped-in horizontal beltline of the Nova. Wheel covers were now none other than those perennial favorites first seen on 1965 Impala Super Sports, on 6.95x14 rims.

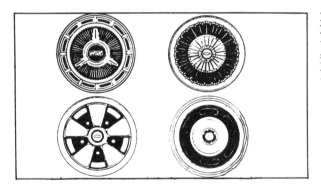

Reaching back to 1965, Chevrolet used that year's Impala SS wheel cover on 1967 Nova SS. Simulated wires lost their knock-off blades this year and mag-style cover was slightly revised as well. Very few Novas were seen with the new disc-brake slotted wheels.

Mild facelift graced 1967 Nova SS. Black-accent rocker panels lengthened body visually. Grille was cleaner this year.

One of the few bright notes for Nova performance enthusiasts in 1967 was the addition of front power disc brakes to the option list. Novas so equipped are instantly recognizable by their fourteen-inch Rally-style slotted rim wheels with trim rings and center caps. The disc brake setup was sold on very few 1967 Novas, only 565 had them. Another new option was Cruise-Master cruise control.

Nova Super Sports featured new upholstery patterning for their all-vinyl interiors; little else was changed. Federally-mandated safety equipment, such as dual master cylinder brake systems, an energy-absorbing steering column and four-way hazard flasher, appeared on 1967 Novas.

For many Nova buyers, there was reason to moan as the hot L79/327 with its 350 charging horses vanished from the engine charts. Chevy II buyers were left with the 275-hp 327 as their top choice. Few took solace in the addition of the 250-cubic-inch Turbo-Thrift six to the option listing for 1967. A number of new rear axle ratios were cataloged for optional installation this year, while transmission choices were in a holding pattern.

The 350-hp 327 was somehow installed in six 1967 Nova Super Sports, and factory literature gives block codes for the Special High Performance Nova 327—certainly one of the rarest Super Sports.

Production of 1967 Nova Super Sports totaled 10,100 units, down more than fifty percent from 1966. Overall Chevy II assemblies totaled 105,858 units for 1967, down by more than 66,000 cars from 1966. The 1966-67 Novas would stand apart from other Nova styles. A new body, which would carry Nova to its last days, was being readied for 1968 introduction.

1967 engine insignia was little changed, but six-cylinder badge now signified optional 250-cubic-inch equipment.

1967 Nova Super Sport interior used new patterns, contrasting color stripes. Powerglide control lever was in console, reverse detent button was built into top of shifter.

CHAPTER EIGHT

The Impala SS Steps Aside
1967–1969

*T*he Caprice, introduced as a complementary line to the Super Sport within the Chevrolet big-car mosaic, continued to steal the scene and sales in 1967. The Super Sport concept, at least as applied to the new larger-looking big Chevrolets, was a wounded duck on the way down. It would take three years to finish it, though. During those three years Impala Super Sports would range from some of the least interesting of all Chevrolets to wear the SS emblems to some of the most rare and fascinating examples of the series.

There were two distinct Chevrolet Super Sports for 1967. Regular Super Sport models continued to feature the bucket-seat, sporty-touch packaging of the original 1962 concept. Trying to have it both ways, the senior Chevrolet line also introduced a car this year done in the same motif as the recently released SS 396 Chevelle. This was the SS 427, a car featuring a trim package built around a specific engine, in this case the Mark IV 427 Turbo-Jet V-8.

Super Sport detailing for 1967 was as thorough as in prior years, but somehow it didn't show up as well. The wide grille was blacked-out horizontally, the black strips following through on the front fender wrap-around trim pieces as well. Super Sport identification was at the left. At the rear there was a small black-accented panel between the huge triple-segment taillights. This panel replaced the bright-metal ribbed panel of lesser Impalas, with the SS emblem to the right, above the lamp bezel. A small SS emblem was affixed low on each front fender, behind the wheelhouse; rear fender panels were clean. Black-accented lower body and rear fender moldings substituted for the higher, bright metal trim strips of conventional Impalas, and wheelhouse moldings were standard with SS equipment. Hub caps were lacking in distinction and not too attractive; they were simply the regular Impala optional full wheel cover with an altered radial insert and plastic center caps carrying the SS logo.

Turn signals on all full-size styles were in slots in the front bumper, while Caprices had running lights built into the fender caps. (These were optional on other series.)

Super Sport Coupe and Convertible models shared bodies with regular Impalas, of course. Although they looked much larger due to the new fluid styling, they were exactly the same length as in 1966 and only 0.3 inch wider. The coupe roof line would be about as close to a fastback design as the large GM cars would ever get. The new roof panel eliminated the traditional 'tulip' (as stylists call it) panel between the lower edge of the back light and the deck lid. The 1967 two-door Impala roof blended right into the deck lid. Total window area was up 173.3 square inches from 1966 as well.

The 1967 AM-FM stereo unit featured an eight-track tape deck in its optimum form. Installation shown is in Caprice.

A four-speed shifter growing out of an SS console was an increasingly rare sight during 1967.

The 1967 color choices numbered fifteen solids with just two two-tone combinations (Granada gold/Capri cream and Sierra fawn/Capri cream). The cars were designed for solid colors, but the stylists had to bow to public pressure and offer black or beige vinyl tops, which were a big fad in 1967, whether they broke the flowing roof line or not.

Convertible tops could be ordered in black, white or a new medium-blue color. Tempered-glass rear windows were now a part of the top assembly, folding with the top. The zippered rear curtain passed from the scene.

Super Sport interiors were offered in what had become the standard vinyl colors. A new parchment-and-black combination was offered with a few selected exterior colors. The 1967 Super Sport buyer had a choice of seats; either Strato-buckets or the new Strato-back bench seat could be ordered. The Strato-back affair had a fold-down center armrest, while the bucket seats featured a center console, housing the transmission shifter. Super Sport identification was found on the glovebox door. Brushed sheet aluminum on the console and instrument panel gave an expansive look.

Chevrolet assured the 1967 new-car buyer (and Uncle Sam) that it was interested in owner and passenger safety by including a host of safety items in the new models. Dual master cylinder brake systems and the energy-absorbing steering column were just two of the twenty-five new safety features built into every 1967 Impala Super Sport.

A new key system, with revised codes, was implemented for greater theft protection, making it "eleven times" more difficult to locate a key that would fit a given lock at random. Rearranged guide slots on 1967 keys made it impossible to use them on previous cars, and vice versa.

Illumination of the ignition switch was accomplished by the use of a light-carrying plastic tube, the first example of fiber optics technology to appear in a Chevrolet.

The buyer with the dollars and desire could still order a responsive Super Sport. For those who opted for less power, the six-cylinder Super Sport Coupe and Convertible models were still offered—only four hundred

Super Sport equipment was further down-graded for 1967, hub caps were same as Caprice, but with different centers. Convertibles were fairly rare.

orders for these came in during 1967. The obvious bulk of the big Impala required at least the standard 195-hp 283 V-8, it seemed. The 1967 Super Sports were about 159 pounds heavier than their 1966 counterparts (and the price had gone up about a dollar a pound, $161 over 1966 list.

Three optional V-8's were offered. The newly-rated 275-hp four-barrel 327 shared a new camshaft design with the 283, giving smoother and more durable operation. The 327 also adapted the sealed large-diaphragm fuel pump used on previous 396 and 427 Turbo-Jet V-8's. The 325-hp 396 (with 61,945 sales) was continued with only minor changes, and the single 427 was down-rated five horsepower for the year, to 385. As installed in an SS 427, the Mark IV big-block was equipped with chrome air-cleaner cover, valve rocker covers, oil filler and engine breather caps. Pressure-sensitive decals applied to the air-cleaner tops carried displacement and horsepower data.

Three-speed transmissions were standard with all small-block V-8's. The 396 and 427 big-blocks required an optional transmission, but the inexpensive M13 three-speed could be specified. Fully-synchro and capable of taking the big-block's punishment, it was a real hindrance in reselling a car, so most of the 699 cars delivered with it were retro-fitted with four-speeds later. The only *cataloged* 1967 four-speed was the M20, which went into about 14,600 full-sized 1967 Chevrolets (option production records show forty-three M21 close-ratio boxes were also installed). A few Super Sports (3,566) had the overdrive unit attached to their base six or 283 V-8 engine. Powerglide was offered for all but the 427, while the well-received Turbo Hydra-matic was offered for both big-blocks; and in response to consumer demand, it was offered with the 275-hp 327 in Super Sport or Caprice cars. A wider range of economy, performance, and special rear axle ratios was offered this year, the application of which

1967 SS console was cleanly designed, with brushed aluminum panel inserts.

1967 Impala SS Sport Coupe featured new fastback roof line.

could greatly vary a given engine-transmission combination's acceleration, top speed and number of miles covered with the 1967 Chevrolet's new twenty-four-gallon gas tank full.

Heavy-duty options included the usual: sintered metallic brake linings, a stronger clutch and other strengthened mechanical parts. New items on the heavy-duty option list for 1967 were led by front disc brakes (which included four handsome Rally slotted wheels in fifteen-inch size with trim rings and center caps), Superlift Air-Adjustable rear shocks and full Superlift shock equipment with automatic level control. A new Special Purpose handling and suspension option, RPO F41, joined the chart and would eventually become highly refined and useful. A gauge package with tachometer was again offered.

Luxury options continued to proliferate for the Caprice, and most were shared with Impala models. An eight-track stereo tape system was built into existing optional sound systems for 1967, which ranged from an AM straight-line radio to AM-FM Multiplex stereo. Cruise-Master cruise control, operated by a button on the turn-signal stalk became a factory or dealer-installed option. An appearance item missing from the charts

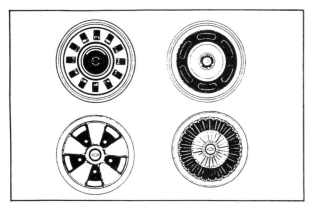

Full wheel covers supplied with 1967 SS Impala were rather homely. Special slotted rims came with front disc brake option. Mag-style covers were slightly changed this year, and the accessory wire cover had a new center.

Ten years separated these two high-performance Chevrolets. The '57 in foreground had caused a sensation with its 283-hp fuel-injected V-8, while 385-hp 1967 SS 427 created little enthusiasm among Chevrolet buyers. The 'factory-fueled' '57 was doing service as a work car when photographed in 1967.

for several years returned for 1967 Impalas and Caprices as fender skirts were once again optional.

On top of this, Chevrolet presented the Impala-based SS 427. It wasn't a great sales success, but is an interesting and rare car today. The SS 427 was a combination of RPO packages (Z24/L36). The Z24 part of the deal started with a specially-domed hood with triple-grid brushed aluminum air ducts near the cowl. Special SS 427 emblems were centered on the grille and deck. The SS 427 had its own unique 427 engine insignia on the front fenders, using large numerals above a big V-shaped emblem with flags. The SS 427 was devoid of side trim except for the engine insignia. Red-stripe 8.25x14 tires on wide-base six-inch rims were standard along with heavy-duty suspension components. Apparently offered for the SS 427 only were (RPO D96) body-side accent stripes that floated on the fender highlight lines.

Powering the special Super Sport was the L36 model 385-hp 427. *Car Life* published a road test of an SS 427 in May 1967. That test machine listed for more than $5,000 full loaded. It swilled super-premium at a steady 10 mpg. The 427 lugged it to 60 mph in 8.4 seconds, turning the quarter mile in 15.75 seconds at 86.5 mph with Turbo Hydra-matic. Top speed was 125 mph.

Just 2,124 SS 427's were counted in total Impala Super Sport production for 1967, which amounted to 76,055 units built for the 1967 model year. Super Sport Convertibles accounted for 9,545, including a few with the SS 427 package. The big 427 was installed in 4,337 full-size Chevrolets.

SS 427 Impala had special filler panel between tail-lights.

SS 427 was new model for 1967. Eyebrow stripes were optional, 385-hp 427 was part of package. Special domed hood had three chrome grids.

Exactly 6,351 big Chevys were delivered with disc brakes during the year, many of them SS 427 Impalas.

Chevrolet's Janesville, Wisconsin, plant had the honor of building the one hundred millionth General Motors Corporation vehicle, a 1967 Caprice Custom Coupe, on April 21, 1967. In a year that had been marked by a twelve percent decline in calendar production, the Nantucket blue Caprice was a welcome reason to celebrate.

The 1968 Chevrolet data book confirmed what declining sales had suggested: the Impala Super Sport was greatly diminished in importance at Chevrolet, as the Caprice luxury models continued to attract thousands of fresh buyers. For the first time since 1963, Impala Super Sports were regular Impala models with optional (RPO Z03) Super Sport equipment. Continued, as an option within an option, was the seldom seen RPO Z24 SS 427 Impala package.

Some sales literature conflict, but apparently the Z06 and Z24 Super Sport options could be ordered on any two-door 1968 Impala, which included three styles for the year. Continued from 1967 were the Sport Coupe (with its zoomy fastback roof) and Convertible. New to the Impala line was the Custom Coupe, with its squared, 'formal' roof borrowed from the Caprice. The Caprice Custom Coupe, at the forefront of Chevrolet styling, became the first big Chevy to discard vent windows in favor of Astro Ventilation, but the Impala Custom Coupe still had the 'ventipanes' to aid air

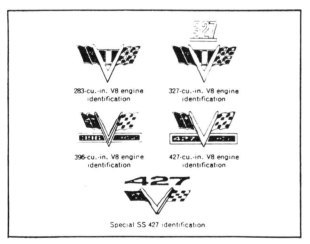

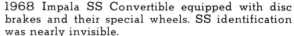

Engine insignia for 1967 full-size Chevrolets. 427 used red filler in bar, while 396 had black. SS 427 had its own fender insignia.

1968 Impala SS Convertible equipped with disc brakes and their special wheels. SS identification was nearly invisible.

circulation. All 1968 Impalas had a raised lip at the rear edge of the hood, which concealed the windshield wiper arms and mechanism and eliminated the vestigial remains of a cowl panel. New side-marker lamps were used front and rear, and new triple-unit round taillights were housed in the bumper panel. Unless optional wheels or covers were specified, all Super Sports came with the full wheel covers optional on other big '68 Chevrolets.

Fifteen solid and six two-tones (recommended mostly for Custom Coupes) were listed on color charts. The all-vinyl interior upholstery patterns included parchment-and-black and Teal for coupe and convertible Impalas. Red vinyl was optionally available on Impala coupes, but was a standard color for Super Sports and convertibles. Convertible tops were white, black or medium-blue, while vinyl roof choices were restricted to white or black.

Under the wide hood of the facelifted 1968 Chevrolets one might find the occasional, but very rare, Super Sport Coupe equipped with a 155-hp 250-cubic-inch six. Impala Custom Coupes and Convertibles required at least the 307 V-8 of 200 hp. The 307 was created by reworking the decade-old 283 Turbo-Fire V-8 block to accept what amounted to a slightly reworked 327 V-8 crankshaft, effectively 'stroking' the motor.

The first rung on the optional V-8 ladder was occupied by a new low-compression (8.75:1) 250-hp 327. Using 10:1 heads and a different four-barrel created the 275-hp 327 which was continued from 1967 along with the 325-hp 396 Turbo-Jet (with 55,190 sales ahead for 1968). The big gun for the bow-tie contingent remained the 385-hp 427 V-8, which would find 4,071 buyers.

Engine identification numerals were housed in the front fender's marker lamp bezel for 1968. SS 427 used same item as any 427 Chevy this year.

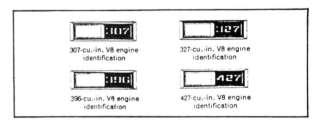

307-cu.-in. V8 engine identification

327-cu.-in. V8 engine identification

396-cu.-in. V8 engine identification

427-cu.-in. V8 engine identification

1968 Super Sport interior was very handsome. New Muncie shifter resembled the forged-blade Hurst-type unit. No reverse lock-out was used.

Six-cylinder and small-block V-8 cars could be had with a full-synchromesh three-speed as standard equipment. Powerglide was optional, as was Turbo Hydra-matic, finally available with any V-8. M20 four-speeds were offered with all V-8's, but the M21, with a 2.20:1 low, was restricted to the 427. M20 installations for 1968 were 6,596; the M21 went into 1,052 cars and 124 M22 "rock crushers" are recorded on the option production list.

Optional rear axle ratios went to the basement at 4.88:1 for drag acceleration. 'Cruise' gears of 2.73:1 were at the other end of the scale, and Positraction was offered with any and all.

The big 427 was supplied with a chromed air cleaner, valve covers and oil filler cap. Heavy-duty shocks, stabilizer bars and special G70x15 red-stripe tires on 15x6 wheels were also included. Essentially, this package made up the mechanical part of the 1968 SS 427 equipment. Trim garnishes included three large horizontal louvers on the front fenders; a revised version of the 1967 SS 427 domed hood, now with four small inlet grids running across the hood near the windshield; and 427 numerals in the front marker lamp bezels (the same as were used on other cars with

Standard 1968 Impala SS cover (upper left) was similar to Caprice, with different center. SS 427 came with small button hub cap (not shown) but buyer could order the full cover at upper right. Rally Wheels could now be ordered on any car, whether it was equipped with disc brakes or not. Wire wheel covers and two mag-style full covers were available as accessories, too.

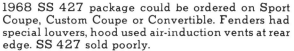

1968 SS 427 package could be ordered on Sport Coupe, Custom Coupe or Convertible. Fenders had special louvers, hood used air-induction vents at rear edge. SS 427 sold poorly.

427 V-8's installed). The SS 427 had the worst of its three years in 1968, with 1,778 built.

Chevrolet offered a wonderful array of options in the late sixties as the 'building block' philosophy permeated its thinking. (The one hundred millionth GM car, that 1967 Caprice mentioned earlier, had fourteen options not offered in 1955, for instance.)

Say you were interested in ordering a new 1968 Super Sport from your friendly local Chevy dealer. There's a new SS on the showroom floor right now, and you stroll in to have a look. Here comes the salesman. As a young sport, you object right off to the 'blah' full wheel covers thrown in with SS equipment. OK, says the salesman, we do have alternatives available at extra cost: choose from the wire wheel cover or one of the two fake mag styles. Should you want power front disc brakes, though, you'll have to settle for the handsome slotted-rim wheels (offered as Rally Wheels for drum-braked cars).

You've already picked the color for your full-vinyl upholstery. Now, do you want Strato-Ease head restraints to cap off your Strato-bucket front seats? Enhance the sports flavor of your SS by adding a plastic Sports Styled steering wheel with simulated walnut rim and special instrumentation which includes a transistorized tachometer and four engine-function gauges.

Comfort and convenience? We've got plenty for you this year, sir. Choose power door locks, four-way power adjustment for your bucket seats, and power windows. We're assuming you want power steering and brakes, of course.

Representative 1968 Chevrolet models from the 1968 *Showroom Album*. Apparently SS and SS 427 equipment could be ordered on the Impala Custom Coupe, with its Caprice roof line. Fastback Sport Coupe could be ordered with regular Impala equipment, too. SS 427 was identifiable from rear by large signature above right taillights.

For year-round comfort you can specify Comfortron Air Conditioning—it'll keep the temperature inside the car at your thermostatically-controlled pleasure. Or, if you just need air for those occasional visits to your aunt in El Paso, you might settle for the much cheaper under-dash Comfort-Car cooler unit.

Well, you've got quite a nice car going here. Why not add fender skirts (unless you are sure you want the wide Rally Wheels, which won't clear the skirts), or how about the new Light Monitoring System instead? Here, you can read about it, from *Finger-Tip Facts*: "Factory installed option (RPO U46) for Chevrolet, Chevelle and Camaro models; standard on Corvette coupe and convertible. System indicates when important lights are burned out. In operation, light is transmitted through a fiber-optics system. Except for Corvette, monitors are located on front fenders and within the rear compartment readily visible through the rearview mirror . . . Front monitors indicate as follows: outer green lens for headlight low beams; center amber lens for parking and turn signal lights; inner red lens for headlight high beam. Rear monitors have center white lens for license plate light and red outer lenses for right and left turn signals, taillights and stoplights."

You'd like concealed headlights, like on that Caprice over there in the showroom? Sorry, they are Caprice-only options.

You'll be spending a lot of time on the road with this cruiser, so maybe you'd want the Superlift air shocks, introduced last year, to help with the luggage or samples. They keep the car at a pre-set level automatically. Just whip into any service station to raise the car with the air hose, or release the air valve to return to normal height.

Okay. Now, you know we're concerned about your safety (someone has to make the payments, after all, heh, heh), so take a look at this list of safety features built into your new Super Sport. We've added shoulder belts for front seat passengers this year. But, you can order shoulder belts for your rear seat passengers, too, if you wish. (Yes, even convertibles can be equipped with shoulder belts.)

Now, sir, you need to pick an engine. Most buyers in your shoes like the 325-hp 396. You might want the 427, but frankly, that's a pretty

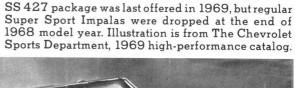

SS 427 package was last offered in 1969, but regular Super Sport Impalas were dropped at the end of 1968 model year. Illustration is from The Chevrolet Sports Department, 1969 high-performance catalog.

expensive and exotic engine, and you might over-rev your air conditioning besides. Oh, lots of people still choose a 307 or 327 V-8, but this Super Sport needs a little more dig than they can provide, so it'll be the 396, then?

You've probably heard about our Turbo Hydra-matic; that's our three-speed automatic transmission designed for Buicks. Almost everyone wants it instead of Powerglide now. We'd better include the Speed Warning Indicator so this brute won't get away from you, don't you think? And, why not add Cruise-Master speed control, too. That way you can set it on seventy and roll all day, relaxing with Burt Bacharach on your AM-FM stereo eight-track unit (right here, RPO U69-U79, with U57 eight-track).

You want me to stop and total this up so far? All right, sir, just a moment while I install a new tape roll in my adding machine . . .

Loaded Super Sports such as that just imagined were quite scarce in 1968, although accessory-laden Caprices were a common sight. (A Caprice Custom Coupe listed for just $198 more than a comparable Impala model, to which $180 would be added for SS equipment, so it was only natural for luxury buyers to opt for the Caprice). Performance enthusiasts were finding all they needed in Chevelle and Camaro models, so hot 1968 Impala Super Sports were also rarely seen. The Impala SS was becoming a car without a market. All varieties of 1968 Super Sports accounted for 36,432 sales in 1968; clearly the end was near for the Impala SS. Chevrolet as a whole posted a good year, rebounding from 1967 with a five-percent increase in sales (but they were still off thirteen percent from the record-breaking 1965 model year). Chevelle, Camaro and Corvette set calendar-year records during 1968, as the sporty muscle and pony car markets flamed to life again. The big Impala, however, had become too large to make a successful 'specialty car.' Chevrolet realized this, and canceled the Super Sport for 1969 big cars, with one rare and interesting exception.

Chevrolet had been merchandising its sport models through multi-line literature since 1967, when it issued a very long and narrow vertical-format brochure for the Camaro SS 350, Chevelle SS 396, Nova SS, Impala SS 427 and Corvette 427. By 1969, they were issuing similar catalogs, but in a more typical format, titled *The Chevrolet Sports Department*, "Where you get the Chevrolet viewpoint on all our sports models." This catalog contains the only widely distributed reference to the swan song model of the Impala Super Sports, the 1969 SS 427. The SS 427 was shown in con-

Final Super Sport used only SS emblem on steering wheel for interior distinction. Ordering optional bucket seats, console and four-speed created an interior worthy of SS 427.

SS 427 used special grille work, SS emblem. 1969 was last year for full-size Super Sport.

vertible form with a very grainy, low-light illustration, and the Sports Department booklet said: "It crosses a luxury car with flat cornering and strong performance. Strictly big-sport class in Custom coupe, Sport coupe and convertible."

The new 1969 bodies, measuring 215.9 inches in length (1.2 inches longer than '68), featured new pontoon-bulge fender lines creating an impression of bulk even greater than was really present.

The SS 427 was distinguished by a black-accented grille with a large SS emblem in its center. Additional SS emblems were found beneath the Impala series identification on the fenders and on the deck lid. G70x15 red-stripe wide-profile tires on fifteen-inch Rally rims were included.

Under the SS 427 hood was a 390-hp 427. Cylinder heads and pistons were slightly modified for this year, accounting for the five-horsepower gain over 1968. Peak horsepower was developed at 3600 rpm, two hundred more than the earlier 427's charted peak.

SS 427 interiors were standard Impala, except for an SS emblem on the steering wheel. Even bucket seats, which featured a console, were optional.

A console for the optional four-speed or Turbo Hydra-matic controls was included with bucket seating. 'Standard' transmission for the 427 was a column-shift M13 three-speed; it is doubtful if any at all were so ordered. Most buyers probably selected one of the four-speeds (2.20 or 2.52:1 low boxes were available) or Turbo Hydra-matic. (Four-speed production was 3,448 M20 boxes and 969 M21's. Not cataloged, the M22 still went into seventy-seven big 1969 Chevys.) Rear axle ratios offered included 3.07 'economy' gears for all combinations. Four-speeds could be ordered with 3.73 gears, and Turbo Hydra-matics with a special 2.29:1 'cruise performance' axle.

Among the options for the year were such goodies as variable-ratio power steering, headlight washers, Comfort-Tilt steering column, Positraction (required with 3.73 gears) and an engine-block heater. A total of 18,308 full-size Chevrolets with LS1 427's were built; an additional 5,582 had the L36 390-hp, including SS 427's, and 546 had the L72 425-hp screamer.

The SS 427 really was a car without a market in 1969. Only 2,455 buyers among the 777,000 customers who selected some sort of Impala for 1969 chose the SS 427; even those few who wanted a Super Sport type big car were becoming wary. Insurance companies were very quick to apply surcharges on cars that were special models. Some buyers, wishing

SS 427 used same engine insignia as any Chevrolet with the 427 V-8 in 1969. Numerals were above front fender marker lamp.

to avoid undue hassle, ordered Impalas with all the traditional SS goodies; even the 427 was sometimes specified.

The 1969 SS 427 is perhaps the most unknown of all Super Sports. However, its scarcity goes unrecognized, so the 1969 SS 427 isn't yet an especially valuable car. A true dinosaur of an automobile, the SS 427 will no doubt be as fascinating to future generations of automotive enthusiasts as certain 'biggest' dinosaurs are to lovers of that sort of biological history.

Apparently the last Chevrolet Impala-based Super Sport was a capable performer. No road tests were published, but *Car Life* did run a very similar Caprice Custom Coupe equipped with a 390-hp 427 through its paces for the June 1969 issue. It found the luxury barge would shoot to 60 mph in 7.7 seconds and give a quarter-mile performance of 89.6 mph in 15.5 seconds. With the 3.07:1 rear axle, the top speed of 126 mph seems modest. The *Car Life* testers raved about the 4,830 pounds of Caprice when discussing its handling characteristics. They applauded the F41 suspension option for making the Caprice's performance in the bends possible. Most of the RPO F41 components were included with SS 427 equipment.

At the 1970 NHRA Winternationals, a big full-size '70 Chevy wagon, running the same 390-hp 427 used in the 1969 SS 427, turned in 13.41 seconds at 103.68 mph to take Top Stock Eliminator (rodders often preferred wagons for the weight bias to the rear).

For the Impala models, the sixties was *the* Super Sport decade. Total Impala Super Sport production fell short of a million units by about 82,000 cars. No doubt several hundred thousand are still around. Perhaps armed with the information found in this book the reader can choose the one he or she wishes to preserve.

Written Off! ▬▬▬▬▬▬▬▬▬▬▬▬▬▬▬▬▬▬▬▬▬▬▬▬▬▬

I'll always remember the night the '67 Chevies arrived. We were hanging around the local Chevy dealer's parking lot, as usual; since our gang drove late-model Chevies, Impala Super Sports mostly, they tolerated us. Anyway, about three a.m. a truck drove up in front of the showroom. It was loaded with '67 big Chevies. We walked out to see them. I can still picture the nose of a new Caprice sticking out of the lower deck of the hauler. Ugly Chinese-lantern parking lights caught my eye at first. The cars seemed bloated, fluid; crisp lines were nowhere to be seen. We all stood around silently, sort of in shock, really. We were Chevy *nuts*; these cars had our favorite name and all that, but it just

wasn't our kind of car, it didn't fit into our world and had no interest for us.

You know, we were getting older, most of us were nineteen or so, and the draft was breathing down our necks. Three or four of the gang had already been sent to Vietnam. Our world was changing, eroding, and those big '67 Chevies brought it all home to us in a single instant. We'd been written off, Chevrolet no longer built cars, big cars anyway, for people like us. It's really funny, but I remember that hot August night in 1966 as a real pivotal point in my life—it was the end of the good years, the *American Graffiti* years, for our bunch.

CHAPTER NINE

Chevelle Ripples Its Muscles
1968–1973

A totally new Chevelle design came to market for the 1968 model year. During its five years of revision it would find tremendous acceptance by a new generation of performance enthusiasts. It would be equipped with some engines that will surely rank among the most powerful ever installed in street-driven automobiles.

Super Sport equipment and the 396 V-8 were again offered only in team form for Chevelle buyers. The SS 396 Sport Coupe and Convertible were classified as distinct models by Chevrolet, although they shared sheet metal and chassis with the complementing Chevelle Malibu models. The 1968 SS 396 used a new short 112-inch wheelbase shared with all contemporary Chevelle coupe and convertible styles (four-doors and wagons used a new 116-inch wheelbase). Tread width was increased one inch, as well.

The 1968 GM intermediate's hardtop body was getting pretty close to a full fastback roof line. An upsweeping curve at the base of the rear side windows gave the new A-bodies a rather distinctive look. The SS 396 and Concours (the luxury line Chevelle, new for '68) used Chevrolet's innovative Hide-A-Way windshield wipers, which were available optionally on lesser Chevelles. All 1968 Chevrolets had side-marker lights for the first time, and engine displacement numerals were carried in the same bezel as the front marker lamp.

El Camino, the popular sport truck from Chevrolet, shared the Chevelle's new styling, using the sedan and wagon 116-inch wheelbase. For the first time it could be ordered officially as an SS 396 (model 13880). Sales of the El Camino SS for 1968 totaled 5,190 units. (Subsequent El Camino SS production figures are counted with Chevelles through 1974.)

Black accents were liberally applied to the new SS 396 for 1968. Grilles were almost completely blacked-out, and a black-filled, bright-outline panel tied the taillights together at the rear. On all but dark-colored Chevelle SS 396 cars, the lower body was painted black, with the band of black sweeping up to the headlamp indentation in the front fender. To divide the contrasting colors, an extra strip of bright metal was added behind the rear wheelhouse on SS 396 cars. Body-side striping was initially listed as an extra-cost option, but was made standard later in the year.

SS emblems were located at front and rear, and SS discs were used instead of Concours identifiers when the cars were delivered with the rather plain full wheel covers used for 1968. The now-traditional twin-dome hood was continued; new styling placed the intake grids nearer the rear edge of the hood.

Series identification for the interior was indicated by an SS emblem on the instrument panel, above the glovebox door. Many SS 396 buyers opted for extra-cost Strato-bucket seats, of course. A console was included with this option. All two-door Chevelles were available with RPO U14 special instrumentation, which included a temperature/ammeter/oil-pressure gauge, tachometer and electric clock.

Chevrolet's fifteen exterior colors were offered on SS 396 Chevelles; five two-tone combinations could also be specified. Ten interior vinyls were offered, including blue and parchment (with buckets only). Vinyl roof colors remained black or white; convertible tops could also be ordered in blue.

SS 396 grille insignia was repeated on fenders, at rear.

El Camino finally received its SS 396 badges in 1968, was actually listed as a Malibu SS 396 model for this one year.

Wearing F70x14 Firestone Wide Ovals on six-inch JK rims, the new shorter and wider Chevelle SS 396 had the look of a tough street fighter, especially when wearing after-market accessory mag wheels. A new, stronger frame was better able to handle the tremendous torque of the big 396's.

For the first time the always-secretly-available L78-type 375-hp 396 option appeared on the back of the order blank. Such an order might still take three or more months to process, but sales increased anyway. A total of 4,751 375-hp 396 Chevelles were built in 1968. Delivered from the dealer such a Sport Coupe would do 0-60 in about 6.6 seconds, break into the fourteen-second bracket at the drags and near 100 mph in the traps in the process.

Specification sheets continued to list the 325-hp 396 Turbo-Jet V-8 as standard equipment for SS 396 Chevelles. The L34 option, the 350-hp 396, was offered (and accounted for 12,481 sales). Backing these engines was the M13 Special three-speed, unless an optional four-speed was specified. It would be either the 2.41:1 low RPO M20 (production of 38,933) or, for the 350- and 375-hp units only, the 2.20:1 low box (RPO M21, 11,208 built. There were 1,049 M22 heavy-duty four-speed 1968 Chevelles). For shiftless types, the old Powerglide or new Turbo Hydra-matic automatics were cataloged.

A limited number of Chevelle enthusiasts continued to look upon the big-block cars with disdain. For them, the L79 with the 325-rated-hp

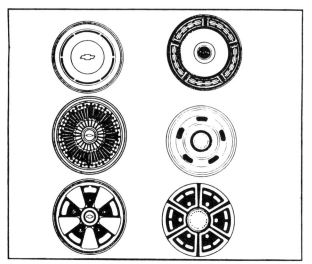

Standard hub cap on 1968 SS 396 was small cap at upper left. Chevelle full wheel covers, with SS 396 centers, were on order, as were wire and two types of mag-style covers. Rally Wheels were offered for all this year.

1968 SS 396 used new 112-inch wheelbase. Convertible is equipped with standard SS 396 wheel covers and optional stripes above lower body trim.

327 was optional again, and found 4,082 Malibu installations. A straight Malibu Sport Coupe, equipped with this potent little V-8 (with its lighter weight, hotter cam and big valves in higher compression heads) was a giant-killer, capable of humbling the 325-hp 396 handily. Of course, a close encounter with an L78-type 396 would be another story.

The revised SS 396 proved to be as popular as the 1967 version. Sales were 62,785 units for the model year, just 300 less than in 1967. A calendar record for Chevelle was also established as 1968 sales sailed over the 400,000 mark. In Baltimore, Chevrolet's assembly plant used a special SS 396 Coupe to commemorate the five millionth Chevrolet assembly made there since operations began in 1935.

Chevelle's styling and the basics of the SS 396 model package were unaltered for 1969, but a major change was made in the car's interrelationship with other Chevelles. For the first time in Chevelle history, the Super Sport equipment became an option package for certain Chevelle models, rather than a distinct series feature. The 1969 SS equipment was ordered as RPO Z25. It was available on all coupe and convertible Chevelles, including the middle-series 300 Deluxe Sport Coupe and the 300 Deluxe Coupe. For the first time in Chevelle SS history, a true two-door sedan-style body, with door pillar, could be ordered with the SS package. In the truck division, the SS 396 El Camino was again offered, with styling changes corresponding to the passenger cars. The El Camino SS 396 was no longer considered a distinct model by Chevrolet.

Styling was refreshingly cleaned-up with a new, blacked-out, grille. At the rear, taillights grew upward, now filling most of the rear fender's end cap. The 1969 Chevelle coupe and convertible models lost their vent windows in conformity with General Motors' decision to eliminate them. A black band across the rear above the bumper still signaled an SS 396 car, as did the SS 396 emblems front and rear and on the front fenders. Bright accents for front and rear wheel openings nicely framed the new and handsome five-spoke chrome Sport Wheels. Tires were F70x14, apparently in white-stripe or white-letter wide-profile trim. Power front disc brakes were standard. Upper-body striping was available in contrasting colors this year.

SS emblems on the steering wheel and instrument panel identified 1969 SS 396 Chevelles on interior surfaces. New Chevelles, along with other 1969 GM cars, used a locking steering-wheel device for anti-theft protection. Bucket seats were still a popular option, and came with a con-

Sport Coupe used new roof line; black-accent rocker and lower fender areas gave illusion of greater length. SS 396 had black band across rear.

sole when ordered. Four-speed and Special three-speed-equipped cars had floor shifters with or without a console, but automatics were always on the column with bench seats and with bucket seats the shifters were on the floor, in a console. For the first time, manual gearbox cars had a safety starter switch, to prevent starting the car with the transmission in gear and clutch engaged.

General sales literature for 1969 indicated that the engine story was unchanged from 1968. Although some head and piston changes were made, the top V-8 was still a 396-cubic-incher rated at 350 hp. It was listed as the optional L34 (17,358 produced), while the 325-hp 396 (59,786 installations) was cataloged as standard with the SS option. The 375-hp 396, though not cataloged, went into 9,486 1969 Chevelles. The heavy-duty Special M13 three-speed manual transmission was also included with SS 396 equipment. Optional was the M20 four-speed (44,950 Chevelle sales), with a close-ratio 2.20:1 box also available (13,786 Chevelles had it) for 350-hp cars. A further 1,276 Chevelles had the strong M22 four-speed. Turbo Hydra-matic was offered for either engine, but the old Powerglide was finally put into well-deserved retirement. About 51,000 of the 1969 Chevelles came with four-speed boxes, and approximately 11,800 had front disc brakes.

Chevrolet remained officially very much out of organized racing of any sort, although a few cracks of light had shown around the sealed doors in 1968. Corvette engineers had been doing some pretty wild things during the 'quiet' years of the mid-1960's; such as the L-88 aluminum head 427 and the *all* aluminum ZL-1. These engines were terribly tempting to Camaro's racing enthusiast engineers, who had adapted the Mark IV big-block to their new sporty car within weeks of its 1967 introduction. The

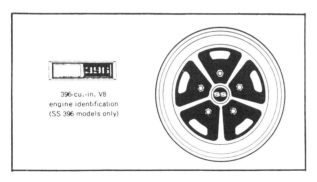

396-cu.-in. V8
engine identification
(SS 396 models only)

1968 SS 396 carried engine displacement numerals in front fender marker lamp bezel (left). Chrome Sport Wheels were included with 1969-70 SS equipment for Malibus.

Handsome chrome Sport Wheels were included with 1969 Malibu SS 396 equipment. Body was essentially unchanged from 1968.

gap between sports car and passenger car thus bridged, it was only a matter of time before exotic big-blocks were fitted to Chevelles, which already had a thing going with the 375-hp 396. During 1969, according to Chevrolet Product Promotion Engineering, quite a few Chevelles and Camaros were delivered with the RPO L72 Corvette 425-hp 427. An additional fifty or so Camaros were delivered with the $3,000-plus ZL-1 aluminum 427 installed. Paul G. Prior, of Chevrolet, told the author: "All three [of the engines described above] were what we called COPO—Central Office Production Order, as opposed to RPO—that's really just a matter of internal paper work; they were available. ZL-1's were limited, but the others were not." No 427 production figures have surfaced, but option production records show 400 1969 375-hp Chevelles had the L89 aluminum head option.

The SS 396 did better as an option than it had as a distinct model. RPO Z25 kits were built into 86,307 Chevelles. The 1969 model year would stand as a high-water mark for Chevelle SS production.

White-letter tires were included with 1970 Sport Wheels on SS Chevelles. Cowl-induction hood option included hood and deck stripes.

Chevelle SS 396 for 1970 benefited from first-cousin relationship to new Monte Carlo, used special round-face instruments, black wheel and column.

One can only try to understand in retrospect why 1970 turned out to be the peak and, for many purists, the last year of the high-performance era. Perhaps it had something to do with our involvement in Vietnam. The big military buildup for that quicksand conflict had begun in 1965, and continued for several years. Thousands of car-crazy young Americans were scooped up as they walked out of their high school graduation and bundled into uniforms. Those 'class of '65' patriots who chose the Navy or Air Force before the draft fell upon them served four-year minimum hitches, as a rule. Many others were drafted in 1967-1968. So they were just coming home about the time the 1970 cars came out. For many of them, *Hot Rod*, *Car Craft*, and *High Performance Cars* had been among their fantasy books in the hootches of Vietnam. These young people, with pent-up emotions and savings accounts, flocked to car dealerships to try and buy the latest and greatest super cars. Chrysler and Ford had fought hard and well for supremacy in the field during the late 1960's, but for those who had been in Vietnam, Chevrolet, the great car of the first half of the sixties, remained their general favorite.

Coincidentally, 1970 was the year the 400-cubic-inch rule for intermediates was finally breached in the GM camp, and it was breached in spectacular fashion. Instead of grabbing the circa-425-cubic-inch big-blocks of large 1965-69 GM cars, the A-bodied mid-size GM juniors moved right into the new generation of 450-plus-cubic-inch V-8's. For Chevelle, it was the new 454-cubic-inch derivative of the Mark IV block. Not just any 454 would power Chevelle in 1970; the top option was the all-out truly muscle-bound LS-6, rated a conservative 450 hp (the same engine was rated 460 hp for Corvette, and even that was probably shy a few ponies of actual gross horsepower). The LS-6 was destined to become a legend.

Ten years later, looking back at the Super Car era, *Hot Rod* and other publications would count the LS-6 Chevelle among the very top members of the Super Car Valhalla, But, even as the LS-6 was first becoming known, it had been recognized as an epitaph to the Super Car era. In 1970, when the cars were brand new, *Hot Rod* said, "The past is gone, the future may never see a car like this." Look at these decade-old road test figures: running standard F70x14 tires, an LS-6 tested by *Hot Rod* clocked the quarter at 108.17 mph in 13.44 seconds. *Car Craft* came even closer to the magical twelve-second bracket, at 13.12 with its LS-6 test car. For comparison, an L88 Corvette had turned in a 13.56-second time at 111.1 mph in a 1969 road test. The LS-6 was not only fast, it was a bargain. Specifying the option added but $321 to the total bill (although various required additional options still made for a pretty expensive Chevelle). On the street, only well-tuned street hemis and the very rarely seen full-race Ford could seriously threaten an LS-6. None of these cars had any

Most 1970 SS Malibus carried the 396 emblem (top) on their front fenders. Occasionally, a 454 with its red-filled numerals would be spotted. A new, gray-finish, Sport Wheel (right) was included with 1971 Malibu SS equipment.

123

business being on the street, anyway, concluded a growing number of insurance companies and legal authorities.

The LS-6 developed its super performance by the use of ultra-high-compression heads (11.25:1) and a very strong solid-lifter camshaft. Most 454 Chevelles were powered by the slightly more tame LS-5 version of the 454, which used 10.25:1 heads for a bit more flexibility as a 'grocery getter.' The standard SS 396 Chevelle engine was moved up a notch, becoming the formerly optional 350-hp 396. The 375-hp version L78 was still offered to anyone who knew enough to ask (and 2,144 buyers did, eighteen of them also ordered L79 aluminum heads). All engines had chrome accents, including valve covers.

During the first few months of 1970 production, the 396 blocks grew to 402 cubic inches. It is believed that cars built before January 1, 1970, had true 396 blocks; while cars built after that date had the 402 with its slightly enlarged cylinder bore. Horsepower ratings were left intact, and even when the 402 went into full model-year production, it would remain known as the 396. Apparently Chevrolet felt it had spent too much money promoting the SS 396 to tamper with the designation. All 1970 big-blocks used 'slim line' spark plugs.

Backing the impressive array of 1970 engines was a job reserved for the strong four-speed and Turbo Hydra-matic transmissions. Both M20 and M21 four-speeds were offered.

The 454 was in short supply during early 1970 (although Monte Carlos were coming through right from the start with the monster block). Original spec sheets for the year indicated that Camaro and even Nova would get their share of the new giant blocks, but they never did.

Since most buyers settled for the 350-hp 396 in 1970, a look at its performance is of interest. *Road Test* magazine (March 1970) had a go

Chevelle featured new frontal ensemble for 1970. Chrome hood lock pins were standard with SS equipment.

with the new SS 396 Coupe normally equipped: 350/396 and Turbo Hydramatic. That test Chevelle ran the quarter in 15.27 seconds at 92 mph. Like other contemporary automotive writers, the *Road Test* crew thought the big-block Chevelle had become a rather good all-around performance car. The SS 396's standard front-disc/rear-drum binders pulled the Chevelle down from 60 mph in 150 feet. Variable-ratio power steering, heavy-duty suspension and F70x14 tires on super-wide seven-inch rims gave the car excellent handling characteristics. Of course, all this GT-type luxury was to be had at additional cost. *Road Test* said the window sticker was $4,433.80, quite a pile of beans over the $2,809 base price of a Malibu coupe in 1970. The SS 396 package alone was $445.55. No one was too worried about gas mileage that first year of the seventies, but *Road Test* still noted that the GT in a muscle shirt gave mileage ratings ranging from 10 to 13.5 miles per gallon.

RPO Z25, the 1970 Super Sport package, consisted of the following features for exterior identification: special domed hood with chromed hood pins, black-accented grille with large SS emblem in center, SS 396 or SS 454 front fender emblems, front and rear wheelhouse moldings, a new black resilient rear-bumper inset panel with the SS emblem and twin rectangular bright-metal exhaust extensions exiting beneath the bumper, which contained new rectangular taillights.

The attractive, chromed five-spoke Sport Wheels with SS emblems in the center caps were again included, with the F70x14 Firestone Wide Oval bias belted tires mounted. A minor distinction for 1970 Chevelle Super Sports was the use of clear lenses over the front parking lamps, while regular Malibus had amber covers.

SS equipment was offered only for Sport Coupes and Convertible models in 1970, leaving what few 1969 SS 396 Coupes that were ordered as the only two-door sedan Chevelle Super Sports. SS equipment, including the hot 454 combos, continued to be listed as optional for El Camino pickups.

New styling would prove to be transitional between the first 1968-69 look and the last 1971-72 design. A new roof shape around the rear side windows was featured. The grille opening was visually separated from the headlights for a new look moving towards the pseudo-Mercedes openings of the new decade.

The 1970 SS Chevelle was the recipient of the first really different instrument-panel design just for a Super Sport. It was completely different from the contemporary Malibu, sharing components with the new Monte Carlo instead. Round gauges were used, and all SS cars had black steering wheels and columns. The wheel had an SS emblem in the center, of course. Optional special instruments were housed in two round bezels flanking the speedometer. It was all very suggestive of the Corvette, and very appealing.

1970 SS Malibu carried black inset panel on rear bumper with SS badge to right. Bright tailpipe extensions were included. Some 1971 SS Chevelles were 454's, with twin bright metal tailpipe extensions included. SS emblem mounted on bumper, as in 1972, also.

Strato-bucket seats were optional, coming with a console for transmission controls. Turbo Hydra-matic consoles used the new safety stirrup shifter, which resembled a giant staple. (The idea was that it would be impossible to impale oneself on the shifter in an accident.)

A very popular 1970 Super Sport-only option was the new Cowl Induction hood (RPO ZL2), which cost an extra $147.45 including the 'trick' black or white wide stripes. (The 'Band-Aid' stripes were optionally available without the special hood, as well.) The Cowl Induction was vacuum-operated, with an air valve at the rear of the hood, under the bulge that flew open when the engine throttle was pushed to the floor. A big rubber seal atop the air cleaner mated with the closed hood to assure induction of only fresh, cool air.

Other new options appeared for 1970, as well. Among them was a power door-lock system (RPO AU3) that could be integrated with the electrically powered Automatic Seat Back Latch (RPO AQ2), which would conveniently unlock the folding front seat backs when a door was opened. European influence surfaced in the RPO CD3 'stalk' windshield wiper control, which was combined with the turn-signal lever. Wiper and washer operation were controlled through a button-and-rotating-knob arrangement on the end of the lever. "A miniature cowl mounted computer programs the type of operation signalled by the driver," the *Sales Album* for 1970 explained. The new Delco side-terminal battery, standard in 1970 on Camaro and Corvette, was optionally available on Chevelle and other Chevrolets. Optional radios received their signals through a windshield antenna for the first time in 1970.

Color choices for the new Chevelles still numbered fifteen, but several new hues were to be found. Metallic earth colors were very popular, in solids and among the seven two-tone combinations. Sport Stripes were black or white, depending on body color. Vinyl tops, if ordered, could be black or white regardless of body color, while convertibles used the same two top colors (soft tops with black tops had black Sport Stripes; white tops mandated white stripes if the option was specified).

The 1970 Chevelle was a tremendous car, and it was well received. But, outside forces were at work, and all was not well in Super Car Land. During 1970, insurance companies, perhaps awakened at last by the in-

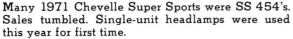

Many 1971 Chevelle Super Sports were SS 454's. Sales tumbled. Single-unit headlamps were used this year for first time.

cessant 'beep-beep' of the Plymouth Roadrunner horn, mounted a surcharge campaign that inflicted immediate pain on the wallets of muscle car owners. Rates soared to such heights that *Car and Driver* remarked, "For some, the cost of insurance was higher than the monthly payment." Safety interests were indirectly influencing the super car future, too. Looking back at 1970, it seems pretty bold of Chevrolet to flaunt such a fast and flashy car as the striped Chevelle SS 454. And there was more bad news coming for the speed enthusiasts: the 1971 advent of regular-fuel compression ratios loomed on the horizon, promising to emasculate the big engines even more (if reducing the power of the LS-6 to a puny 425 hp can be called emasculation, indeed). Perhaps it was just as well. A car capable of 110 mph in less than fourteen seconds was too much for even the most capable driver to handle everywhere; and unless the owner lived in Nevada, it probably had too much power to be used safely on the street on any occasion. A backing-off was inevitable. The insurance companies and the Environmental Protection Agency (EPA) made handy 'bad guys,' and were shouldered with the blame.

Chevelle Super Sport production for 1970 receded to a still-respectable 53,599 units. Of these 8,773 were SS 454's. (4,475 with RPO LS6.)

The frontal ensemble of the 1971 Chevelle was a splendid example of GM Design's ability to make considerable revision in a design, while maintaining an appearance of gentle evolution. The 1971 Chevelles were the first of their kind to use single-bulb headlamp units, achieved by adapting Camaro/Nova's big seven-inch units. The parking/side-marker lamp units were doubled and stacked on front fender caps. The grille lost its distinctive body-color horizontal division, using a chrome bar in its stead. SS cars had black-accented grille inserts. At the rear, taillights underwent cell division, splitting into two round units at each bumper end.

The RPO Z15 SS equipment package for Chevelle Sport Coupes and Convertibles remained basically intact from 1970. SS emblems on the grille and front fenders were unchanged in location. At the rear, the SS emblem was centered on the new deeper rear bumper. There was no black accent panel this year. Super Sports continued to feature bright wheelhouse moldings, without corresponding rocker panel trim. New, really 'tough' looking 15x7 five-spoke gray-finish mag-style Sport Wheels

Mid-year 1971 competitor for doing battle with Plymouth Roadrunner was the Heavy Chevy, featuring blacked-out grille, decal identification and stripes, Rally Wheels. Any V-8 except 454 could be specified.

with F60x15 white letter tires were featured. Power front disc and rear drum brakes were included in the $357 SS package. The domed cowl-induction-type hood, without the actual rear-edge flap was included with chrome lock pins and all SS Chevelles had a left-hand remote control Sport Mirror as standard.

Inside, the SS was virtually identical to its 1970 counterpart. A new black steering wheel with SS emblem and black steering column was used in all Chevelle Super Sports. The nicely detailed, round-face instrument panel was continued. One change, a harbinger of coming times, was the adaptation of European-style 'function symbols' for headlight, cigarette lighter and radio knobs.

Twin chrome exhaust outlets beneath a 1971 SS rear bumper attested to the presence of a 454 V-8, as did the addition of red-filled 454 numerals below the fender SS emblems. Chevrolet's 1970 *Sales Album* listed both the "Chevelle SS" and the "SS 454" as RPO Z15 options. Apparently the difference was all under the hood, although some magazine articles stated the Sport Wheels came only with the 454.

The SS 454 cars were equipped with a 365-hp version of Chevrolet's biggest V-8. It managed to rate five more horses than the 1970 version following the rather drastic cut in compression ratio from 1970's 10.25:1 to 1971's 8.5:1, by the use of a new head design and revised camshaft.

During the year General Motors switched to advertising *net* horsepower ratings for their cars' engines, which amounted to 285 for the 365-gross-rated-hp 454. The old ratings had ostensibly represented figures generated by an engine running unencumbered on a dynamometer. The new 'net' figures were garnered by testing engines as installed with exhaust system and accessory drives in place and taking their toll. Either way, the 1971 SS 454 was an LS-5 engine. Production records indicate 9,502 were installed (possibly including SS 454 Monte Carlos). The total number of RPO Z15 SS-equipped Chevelles was 19,293.

Chrome dress-up items hadn't been outlawed, though, and the SS 454 featured plated valve covers, oil filler cap and air-cleaner cover. Transmission choices were either the growling M22 four-speed, with its extra-duty gears; or Turbo Hydra-matic. The 1971 Chevelles and Monte Carlos accounted for 9,786 M20 four-speeds, and 3,035 SS 454's had M22 heavy-duty boxes.

Not on most availability charts, but still around, was a 1971 version of the 454 LS-6. It was the only Chevrolet engine to be allowed a compression ratio of more than 8.5:1 for 1971, with its 9.0:1 heads. According to records, though, only Corvettes—188 of them—were so equipped.

During early 1970, enthusiast magazines had been full of rumors about a new 454 that would upstage the LS-6. Among the rumored specifications for the so-called LS-7 V-8 was a compression ratio of 12.5:1, ZL-1-type aluminum heads and many more modified or lightened parts. It was a Corvette project, but it might have spread quickly to Camaro and even Chevelle in the atmosphere at Chevrolet as the new decade began. The LS-7 project's chances dimmed quickly as 1970 progressed, and it finally died in the crossfire between safety/emissions troops and the engineers. Reportedly, it did appear, dismembered, in the 1971 service parts lists for specialty applications. In other words, if you had enough dollars and contacts, you might have been able to piece together an LS-7 454 Chevelle in 1971. Whether anyone did or not is unrecorded by the sources used for this book.

The plain Chevelle SS was offered with, according to the *Sales Album*, either 245- or 270-hp Turbo-Fire 350 V-8, or the 300-hp Turbo-

Jet 400 V-8 (which was the 396 cum 402—not to be confused with the Turbo-*Fire* 400 small-block offered in the full-size Chevrolet line). These engines were devoid of special trimmings. The *Sales Album* was very confusing on engine availability, and some dealers told customers it was the 454 or nothing, since all the 'up-front' material showed SS 454 Chevelles, while the lesser Chevelle SS was mentioned way back in the Model Options section.

Exterior colors for 1971 still numbered fifteen, but only six two-tones were now offered. Vinyl tops proliferated; black, dark blue, dark brown, dark green and white were the choices. Convertibles, already being increasingly ignored, had to get by with black or white top fabrics. For the first time, a power top was standard on Chevelle convertible styles. The popular Cowl Induction hood and Sport Stripe option was virtually unchanged from 1970; stripes were again black or white.

Chevrolet threw a new model option into the muscle car fray during the middle of the 1971 model year, continuing it through 1972. Dubbed the Heavy Chevy (RPO YF3), it amounted to a Chevelle version of the concurrently introduced Rally Nova. What you got besides the oh-so-clever name in this cheapened SS was a black grille à la SS, but without the emblem; the Super Sport's domed hood and lock pins; current-type Rally Wheels in 14x6 size with bright lug nuts; and special body highlight striping and decal identification. The Heavy Chevy was identified exclusively by the use of decals which spelled out the name in black block letters on the front fenders and at both ends of the car. Engines ranged from the 307 Turbo-Fire V-8 to the 400 Turbo-Jet. Cowl Induction was available optionally, but without the stripe kit.

Production figures for the 1971 SS 454 Chevelle bear out its obvious scarcity. Less than half of 1971 SS Chevelles were 454's. Obviously, not everyone wanted so much muscle. The number of Chevelle SS Sport Coupes and Convertibles built with smaller V-8's is not on record at Chevrolet. Production of 1971 Heavy Chevy Sport Coupes was 6,727.

To the eye, the 1972 Chevelle Super Sport seemed to be almost identical to its 1971 counterpart. New single-unit turn-signal/marker lamp units on the front fender edges distinguished that aspect, but there were no changes at all to the rear. Once again SS equipment was offered for Sport Coupe and Convertible Chevelle models.

Last Chevelle convertible was in 1972. Versions equipped with SS 454 were very rare, are avidly sought by collectors today. Cowl-induction hood no longer included Sport Stripe treatment.

SS Convertible

The hefty-looking gray-finish Sport Wheels, executed in classic mag wheel design, continued as SS equipment, shod with 15x7 low profile, white-letter tires. A new Sport Mirror was included on the driver's side. Most 1972 Chevelle Super Sports were much more docile than their 1971 counterparts, however; few appeared with the 454 numerals beneath the SS fender insignia this year. Chevrolet further expanded the engine/power train combinations for this final year of the popular body style used since 1970 to include any V-8 offered for Chevelle! You could order this muscular-looking street machine with a 130-hp 307 if you desired. Two 350's, rated at 165- and 175-hp were again offered, as was a revised 240-hp LS-3 Turbo-Jet 400 (still the 396-402 in reality). Restricted to SS Chevelles only was the LS-5 version of the 454, hanging in with a 270-hp rating.

Opening up the SS to smaller engines allowed the use of lighter-duty transmissions. Powerglide even rejoined Turbo Hydra-matic on the optional automatic chart. Unless an optional transmission was chosen, 307's and 350's came with a three-speed manual (with floor shift on the 350's). The heavier-duty Special three-speed could be specified, with floor shift, for the 240/402 combination; while the current wide-ratio four-speed was offered for the 175/350 and 402. LS-5 cars were all equipped with M22 'rock crusher' four-speeds, according to availability charts. Front power disc brakes and heavy-duty suspension came with all SS Chevelles. 1972 Chevelles with M20 four-speeds numbered 10,201 (not all were Super Sports) but only 1,513 had M22 'rock crushers.'

The Heavy Chevy was offered again as a lower-cost muscle-type car in the Chevelle line for 1972. It was substantially unaltered from 1971 Sales climbed in this full year of production to 9,508.

California Chevelle enthusiasts had an especially bad year as their state's tough emission laws kept several Chevelle engines out of the state. The base 307 and the '400' 402 were not allowed, nor was the 'king rat' 454, leaving California Super Sport buyers with their choice of the 350 V-8's. Changing times were further reflected in the axle-ratio availability charts. The lowest factory-installed gear set offered for the 1972 Chevelle was the 3.31:1 'performance' axle, a far cry from the multiple listings of just a few years back with ratios as low as 4.88:1 (these gear sets were still available through Chevrolet service parts counters, however).

1972 Chevelle SS had the husky look of 1971 SS 454, but carried anything from 307 V-8 to LS-5 big-block. New styling feature for '72 was single-unit parking lamps.

Chevelle was a popular intermediate car in 1972, but Super Sport sales were only 24,946 units, and even this was due for the most part to the increased availability of smaller V-8's with the package. The 454 was fitted to 5,333 SS 454 Sport Coupes and an extremely limited number of Convertibles. The 1972 SS 454 Convertible, representing the last of the Chevelle convertibles, has become an especially sought-after automobile.

Chevelle was totally redone for the 1973 model year, featuring all-new sheet metal on a one-inch-longer wheelbase (113-inches) for two-door models. Rumored for 1972 introduction, the new A-body by Fisher was delayed a year by the engineering crises of the new decade's first years, especially the rushed conversion to no-lead or low-lead regular-fuel engines in 1971—all of which followed on the heels of the long and disruptive United Automobile Workers (UAW) strike in the fall of 1970.

The 1973 coupe bodies were no longer pillarless hardtop styles, but did use doors with frameless windows. Given the deepening energy crisis of 1973, and the increasing cries of the safety legions, the Super Sport Chevelle may have been born of uncertainty, but at least it did get into production (unlike the Camaro SS, which had passed from the option list at the end of 1972). Even more remarkable was the addition of a new Super Sport model that would make 1973 a year unique in Super Sport history. This was the only year, ever, that a Chevrolet lover could buy an SS *Station Wagon*.

Unusual Super Sport was 1973 Chevelle SS wagon. This one was equipped with 454, as identified above marker lamp.

Chevelle Super Sport lasted into new body era, featured distinctive stripe kit in 1973.

This was accomplished by ordering a Malibu wagon with any optional V-8 and the RPO Z15 Super Sport package. Included was a black-finished grille with SS emblem; left- and right-hand Sport Mirrors (remote control on the left); SS emblems on front fenders, interior front door panels and steering wheel; and the double-S insignia at the rear on the liftgate. Lower body-side and wheel-opening stripes were keyed to the body color, and replaced the lower body bright moldings of conventional Malibus. SS wagons had a special rear stabilizer. These wagons shared the special Super Sport instrument cluster with black bezels.

All SS Chevelles for 1973 were supposed to be equipped with 14x7 Rally Wheels, according to some sales literature. The *Sales Album* for the year shows an SS wagon with the new Turbine I wheels, however, and their availability is listed in one section of the data guide, but denied in another. G70x14 white-letter tires were specified, and all SS Chevelles had large, front-stabilizer bars.

The other 1973 Super Sport, the Malibu coupe equipped with SS package, used the same parts as the SS wagon, but carried its rear SS emblem on the bumper. Super Sport Coupes also had black-accented taillight bezels. Total SS option sales for 1973 were 28,647 units.

Three optional V-8's were listed for the SS buyer's consideration (those who chose the new luxury Laguna model had the same choices). A 165-hp 350 was the basic engine, while the contemporary version of the L48 four-barrel 350 or the 454 Turbo-Jet (LS-4) could also be specified (as it was by 22,528 1973 Chevelle buyers). Regular-gas compression ratios and a further tightening of emissions standards cut the big-block's net horsepower to 245 at 4000 rpm this year. Turbo Hydra-matic, increasingly popular, could be ordered with any engine, while the M20 four-speed could be chosen for the L48-type 350 and the M21 close-ratio box was offered for the LS-4 big-block. Four-speed sales plummeted to 3,879 M20's and 1,685 close-ratio M21's. No three-speeds were cataloged, suggesting that all 350 two-barrel Super Sports were equipped with a Turbo Hydra-matic.

A new optional Strato-bucket seat, that could swivel to the side for entering or exiting the car, was offered. Prospective buyers had to take the swinging buckets to get a console. Special instrumentation, including a tachometer, was available for all engine combinations offered in Super Sports.

Although popular history will always record 1972 as the last year of true muscle cars, Chevelle Super Sport production increased by nearly 4,000 units in 1973, reaching a total of 28,647 cars. The original Arab oil embargo that summer dampened any hopes that the increased sales figures might prompt a rebirth of factory interest in big muscle-type cars and the Super Sport was dropped from Chevelle's option list for 1974.

Super Sports were gone from all Chevrolet passenger-car lines except Nova when the 1974 models rolled into the showrooms. Chevelle, though, provided a successor obviously related by heredity to the SS. The Laguna Type S-3 was a special model capping Chevelle's prestige line. The Type S-3 featured many SS trademarks, including special grille patterning, special 15x7 Rally Wheels, added interior features such as the swing-out Strato-bucket seats, and performance-tuned suspension parts. Laguna's S-3 was built only in Antique white with dark-red vinyl roof and striping during the late 1973 production months of the 1974 model year; later other combinations were made available.

Laguna S-3 buyers could still have the 454 Turbo-Jet V-8 installed, giving them an engine rated at 235 net horses. Two- or four-barrel versions of the 350 V-8 were also offered.

For 1975, the Laguna Type S-3 featured a new roof line with louvered appliqués over the rear quarter sail panels. A new, resilient-type front end with color-accented bumper (and a mate at the rear) added real distinction. Special wheels were part of the package, but, inside, the Strato-bucket swing-out seats were now optional.

A wild graphics package was created for the 1975 Laguna Type S-3. Bumpers, vinyl top and stripes contrasted with body colors of black, bright metallic blue, metallic orange, silver or Antique white. The detailing of the 1975 S-3 was largely unappreciated as the car attracted just 7,638 customers. Only a very few S-3 buyers chose the 454 V-8, which had been whittled down to a blanched 215 net horsepower; most used one of the available 350 V-8's, or the newly revived 400-cubic-inch small-block four-barrel V-8 rated at 175 hp.

Laguna Type S-3 cars continued into 1976 with only minimal changes, but the 454 had finally checked out, leaving the 400 small-block V-8 as the top engine choice.

Chevrolet abandoned any sort of sports package for the 1977 Chevelle, while concentrating on the new down-sized 'regular' Chevrolet line. Demand for a sports-type Chevelle was still there, though, and a Wichita, Kansas-based custom outfit, Special Editions, Inc., decided to fill it. They put together a handsome Special Edition package for the last big Chevelle, using front and rear spoilers, Turbine II Wheels, and stripes running along the upper fender and door edges to the roof, where they swept up and forward on the sail panel. Special duct-type fillers were used in the quarter-window openings. Identification was made by decals, with Chevelle SE spelled out neatly just below the spoiler at the right rear and additional decal badges on the front fenders. The kits were applied to Antique white,

Chevelle SE package included front spoiler, removed from Ron Lee's otherwise original example. This was first one of approximately 50—all others had orange stripes instead of red. Turbine Wheels, Sport Mirrors, F60x15 tires helped create cosmetic muscle image. Engine was 350 four-barrel.

Super Sport survived as an El Camino deluxe package through the turbulence of the seventies, even when Chevelle was down-sized. SS package is still offered for El Caminos.

silver and black Chevelle coupes. About fifty were built. The 1978 down-sized Chevelle wasn't nearly as adaptable to sports-styling kits; so the 1977 Special Editions remained as the only testimony to their ideas. These cars look 'factory' and are still the source of much excitement and confusion when spotted by an unknowing enthusiast passing through the central U.S.

Although the last Chevelle Super Sport passenger car was built in 1973, Chevrolet's truck operation continued to offer Super Sport trim as part of an option package for their popular El Camino sport pickup for the rest of the seventies and into the 1980's. These El Caminos continued to share frontal sheet metal and trim with contemporary Chevelles.

Chevrolet production records indicate 4,543 of the 1974 Super Sport El Caminos were built. Production for the following year slid to 3,521, but a recovery began in 1976 when 5,163 were built. The 1977 production number was fairly constant, at 5,226, but then the El Camino Super Sport, like the Z-28 Camaro and Pontiac Firebird Trans Am, underwent an amazing resurgence in popularity. Sales for 1978 were 12,027, and another 11,371 El Camino Super Sports were built in 1979.

Performance Terms

Chevrolet's over-the-counter speed and handling parts program brought thousands of home-brewed car builders into Chevrolet parts departments seeking the good stuff. These enthusiasts spoke a language of their own, so Chevrolet compiled and issued, in 1971, a five page "Performance and Competition Terminology" glossary for field distribution to counter men.

Armed with the translator's guide, the Chevrolet parts man might be able to decode the requests of a customer who came in to 'eyeball' a 'bumpstick' for his 'beast's' 'big-bone bent eight,' so that he might 'cut a fat one' to become 'Hot Shoe' while 'wailing' at the local strip.

In plain English, the customer wanted to look at a camshaft that would fit his over-bored Chevrolet V-8, so that he might find increased performance and make enough good runs to become top driver in the quarter-mile standing-start elapsed time and speed trials at the nearby drag racing establishment.

CHAPTER TEN

New Novas, Old Themes 1968–1976

*T*he Chevy II Nova for 1968 might be called the first passenger car of the seventies. It represented a clean break with the past, and its new basic body would last for eleven model years (and would eventually be shared with Buick, Oldsmobile and Pontiac models). In standard form the Nova would be the most unlikely car in the country to attract a car enthusiast's attention. Dull, drab, available only in two- or four-door body styles, the basic Nova was strictly transportation. That there was a Nova Super Sport was remarkable in itself; that Nova Super Sports were truly satisfying performance cars was more an accident of chance.

Fortunately, the 1968 Nova was designed concurrently, and with a great deal of interfaced technology, with the first Camaro. Thus the plain Nova shared some of the same attributes that went toward making the Camaro a really sporty performance car. The Nova would also share many of the special speed and handling parts created for the Camaro, which was only natural in the environment within Chevrolet Engineering in the late 1960's. Cross-breeding was a favorite pastime, especially when it promised a lighter, faster result.

So it came to pass that the 1968 Nova Super Sport option shared the SS 350 Camaro's zippy 295-hp V-8 (a Camaro exclusive in 1967). Styling turned out a trim package to complement the engine that, although made up of traditional Super Sport items, seemed a little too calm for a car of the SS 350 Nova's capabilities. A black-accented grille, black-filled rear deck panel and even a special hood with a pair of bright-metal simulated air intakes, were used. SS emblems front and rear, and a truly sedate Super Sport side identification (the words were spelled out in block letters just behind the front wheels) completed the exterior SS package.

Nova SS cars came with E70x14 Uniroyal Tiger Paw tires, but hub caps were the plain, standard Nova style. Simulated magnesium wheel covers, imitation wire jobs or Rally Wheels were offered. The Rally Wheels really helped the car's appearance.

The deluxe Nova steering wheel was part of the SS package, and it mounted an SS emblem for the occasion. SS cars also had hood insulation to help muffle the rumblings of the rather potent 350 V-8. Only 4,670 SS 350 Novas were sold in 1968.

Chevrolet's standard three-speed transmission came with the L48-type 295-hp 350 V-8, unless one of the optional transmissions was specified: the M13 heavy-duty three-speed, the M20 four-speed or Powerglide automoatic. 1968 Novas with M20 four-speeds numbered 5,399; an additional 1,495 had the close-ratio M21 and 167 had heavy-duty M22 transmissions.

That was about it if you ordered a plain Nova SS (which, incidentally, was the first two-door-with-a-post Super Sport). If you wanted more pizzazz you had to consult the option list.

Attending to the exterior first, you would probably choose the Custom Exterior (RPO ZJ2), which included roof drip moldings, ribbed body-sill and rear lower fender bright strips, side-window moldings and a wide black accent band along the lower body.

That settled, you would at least want to know what kind of deal you could get on the RPO A51 Custom Interior with Strato-bucket seats (or ZJ1 with bench seat). This included "luxury seat and sidewall trim with bright accents, ashtrays and rear armrests, carpet floor covering, bright rearview mirror support, door jamb light switches, glovebox lamp, illuminated heater control and a luggage compartment mat." Your salesman might mention that all Novas were coming through with carpeting as standard, now that production was actually under way.

Strato-bucket seats came in black, dark blue or gold. If you opted for a four-speed or Powerglide, a console was included with the buckets. A nice finishing touch would have been the RPO U17 Special Instrumentation group consisting of an instrument-panel-mounted tachometer and a handsome four-gauge unit cluster on the console for monitoring vital engine functions. The gauge cluster was another example of Nova's beneficial close relationship to Camaro, since it was virtually identical to the cluster designed for the sports car.

The Nova, with its long hood and wide-stance tread (courtesy of a preliminary design requirement that the Nova use Chevelle's rear axle),

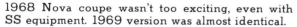

1968 Nova coupe wasn't too exciting, even with SS equipment. 1969 version was almost identical.

took on a different look altogether when equipped with enough SS and Custom features. Any 1968 Nova SS is a rare sight today, but one special version is almost unknown.

In rodder's slang, it was a 'sleeper.' An innocent-looking folksy car rolls up beside you on a red light. You didn't even give it a glance as you zap your throttle and watch the tach respond. Then: green light! The commuter special vanishes in a cloud of tire and exhaust haze as you mash your foot feed against the floor pan. You've just been had!

Late in the 1968 model run, Chevrolet released a few hundred of the decade's greatest sleepers. These little giant-killers were Nova SS Coupes equipped with the RPO L78, solid-lifter cam, 375-hp 396. For just $500.30 you could have this fearsome engine installed in a Nova. Other extras of the performance and comfort type could push the total tab to the $4,000 roof rather quickly.

Exactly when the SS 396 Nova became available is not known. Road tests on the little stingers came out in August 1968. Chevrolet engineers had immediately seen the potential of mating the Nova and the 396, but some sheet metal reshaping and fabrication of necessary headers had taken quite a bit of time. Still, of the rather small 5,571 run of the 1968 Nova Super Sports, 667 were equipped with the L78 option. An additional 234 Nova SS cars had the L34-version 396, rated at 350 hp (this was the top *listed* engine for the larger Chevelle). An L78 Nova 396 could shame just about any four-passenger Chevrolet built in 1968. The only family competition that could unseat such a Nova was a white-hot Corvette or one of those super-rare drag-only L72-type 427 Camaros or Chevelles. Right out of the showroom an L78 Nova 396 could be expected to crack 100 mph in about fourteen seconds, and the potential was tremendous for even more speed, since all sorts of 'trick' parts for the 396 block were offered by Chevrolet and specialty manufacturers.

The SS 396 Nova was identifiable on sight only by the small 396 numerals placed in the front side-marker lamp bezels. The sound of the big, solid-lifter-cam engine, exiting its exhaust through big pipes, was another giveaway. Few survivors of street encounters with one of these beasts soon forgot it.

The Chevy Nova SS (the 'II' was dropped from the name) for 1969 was given little attention in Chevrolet's Sports Department literature. In

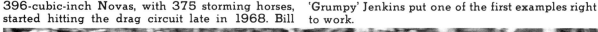

396-cubic-inch Novas, with 375 storming horses, started hitting the drag circuit late in 1968. Bill 'Grumpy' Jenkins put one of the first examples right to work.

the specialty performance cars brochure, for example, it was given last-chapter billing and had to share its color page with a Corvair Monza coupe, which prophetically was shown on its way out of the picture (Corvair production would end on May 14, 1969). Nova had a good sales year anyway, with calendar sales up more than forty percent and a model year total of 268,011. Super Sports accounted for 17,564 units, a three hundred percent increase over 1968 production.

Nova Super Sports for 1969 were almost unchanged from 1968, right down to the SS lettering and black-accent body trim. Red-stripe wide-profile tires were again included with SS equipment. All SS Novas had black steering wheels with an SS emblem in the center.

A glance at the spec sheets showed a five-horsepower gain for the 350 V-8 included with RPO Z26 Super Sport equipment. The new 300-hp rating was only part of the story, however. For 1969, the 350 (RPO L48 by its own option code) was literally a tougher engine physically. A new strengthened 350-cubic-inch block was used, with stronger main-bearing bulkheads. The main-bearing caps were now fastened by four bolts instead of two.

To handle the new 350's torque, all Novas so equipped used at least the Special three-speed manual box with floor shift (and console, if bucket seats had been specified). All three four-speeds were available on order, along with Powerglide, and, for the first time in Nova history, Turbo Hydramatic. Sales of four-speed boxes in 1969 Novas were 10,036 M20's, 3,751 close-ratio M21's and 682 heavy-duty M22's.

Nova Super Sports had special front suspension components including stiffer front coil springs and a stabilizer bar. Multiple-leaf rear springs of heavy-duty design were used at the rear.

Single-disc power front brakes were included with the 1969 Nova Super Sport at no extra cost, but the usually complementing Rally-type wheels were apparently no longer included and had to be ordered as an extra-cost option. Mag-spoke and Sport-style wheels were offered to Nova buyers who wanted something special besides Rally rims. Standard dog-dish hub caps came on an SS Nova unless something else was optionally ordered. For the first time, the Nova buyer could enjoy factory AM-FM radio reception in 1969.

Though not listed in Nova specifications generally published for 1969, the 396 Turbo-Jet continued to find its way into an increasing number of new Nova Super Sports. Both the hot, solid-lifter 375-hp L78 and the fairly potent 350-hp L34 were again quietly available. Details on additional performance equipment added to Nova Super Sport chassis when the 396 was used are not clear, but it was agreed that the Nova was completely capable of handling the big V-8. Production of 396-equipped Novas shot up drastically as the option became available for the first full year. In 375-hp form, the 396 powered 5,262 of the 1969 Nova SS Coupes (of which 311 had RPO L89 aluminum heads). An additional 1,947 were equipped with the 350-hp 396.

Nova SS carried displacement numerals in front marker unit for 1968. Late in the year street-wise enthusiasts learned to watch for 396 numerals in place of 350 identification.

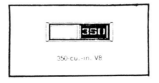

350-cu.-in. V8

Exterior styling changes for 1970 Chevy Nova models were very minor, but at least they made it easier to differentiate the new cars from the previous year's models than had been the case in 1968 and 1969. A new grille, with a slightly different texture was used. At the side, a group of vertical 'hash marks' on each front fender was a sure sign of a 1970 Nova, and at the rear, taillights and backup lights were integrated into one unit. Side-marker lamps were redesigned, and big '350' numerals above the front-marker lamps now identified a Nova carrying the healthy small-block V-8. Standard interiors were revamped and offered in new colors. Variable-ratio power steering joined the comfort and appearance items on the Nova's option list.

The Super Sport equipment option for 1970 was again unchanged in most respects. The blacked-out grille, black-accented rear deck panel and domed hood with simulated air intakes continued. SS emblems were located front and rear, but there was no identification on the body or fender sides this year.

The E70x14 wide-profile Uniroyal Tiger Paw tires on 14x7JJ rims continued to be supplied with RPO Z26, but they were of the white-stripe variety for 1970, and were mounted on seven-inch rims. Rally Wheels were a popular option, but the Chevelle's handsome five-spoke chrome Sport Wheels were also available at extra cost.

Many Nova Super Sports had either the RPO ZJ5 Exterior Decor or RPO ZJ2 Custom Exterior option package. The Custom Exterior group included body accent stripes and accented lower body moldings, while the less expensive Exterior Decor group used full-length mid-body moldings with vinyl inserts. Both options added bright side-window moldings to the Nova coupe body.

A black steering wheel with SS emblem was installed on all SS Novas, regardless of interior color.

The heart of the 1970 Nova SS base package continued to be the reasonably strong 300-hp Turbo-Fire 350 V-8. As delivered in a Nova SS, it had a chrome-finish air cleaner and oil filler cap, and finned aluminum valve covers. Dual exhausts, special underhood insulation, heavy-duty clutch, special front springs and—in cars using optional four-speed or Turbo Hydra-matic—heavy-duty universal joints and the big 8.875-inch rear-axle ring gear were part of the SS 350's modifications.

Transmissions were cataloged as required options only for 1970, the buyer able to choose between the 2.52:1 low four-speed, Powerglide

1970 Novas are readily identified by hash marks on front fenders. SS Coupes used 350 V-8 as standard engine.

and Turbo Hydra-matic. The four-speed came with 3.31 rear axle gears, Powerglide with 3.08 and the Turbo Hydra-matic with 3.07 cogs. Positraction was optional with any gear set, and any of Chevrolet's numerous parts-catalog gears for special purposes could be installed by the dealer or owner. (Torque-Drive, the driver shifted super-cheap Powerglide adaptation, wasn't up to the V-8's torque, apparently, since it was restricted to six-cylinder Novas.) Among 1970 Novas, 13,198 had RPO M20 four-speeds and 3,448 had close-ratio M21 transmissions.

Although sales literature and even the Motor Vehicle Manufacturers' Association (MVMA) specs for the Nova didn't indicate it, the Turbo-Jet 396 (now displacing 402 cubic inches) was still creeping into a few Novas, just as it had in 1968 and 1969. During 1970 350-hp (L34) sales were 1,802 while 375-hp (L78) versions enjoyed greater popularity, with 3,765 built.

Popular options for the SS continued to include bucket seats, tachometer, gauges and other performance items.

The Nova SS was increasingly popular with the low-budget drag racing crowd. It was good, basic hot rod material; a traditional two-door coupe unadorned with frills. Its strong 350 V-8 just happened to be a small-block Chevy, which was the heart of an entire speed parts industry, manufacturers issued a never-ending flow of special manifolds, carbs, headers, distributors and other goodies for these popular and plentiful engines.

The raised rear end of a 1970-style Nova coupe, with rear tire wells stuffed full of giant, wide rubber, continues to be a familiar sight on the Main Streets of America when the kids take over on Friday night. Could it be, as one automotive editor has suggested, that the lowly Nova will turn out to be the '40 Ford or the '57 Chevy of the current generation?

The simulated fender louvers of the 1970 Nova went away for 1971. Higher output single-unit headlamps replaced previous bulbs, but did not change the car's appearance. New standard hub caps, resembling

Nova SS for 1970 could be ordered with several styles of hub caps and wheel covers, but came with standard small cap unless extra-cost covers were ordered. Only SS could be ordered with Sport Wheel chrome five-spoke rim.

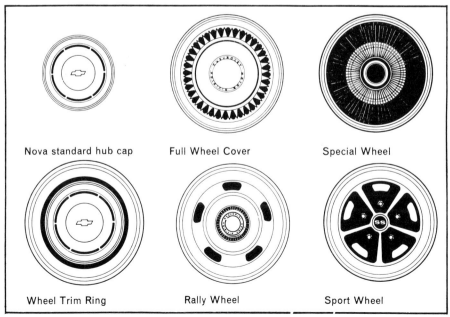

| Nova standard hub cap | Full Wheel Cover | Special Wheel |
| Wheel Trim Ring | Rally Wheel | Sport Wheel |

'baby moons,' with a Chevy bow-tie stamped in the center, appeared. To give some variety to the many thousands of Nova coupes cruising American highways, eleven new colors were offered for 1971. At the rear, slightly larger backup lamp inserts were centered in the taillight lenses.

An unchanged format was pursued for the RPO Z26 Nova SS option. Blacked-out grilles and rear panels continued as visual identifiers of these cars, with SS emblems centered front and rear. Wide-profile E70x14 tires continued from 1970 as part of the SS equipment, as did the exterior trim groups. The Custom Exterior did have new-style body sill moldings for 1971, which were in effect rocker panel moldings with an extension behind the rear wheelhouse. A new Rally Wheel was issued and achieved considerable popularity on Novas. (During late 1971 the Rally Nova would bow, using special upper body stripes, a blacked-out grille, decal identification and the Rally Wheels. A 245-hp [165 net] 350 V-8 would be included.)

Strato-bucket seats were optional when the Custom interior was ordered. Nova had four steering wheels for 1971; the SS came standard with the second-from-the-top version, which was the Deluxe wheel with an SS emblem. A popular option was the Sport Wheel, using four spokes. All Nova steering wheels were black this year.

The popular 350 V-8 appeared in a new regular-fuel version to power the 1971 SS 350 Nova. Gross rated horsepower went down to 270. Using the Society of Automotive Engineers net rating being phased-in during 1971, the engine was a 210-hp unit.

Some of 1970's extra mechanical and suspension features were gone for 1971, including heavy-duty front springs and even the chrome engine garnishes. Transmission choices were simply the standard manual three-speed, optional M-20 four-speed (3,950 built) or Turbo Hydra-matic. Gone forever was the potent 396 V-8.

Super Sport buyers were few in Chevrolet showrooms during this anti-performance year. Nova SS production declined by more than 12,000 cars from 1970. There were just 7,016 Novas built in 1971 that carried the SS logo.

The Nova SS began its fifth year without any major structural or appearance change as the 1972 models made their debut. Although Chev-

Little change was made to Nova for 1971. For SS package, 350 V-8 was standard, now tuned for regular fuel.

elle now offered SS equipment with any V-8, Nova continued to build the RPO Z26 Super Sport equipment option around the 350 four-barrel V-8 now rated an even 200 net hp. Transmission choices were simplified: either the extra-cost four-speed or the optional Turbo Hydra-matic. Dual exhausts, special suspension components and power front disc brakes were part of the SS equipment. The E70x14 bias belted white-lettered tires came on all 1972 Nova Super Sports. They were announced as part of the deal, later they became required options. One of the Nova's exterior trim packages was usually chosen by the SS buyer; this year cars with Custom exterior trim had black accent stripes above the rocker panel chrome on all but dark colored cars.

Chevrolet spent relatively little advertising money on the Nova SS. It really wasn't necessary, as the popular Novas appeared in dozens of speed equipment manufacturers' ads in the numerous performance enthusiast magazines crowding the nation's newsstands in the last glowing hours of the super car age. *Hot Rod* magazine and Lee Filters paid the 1972 Nova SS its just homage by offering a slightly modified red coupe as first prize in a national contest that year. That Nova, a *Hot Rod* project car built to a goal of providing reliable street operation with respectable drag potential, was typical of hundreds of Novas on the street already.

Actually, the 350 four-barrel V-8 was no slouch in a 1972 Nova as it was delivered. *Hot Rod* clocked a 15.42-second run, at 88.40 mph in the quarter, without doing a thing to the car. By the time the contest was announced a good set of headers and a few speed tricks had brought elapsed times down to 14.60 seconds and pushed the quarter-mile trap speed to 93.65 mph.

Hot Rod staffer Tom Senter took a long look at the project Nova and its numerous brethren, forming the conclusion that here might indeed be this generation's '57 Chevy. Another prediction, that the 1973 Nova would be all-new, wasn't so accurate.

Demand for sporty, performance-type cars rebounded in 1972. Nova Super Sport Coupes shared in the revival, with 12,309 copies sold.

The Rally Nova Coupe continued in production during 1972 after its late 1971 debut. Any available power train was offered in the Rally Nova, which featured broad, tapering stripes extending the full length of the body and around the rear panel. A blacked-out grille (à la Super Sport) was used. The current-style Sport Mirror was included for left-hand installation, painted body color. Rally Nova equipment included 14x6 Rally Wheels, which were optional on Nova Super Sports. Some special suspension parts were included as well. 1971 Rally Nova production was 7,700; the package caught on big in 1972, with 33,319 sold.

Fresh styling marked the 1973 Nova SS, which found a tremendous reception in the market, with sales amounting to 35,542 by the end of the year, making it the top Nova Super Sport year of the decade. Blunt, front fender edges relieved the stark mass of new impact-resistant bumpers. Nova finally did away with vent windows. Underneath, it was basically the same car. For the first time since 1967, Novas were offered in two series, Custom and plain Nova. Three styles were offered: a coupe, hatchback coupe and sedan.

The Nova Super Sport option survived, but was hidden away in the "Nova Selected Options" section of the 1973 showroom book, and even there it was merely described, not illustrated. The 1973 Nova SS was a blend of 1972's SS and Rally Nova features. Any engine/transmission combination offered for Nova was acceptable. Exterior detailing included black or white stripes, the traditional black-accented grille, and a black panel on the rear. SS identification appeared front and rear, on the front fenders, and on the black steering wheel. A left-hand remote control Sport Mirror and complementing manually adjusted right-hand mirror were included. Rally Nova's 14x6 wheels, with special center caps, became part of the SS option this year, but front disc brakes returned to the option list. White-letter E70x14B bias belted tires were optional at extra cost, and came with 14x7 wheels when ordered. Sales were strong, stopping at 5,542. There was no 1973 Rally Nova option.

Strato-bucket seats were optional, and gave the buyer the right to also specify a floor console, and if he wished to spend even more, a gauge cluster. On cars equipped with the cluster, a tach/clock unit replaced the fuel gauge on the dash which moved down to the console gauge group.

Engines for the 1973 Nova SS went from the 250-cubic-inch six to the 350 four-barrel V-8. The L48 received another cut in horsepower, as emissions regulations continued to strangle it. Net horsepower was now 175. Power disc brakes for front wheels were required with the 350, as was either the M20 four-speed or Turbo Hydra-matic.

A new rarely seen optional Sky Roof (RPO CF1), introduced in mid-1972, was offered again for 1973. This was a vinyl roof insert that rolled back to give a view of the sky.

Nova Super Sport sales started strong as the Chevrolet compact entered the 1974 model year. Adverse economic conditions slowed the pace as the year progressed, however, and sales took a downturn. Still, there were 21,419 Nova SS Coupes built in 1974.

Sheet metal styling was virtually unchanged on the 1974 Nova, but a new graphic approach gave the car a really new look. Contrasting paint

Sliding sunroof came out during 1972, was continued for 1973. SS package for 1972 was again basically untouched.

and decal areas spread across the Nova Super Sport's surfaces this year. Black accents were used not only on the grille, but around side windows as well. Large Nova SS decals were used on front fenders, while traditional SS emblems appeared on the grille and steering wheel. Dual Sport Mirrors, finished in flat black, were standard, as were Rally-type 14x6 wheels. The new stripes, in black outlined with gold or gold outlined with red (depending on body color), raced along the hood and deck lid.

All available Nova engines were again offered, but the SS option did include heavy-duty suspension components with larger stabilizer bars and stiffer springs. The top engines were still 350 four-barrel units, but now there were two RPO numbers: L48, gaining back a few of its lost ponies at 185 net hp; and the California-only LM1 of 160 emaciated horsepower, resulting from a detune to meet that state's emission requirements. Required options with the L48 350 were power front disc brakes and either the M20 four-speed or Turbo Hydra-matic.

Gone from the 1974 option list was the mid-1972 and 1973 sliding sunroof. Variable power steering, with special SS ratios (14.2:1 to 10.2:1 for the SS compared to 18.9:1 to 13.5:1 for regular Novas) was an increasingly popular option. A full traditional SS interior could still be ordered by purchasing extra-cost optional bucket seats, console and gauges.

During 1974 Novas were offered, along with Vegas and Impalas, in special Spirit of America trim. These cars were white, with special red and blue stripes. Identification was by decal on Novas and Vegas, while the Impala coupes had gold medallions. Rally Wheels and bucket seats were included, but apparently the Spirit of America package could not be combined with SS equipment on the Nova.

Novas used totally new sheet metal for 1975, though the basic design package continued intact. A new roof line, using a new windshield which eliminated the rounded corners of previous Nova windshields gave the car a really fresh look. Front and rear ensembles were redesigned to bring the car up-to-date.

A new top series of Novas was introduced for 1975. The new Nova LN models were the nicest yet. Going another round was the SS package. This year it had black accents on the new roof pillar louvers, as well as on the grille and around side windows. Black Sport Mirrors were standard, and large SS identification symbols were used on the front fenders and deck, while a smaller emblem provided frontal recognition. Contrasting lower body stripes were part of the year's graphics package—dual stripes

New styling came in 1973, with elimination of vent windows. SS Novas used stripe decals, which were revised for the 1974 edition shown.

Nova SS Coupe

in red, silver or white, depending on the body color. Rally Wheels with trim rings and SS center caps were used on SS cars. Inside, the neat Sport four-spoke steering wheel was installed, with an SS emblem on the horn button.

The SS package was offered with any engine. Standard Nova power plant for 1975 was the 250 six, with three V-8's; the new 4.3-liter engine and two- and four-barrel versions of the 350. The top V-8 was now the LM1 with catalytic converter and unleaded-fuel capability. The very word horsepower was stricken from the Chevrolet *Sales Album* this year; the LM1 now had a 'power rating' of 155. The M20 four-speed or Turbo Hydramatic were required options for LM1 (in California, even the four-speed was forbidden). Special suspension (RPO F40 for other Novas) was included, but the heavy-duty Sports Suspension, RPO F41, was optional. Manual front disc brakes were standard on all 1975 Novas, but the power unit was still offered, optionally. The new Turbine Wheels were excluded from Nova equipment in parts of the *Sales Album*, but listed as available elsewhere. The sun was really setting on the muscle car era in 1975. Nova Super Sports suffered from the general decline in performance interest, as sales fell to 9,067 units.

There was a 1976 Nova Super Sport, although it was almost a secret. The 1976 *Passenger Car Buyers Guide (Showroom Album)* devoted exactly one line to the Super Sport, stating under the "Option Availability" listing that SS equipment was offered. The final passenger-car Super Sport (El Caminos would continue to feature SS kits for the rest of the decade) consisted of a Nova coupe with special paint and decal detailing. Most of the former goodies were still available, though, and many of the small number (exact figures are unavailable) of 1976 SS Novas built were equipped with bucket seats, an improved 350 V-8, four-speed, gauges and special wheels.

By 1977 there was no further mention of SS equipment being offered for the Nova, although the 350, and other performance-type options, remained on the list.

A half-hearted effort to revive a sporting Nova came in 1978 with a regenerated Rally equipment package approximating the 1971-72 Rally Nova's kit. The Nova passed away quietly during the 1979 model year; there was no fanfare when the last Nova was built on December 22, 1978. The basic Nova package had lasted for eleven years, accounting for more than 3.5 million sales. Today only the 396-engined 1968-70 versions of the last type of Novas are avidly sought by collectors. But, then, there was a time when no one wanted a 1957 Chevy as a collector car, either.

Final Nova Super Sports were in 1975 and 1976, used special paint, black accents around window area. This is 1975 version.

The Super Sport phenomenon was not confined to the United States, or the North American continent. Super Sport trim and performance packages were marketed on General Motors cars built in Canada, Australia, South Africa and Brazil.

Canadian Chevrolet enthusiasts could order Super Sport equipment or models concurrently with Chevrolet customers in the United States. In addition a Super Sport version of the Canadian Acadian, based on the Chevy II, and the similarly-equipped Chevelle-based Beaumont SD (Sport Deluxe) were offered to Canadians exclusively. Pre-1971 Canadian Pontiacs used Chevrolet power trains in most instances, although the sheet metal was virtually identical to U.S. Pontiacs. The Canadian collector might, then, find an occasional, very rare Pontiac equipped with a Chevrolet big-block V-8. Apparently 409-cubic-inch Canadian Pontiacs using the same horsepower ratings as U.S. 409 Chevrolets were built during 1963-65. Most of the 1965 Mark IV big-block engines were used in Canadian

Pontiacs as well, including the 427's of 1966-69 and the 454 of 1970. Acadians and Beaumonts, merchandised by Pontiac dealers, used Chevrolet power-teams as well. The Canadian full-size Pontiac's equivalent of the Chevrolet Super Sport was known as the Parisienne Custom Sport and featured all the hallmarks of the Super Sport, including bucket seats and special trim.

Holden's Ltd., the General Motors' Australian operation, produced Holden Super Sports during the sixties and seventies. GM do Brazil still offered an SS package for its small sedans as late as 1979. In South Africa, GM produced a handsome two-door hardtop Chevrolet SS in the early 1970's. It featured many of the contemporary U.S. Nova Super Sport's features, including 307 or 350 V-8 power, four-speed transmission, bucket seats, wire wheel covers, red-stripe tires, special blacked-out grille, black accents and SS emblems. Optional automatic transmissions were Powerglide and Tri-matic.

Acadian was very similar to 1970 Nova SS, but no longer used split grille as had previous Acadians. Pontiac dealers sold them in Canada.

1971 South African 'Chevrolet SS' Sport Coupe resembled Nova, but was true pillar-less hardtop style. 350 V-8, four-speed or automatic, bucket seats, red-stripe tires were among the goodies.

CHAPTER ELEVEN

Camaro Fields a Super Sport
1967–1972

Rumors of a General Motors response to Ford's highly successful 'pony car,' the Mustang, were widespread through spring 1966. Chevrolet confirmed it would be building such a car, code named the Panther, as early as April of that year. The Panther became the Camaro at the last minute, and was announced as such through a novel conference-call press meeting between top Chevrolet executives and more than one hundred newspaper reporters on June 29, 1966. Camaros appeared in Chevrolet showrooms on September 21.

Avoiding the obvious, the 1967 Chevrolet *Engineering Features* book compared the new car to the contemporary Corvette. The new car's styling was ". . . proportioned in a long, low silhouette featuring a long hood line and relatively short rear deck," the book said. Shifting the Camaro's wheelbase rearward created a frontal overhang of 36.6 inches, a styling touch that would recur through the next decade. The styling theme was described as ". . . smooth, horizontally accented surfaces blended together to an aerodynamically functional shape."

Computer technology was used extensively in developing the Camaro. Handling analysis, design parameters, aerodynamic qualities, even the volume of the gas tank were all determined with extensive computer assistance.

As it was initially announced, the Camaro featured a single Super Sport option package, built around the new 350-cubic-inch V-8. Shortly after introduction, a second engine was offered with SS equipment, then some of the Super Sport's distinguishing trim pieces became available on any Camaro. To add to the confusion, the SS packages could be combined with Rally Sport equipment. According to Mike Lamm, in his book *The Great Camaro*, there were no less than eighty-one RPO factory options and forty-one additional dealer-installed accessories available for the new Camaro. It was the building block philosophy in full bloom: sell a basic car and let the customer create his own personal blend of show and go.

The 1967 Camaro SS 350 was a fairly defined package as released, using the 350 V-8 as a nucleus (eventually the 350 would power the majority of Chevrolets and millions of other GM cars as well, but it was a Camaro exclusive in 1967). The Camaro SS 350 engine was created by stroking the crankshaft of the existing 327-cubic-inch Chevrolet V-8 0.23 inch. Bearing surfaces were correspondingly enlarged. The SS 350's single-snorkel air cleaner was fitted with a chromed cover plate carrying an engine identification sticker. Plating was also used on rocker covers and the oil filler cap. Dual exhausts with resonators were standard on this 295-hp engine.

Thus, as originally announced, the SS 350 was executed in the same manner as the contemporary Chevelle SS 396 and Impala SS 427. SS 350 equipment added $210.65 to the price of a 1967 Camaro Sport Coupe or Convertible. Included for the extra charge were beefed suspension components and D70x14 Wide Oval red-stripe tires on six-inch special rims. A Camaro version of the Chevrolet simulated air-intake hood with raised center area gave the SS 350 external distinction, as did a blacked-out grille with an SS 350 emblem in the center. The SS 350 had the soon-to-be-famous 'bumble bee' striping encircling the jet-aircraft-inspired frontal grille intake. (Later in the year, the bumble bee stripes would be available on lesser Camaros, as well.) Additional SS identification was found on the front fenders and on the fuel filler cap centered in the rear body panel. The SS 350 filler cap had a retention cord, unlike other Camaros. An SS

Bumble Bee stripe was part of 1967 SS package. Many coupes had vinyl tops.

horn button cap was fitted to the steering wheel of RPO Z27 SS 350 Camaros.

Camaro sales literature encouraged the addition of Rally Sport equipment (RPO Z22, $105.35) to cars with SS packages. These cars had full-width black grilles with headlamps hidden behind electrically operated doors. Parking lamps moved to the valance panel beneath the grille opening, as did the backup lamps at the rear. All-red taillamp lenses, with black-striped bezels, replaced conventional Camaro units on cars with Rally Sport equipment. 'Twinline' body pinstriping, anodized rocker and wheelhouse moldings, and bright drip strips (on coupes) were also added. Rally Sport identification was superceded by SS emblems on cars with both option groups.

The new front wheel disc brakes from Chevrolet were fairly popular on 1967 Camaros; special vented wheels, optionally available as Rally Wheels on drum-braked Camaros, were included. Buyers of drum-braked Camaros could specify fake mags, full discs or wire wheel covers optionally.

Inside, bucket seats were standard, although the Strato-back bench seat was optional. A fold-down rear seat (RPO A67) was also offered. Standard interiors came in four solid vinyls, while the optional Custom interior group featured two-tone seat panels along with plusher embossed vinyl, deluxe steering wheel, rear seat armrests with ashtray, and courtesy lamps (for the coupe). Underhood insulation was also specified, but it was part of the SS package anyway.

The ultimate Camaro interior included the Special interior group's chrome-finished plastic windshield-pillar moldings, roof rail trim and bright-outlined pedal pads. Deep twist carpeting was standard on all Camaros.

Camaro's instrument panel used two elliptical bezels to house most instruments. A brake indicator lamp served as an early warning system for brake failures, and as a reminder that the emergency brake was set.

1967 Camaro Special Interior Group, found on many SS Camaros.

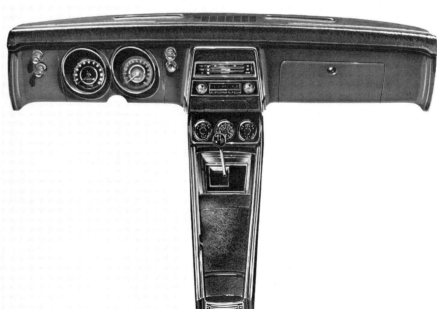

Powerglide and standard three-speed Camaros used a column shift, while heavy-duty three-speed and four-speed (and later Turbo Hydra-matic) cars had floor-mounted control levers which called for the addition of the extra-cost illuminated floor-tunnel console. Many SS 350 Camaros were equipped with the RPO U17 gauge console. Three faces showed fuel, temperature, oil pressure and ammeter readings for the engine, plus the clock. A tachometer replaced the regular instrument-panel gauge cluster in the right-hand bezel, and a low-fuel lamp replaced the oil warning lamp on the dash.

SS 350 Camaros had hardly gotten to the street before they were eclipsed by the introduction of the big 396-cubic-inch V-8 to the Camaro line, in 325-hp (L35) trim (4,003 sold). Turbo Hydra-matic or four-speed transmission was a required option for the 396. Introduced to Camaro in November 1967, the SS 396 Camaro used the familiar large 396 V-shaped insignias on its front fenders. It was a direct response to Ford's inclusion of its 390 on Mustang's option list. By mid-winter, L78-type 375-hp 396 Camaros were being delivered—1,138 were built for the year. Engine codes for 350-hp versions were also released but apparently none were built. Bill

Model holds air cleaner displaying the multitude of engine identification decals that might be found under the hood of 1967 Camaro—everything from six-cylinder to 396 Mark IV V-8.

Super Sport and Rally Sport equipment options were often combined, as on this 1967 convertible. SS emblems were used when cars carried both option packages. Hidden headlamps were part of RS equipment.

'Grumpy' Jenkins and other drag racers cleaned house with the hot solid-lifter Camaros for several seasons. Jenkins took the Pro Stock Eliminator crown at the 1968 NHRA Gatornationals, hitting 138.46 mph in 9.905 seconds with his Camaro.

Actually, the 325-hp 396 wasn't that much quicker than its 350 counterpart. 1967 road tests indicated the 350 Camaro could run the quarter in 15.8 seconds at 89 mph, with 3.55 gears. A 325-hp 396 tested by *Car Life* at GM's Mesa, Arizona, proving grounds managed to do the same run in 15.1 seconds at 91.8. The *Car Life* crew also got a chance to ride in a 'pet' engineering Camaro packing a 427—it made the quarter mile run in 13.5 seconds at 99.5 mph. It would never become an official production car, but several Chevrolet dealers, among them Nickey of Chicago and Dana of Southgate, California, started offering 425-hp 427 Camaros built in their own shops shortly after the Mustang Shelby GT 500 came out. These $4,500 Camaros could top 100 mph in the quarter-mile acceleration run with ease. Production was very limited, of course.

Despite its indisputable potential for drag racing, the 396 Camaro was quickly eclipsed by its rarely seen brother, the Z-28, which actually preceded the 396 in availability and continued in quiet production throughout the year. What it did to the SS 396 Camaro might be compared to the local kid who was getting close to a state track dash record, only to have his smaller brother come along, grab a lot of glory and attention in gymnastics and then match him almost step-for-step on the straight track. The Z-28 was that kind of kin to the SS 396; out-handling and often out-running the 396 with its super-potent 302-cubic-inch V-8.

Camaro closed out its first sales year reporting 195,765 cars sold, of which 25,141 were convertibles. SS equipment was installed on 34,411 Camaros with the 295-hp SS-only 350 numbered 29,270 Camaros while 64,842 had Rally Sport trim (including 10,675 convertibles). An SS 396 Camaro paced the 1967 Indy 500 in May; a nice tribute to the new car. About one hundred pace car replicas were built, with little fanfare.

1968 Camaro Custom Interior group used sawtooth accessory gauge unit, instead of round units used for 1967.

Little change was made for Camaro's second year as far as first impressions went. But there *was* news for 1968, and quite a bit of it at that. Revisions in bearing surfaces created a stronger base 350 V-8 for Super Sports. The 325-hp 396 (RPO L35) was offered.

The basic Super Sport equipment (RPO Z27) again combined special trim items with the L48 Camaro 350 or optional 396's. There was more variation between 350 and 396 cars this year. Both used the 1967-style bumble bee stripe around the grille, with engine identification in the stripe's opening on the front fenders. Camaro SS emblems were aft of the wheelhouse, with another SS emblem centered in the standard Camaro grille. A black-filled SS fuel filler cap was used. SS 396 Camaros had eight-grid chromed hood inserts on their raised center hoods, while SS 350's kept the 1967-style trim. A flat-black rear panel was fitted to 396 Camaros (except on black cars).

Both 350 and 396 V-8's had chrome garnishes when installed in SS Camaros. Bright air-cleaner intakes, valve rocker covers and oil filler caps were used. Special suspension components, and the popular red-stripe wide-profile tires on wide-stance rims were continued as standard SS items. RPO L48 350-engined Super Sports declined to 12,496, while the 325-hp L35 396 jumped to 10,773. The L34 350-hp engine accounted for 2,579 more and 4,575 buyers picked the RPO L78 ground pounder. Then there was RPO L89—an aluminum head version of the 375-hp V-8. Sales were 272.

Super Sport trim was revised in January 1968 with the inclusion of four new colors: Corvette bronze, LeMans blue, British green and Rallye green. A new, modified frontal stripe was introduced, too. It crossed in front of the hood, dropping onto the front fenders to the mid-point, where it swept rearward in a tapering flight to the door panel.

Super Sport equipment could be ordered on a plain-Jane Camaro for 1968, but most buyers added one of the two additional optional trim groups. RPO Z21 was a style trim group, which included belt reveal moldings, wheelhouse trim and bright drip moldings on coupes. These features

Stock 1968 Camaro Super Sport with Rally Sport equipment was shown at that year's New York Auto Show. Optional wheel covers weren't too popular.

1968 nose stripe no longer encircled grille, but RS cars still had hidden headlamps.

were also included with the more deluxe Rally Sport option (RPO Z22). The RS package again offered concealed headlamps behind a special grille, with parking lamps (and rear backup lamps) dropped below the bumpers. Dual-unit special taillamps were used, with black-accented lower body side moldings and a fine-line belt molding completing the treatment (black cars had contrasting lower body accents, however). Cars with SS and RS equipment carried SS emblems front and rear, but used Rally Sport script over the SS insignia on front fenders this year.

Six types of hub caps and wheel covers were offered on 1968 Super Sports, ranging from the standard small Camaro cap to an imitation wire and two simulated magnesium wheel covers. Offered only on SS cars was a full SS cover reminiscent of the 1964 Impala SS cover. Standard SS 350 tires were 14-inch red-stripes on 14x6 rims. Rally Wheels continued as part of the power front disc brake option, and they were available in fourteen- or fifteen-inch sizes, with different center caps than had been used in 1967.

Vinyl tops in black or white, and convertible tops in these colors plus medium blue could be ordered. Body pinstripes, part of the 1967 Rally Sport group, were now optional on all models in black or white.

Bucket seats continued as standard with all interiors, and the Strato-back bench was again optional. Custom upholstery trim included a dash pad this year. On the instrument panel itself, silver gauge faces replaced the black-background units of 1967. Redesigned gauges in a four-unit 'sawtooth' housing located far forward on the console were used for the RPO U17 gauge package this year, in conjunction with a new console. Cars so equipped had the new Tick-Tock Tach clock/tachometer unit in the right-hand instrument bezel.

Super Sport Camaros equipped with Turbo Hydra-matic had a new stirrup shifter on the console, designed for safety considerations, according to sales material.

Looking at a 1968 Camaro, the deletion of vent windows and addition of side-marker lights are the quickest methods of distinguishing it from a '67. Astro Ventilation, using vented balls to duct air through the instrument panel to exhaust-vent pressure valves in the door jambs, replaced the traditional vent windows.

Camaro production totaled 235,147 cars for 1968. Super Sport equipment was ordered for 27,844 of these, and 40,979 had Rally Sport trim. The total number of convertibles built in all forms was 20,440.

1968 Camaro SS engine numerals were mounted at front edge of fender, indicated 350- or 396-cubic-inch V-8's. Standard 1968 SS hub cap was small type, but a special SS full wheel cover could be ordered this year. Accessory covers were wire, two simulated mags. Rally Wheels could be ordered for drum brakes, came with power front discs.

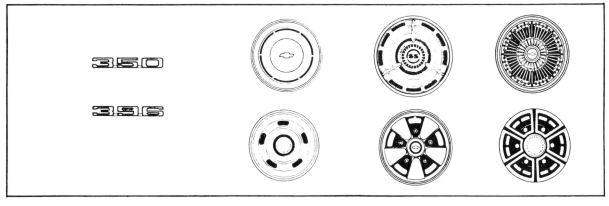

New styling graced the 1969 Camaro. Squared wheelhouses, with slight flares, helped generate a more muscular, slightly larger look. The RPO Z27 Super Sport equipment option was revised to accommodate styling changes. All 1969 SS Camaros had black rear cove panels and the eight-segment waffle-pattern hood inserts of 1968's 396 Super Sports. On body sides, triple simulated rear brake cooling slots, outlined in bright metal, were stamped in just ahead of the wheelhouse.

Camaro offered four striping packages for 1969; one of them, RPO D90, was included with the SS package. It featured a stripe that shot up the leading edge of each front fender, then zoomed back along the fender peak and door. Complementary stripes trailing from the wheel opening brows were listed as unavailable with the SS D90 stripes, but photos do exist of cars so striped.

Engine identification was now ahead of the front fender marker lamp; SS emblems were located on the grille, below the Camaro script

First-series Camaros were very popular with drag racers, using everything from the 302 small-block Z-28 V-8 to the mammoth 427. This SS/F stocker is a Bill Jenkins-prepped Z-28 driven by famed Chevy handler Dave Strickler.

1969 Camaro Coupe with SS equipment. It would be a one-year style, but it would be a long year.

aft of the front wheelhouses, and at the rear. An additional SS insignia was found on the steering wheel.

1969 SS Camaros continued to use 350 Turbo-Fire or 396 Turbo-Jet V-8's. New four-bolt main bearings were used for the strengthened 350, newly rated at 300 hp. Cataloged only in 325-hp tune, the 396 was readily available in 350- and 375-hp stages by special order. (1969 Camaro 396 installations were 6,752 L35, 2,018 L34 and 4,889 L78 units.)

Car Life tested a 375-hp Camaro for the May 1969 issue. They were displeased. "At the mere suggestion of work the (rear) axle hops, judders and bucks . . . starting, stopping or turning, whatever the rest of the car wants to do, the rear suspension won't let it do it," they complained. Still, their test car's $318 optional solid-lifter V-8 propelled it to 98.2 mph in 14.77 seconds during quarter-mile runs, with a 3.73 axle. After-market traction bars and other modifications added speed and deducted seconds readily.

Two optional air-induction packages were offered, a cowl-plenum cold air system originally seen on 1968 Z-28's and the raised-panel cowl induction unit used on the contemporary 1969 Z-car. Z-28-type rear spoilers, or after-market imitations graced the decks of all sorts of Camaros (and every other type of car) this year. An SS Camaro equipped with seven-inch Rally Wheels (part of power front disc brake equipment), spoiler and cowl induction hood looked like a Z-28. A total of 206 Camaros, all Z-28's, had RPO JL8 *four*-wheel disc brakes this year.

The Super Sport seven-inch standard wheels, with F70x14 white-letter tires, could be ordered with Rally Wheel trim rings, which, in combination with the standard Camaro hub cap, gave a pleasing deep-reverse look featured in several 1969 ads.

Rally Sport equipment continued as a popular addition to SS equipment. Rally Sport Camaros had the following special features for 1969: hidden headlamps (with louvered doors in case of malfunction), headlamp washers, single-unit taillamps with separate backup lamps below the bumper and black-painted rocker panels (except on dark colored cars). Wheelhouse moldings, brow stripes and plated headlamp bezels made up the 1969 Style Trim group.

Fourteen new colors, plus four carry-overs from 1968 were concocted for the 1969 Camaro. Six two-tones were cataloged. Stripes were now offered in red, in addition to black and white.

Square gauge bezels replaced the round instruments of previous Camaros. The entire assembly was closely related to the contemporary

Camaro SS for 1969 could again be combined with RS option. New RS headlamp doors had slits so lamps could be seen even when doors were closed.

Sport Wheels and F70x14 Uniroyal Tiger Paws were optional.

Chevy Nova, except for the panel padding. Interiors came in three stages: standard, Special or Custom, in ascending order of cost and luxury. All used bucket seats up front; the Strato-back bench was discontinued. Custom seats could be ordered with hound's-tooth-weave black and white inserts with either black or ivory vinyl surrounds. Additional hound's-tooth patterns in yellow or orange were added to color and trim listings mid-year.

Camaro was again selected to pace the Indianapolis 500 Memorial Day Race, for 1969. The pace car was a Super Sport with Rally Sport trim, running the 325-hp 396. Orange Z-28-style hood and deck stripes were used. Chevrolet dealers benefitted from a pace car replica promotion, selling 3,675 convertibles trimmed like the actual pace car. Interiors of these cars were done with orange hound's-tooth inserts in the Custom vinyl trim.

Full-bore drag racing in 1969 was represented by Bill Jenkins's 427-cubic-inch-powered Camaro pro-stocker.

Bill 'Grumpy' Jenkins and Dave Strickler operated a mobile Chevrolet Hi-Performance Clinic for drag racers on the NHRA circuit. Strickler's SS/J Stock 1969 Z-28 was campaigned at the same time.

Offered concurrently with the pace car replicas, a number of Camaros were sold with the Pacesetter Value Package, a special deal from the Chevrolet Sports Department, featuring the 350 V-8, power front discs with Rally Wheels and whitewalls.

Chevrolet's ad agency, Campbell-Ewald, pursued the sports tie-in avidly in 1969, even recruiting ski star Jean-Claude Killy to cuddle a snow bunny next to a Camaro SS/RS Convertible for a magazine advertisement.

An unusually long production period prolonged the 1969 Camaro's life beyond the normal twelve-month duration, continuing past the autumn introduction right up to the last day of the year. This was done by the dictate of John Z. DeLorean, who had been recently placed in the top slot at Chevrolet. Various reasons were given for DeLorean's decision: strikes in early 1969 had created a pent-up demand for Camaros; the 1970 bodies needed extra refinement time; federal mandates were interfering with the normal scheduling.

When the rest of the Chevrolet passenger-car line went into production for 1969, the 396 actually grew a little, becoming a 402-cubic-inch V-8. The new '396' was phased into Camaro production during the last months of 1969's long run.

Some of the most exotic of all COPO Camaros were built during 1969. Factory orders for the nation's top drag racers included Camaros with L72-type 425-hp 427's and even an incredible run of fifty ZL-1 aluminum-block 427 Camaros were reportedly assembled. Running parallel to factory efforts were custom installations of 427's with all sorts of super-exotic speed goodies into Camaros and other lightweight Chevrolets by several Chevrolet dealers and race preparers. Nickey in Chicago, Baldwin-Motion Performance on Long Island, Bill Thomas in Los Angeles; all would gladly build you a custom-tailored street terror if you had the bucks to pay for it. These multiple efforts undoubtedly resulted in several hundred 427 Camaros during 1969.

Jean-Claude Killy, sixties ski super-star helped sell 1969 Camaro SS Convertibles. Car used in ad had Rally Sport package, too.

Most Camaro buyers preferred the mild stock versions, however. Even these were fairly competitive. An SS Camaro with the 350 V-8 might approach 90 mph in the quarter, in less than seventeen seconds, right out of the showroom.

With its new styling, the 1969 Camaro was the shortest (at 186 inches overall) of the four-passenger pony cars. Camaro set another model year production record for 1969, thanks in part to the extra-long model year, no doubt. Sales hit 243,085, of which 34,932 had Super Sport equipment and 37,773 were equipped with Rally Sport items (no number for cars with both options is available). Camaro convertible production in all guises totaled 17,573. SS 396 Camaros were an uncommon sight, as just 2,018 were built in both body styles.

Chevrolet Product Promotion Engineer Paul G. Prior says there isn't any such thing as a '1970½' Camaro, since there were no early 1970 Camaros. Production of 1969 Camaros continued through the last day of that year, Prior says, and 1970 production began when the workers returned from the New Year holiday. But the introduction wasn't until February 15, 1970, and by the time cars became available nationally many enthusiasts felt they were looking at a 'mid-year' model—for 1970½.

The new Camaro made its debut with the 1970 Corvette. More than one and a half million potential buyers crowded Chevrolet showrooms for a look at the new cars during the introduction. What they found was a different Camaro coupe (no convertible was offered) that was almost a clean break with the past. Except for the 108-inch wheelbase, the famed Chevrolet engines and the Camaro script nameplates, it was virtually a new car. The 1970 Camaro represented a maturation for Camaro; a turning away from the pony-car-cum-muscle-car image. It was, obviously, as *Road & Track* said, "the first effort since the 1963 Corvette to create a real American GT."

Standard Camaro SS engine in 1970 was 300-hp 350 Turbo-Fire V-8.

This new Camaro design would survive eleven incredible years, including a decade that turned the automotive industry upside down, without serious alteration of its basic structure and appearance. Nearly abandoned in 1972, it and its corporate sister, the Pontiac Firebird, would be revived to become perhaps the most recognized American passenger automobiles of the seventies (we're not counting the Corvette here).

The early *Road & Track* rejoicing signaled the advent of the first car to be produced in America for nearly a decade that could truly catch the fancy of the elitist automotive press. Here was an American design capable of luring eyes and dollars away from the traditional strongholds of refined design in Europe.

Somehow the Super Sport image, with its connotations of drag racing and down-and-dirty street racing, seemed to clash with the restrained mood of the 1970 Camaro. Yet, there were 1970 Camaro Super Sports, and they were very good cars.

The 1970 SS package continued to carry the RPO Z27 option number and included the 300-hp Turbo-Fire 350. The L-34 version of the 350-hp 396 was available optionally, but only 1,864 Camaros had this engine; a further 600 375-hp L78 big-blocks were sold. A black grille with full-width bumper and parking lamps below was included. Hide-A-Way windshield wipers, bright hood rear edge molding, SS emblems with engine displacement numerals on the front fenders, an SS emblem for the grille and one

Showroom Album silhouettes for 1970 illustrate different appearances created by addition of Style Trim Group (center) or Rally Sport option (bottom) to basic Camaro with SS equipment (top).

Camaro SS in 1970 came with baby-moon-type standard cap, full cover and heavy wire 'Special' cover were optional. New-design Rally Wheel was also available.

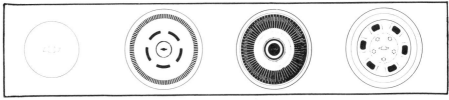

for the steering wheel completed the grouping. The popular spoiler was available at additional cost. Power front disc brakes up front, seven-inch wheels mounting F70x14 bias belted ply tires and some suspension modifications were also part of the SS deal. Standard dual exhausts had bright metal outlet extensions on SS cars, and the 396 Super Sport Camaros had a black rear deck panel.

The addition of Style Trim group Z21 added bright moldings around windows, color-accented door handles and bright accents on parking lamps and taillights.

A totally new Rally Sport package (RPO Z22) gave the Camaro SS a truly distinctive frontal appearance without resorting to hidden headlamps. RS trim was available for cars ordered with Super Sport or Z28 equipment. It used a special black grille with silver accent, and a resilient vertical center bar. The grille frame was also impact-absorbing. Bumperettes flanked the grille, with the license mounting low on the right. 'Roadlight-styled' parking lamps went into the space between the headlights and grille.

Camaro Super Sports could be ordered with any type of available wheel cover, from the small new baby-moon with a bow-tie, to the latest style Rally Wheel. The big Chevy's full wheel cover, and the Z-28's special mag spoke wheel were not available.

Underhood garnishes continued to include plated air cleaner tops and oil filler caps. The 350 cars had finned aluminum rocker covers, while the 396's had chromed covers. Heavy-duty suspension parts included special springs, and on the 350-hp 396, heavier shocks, special multiple-

Rated one of the ten best cars in the world by a prestigious auto magazine, the 1971 Camaro SS (shown with Rally Sport frontal group) was coolly received by U.S. car buyers. Second year for classic design was little changed from 1970, which got off to a late start with a February 1970 introduction.

leaf rear springs and extra-duty motor mounts. The additional suspension tuning could be ordered on SS 350 Camaros, or any other model as the F41 suspension option.

A four-speed gearbox was required, at least, with SS Camaros (396 buyers could specify the close-ratio 2.20:1 box). Turbo Hydra-matic was also available. Rear axle ratios were as low as 4.10:1, which required Positraction, as did the more frequently seen 3.73:1 gear set. With Turbo Hydra-matic, cruise performance gearing of 3.07:1 was offered.

Opening the long door of a 1970 Camaro revealed new, deeply contoured Strato-bucket front seats with low-profile head restraints; in the rear area were individually contoured and cushioned semi-buckets with a full-width backrest. Cloth or vinyl Custom interiors were available.

Special instrumentation with tachometer, transmission lever console, Comfort-Tilt steering column, AM/FM radio and various other luxury/convenience options were available.

Dress-up options for the exterior were deluxe front and rear bumpers, with rubber insert strips; and rear bumper guards. New Sport Mirrors were offered, as were vinyl tops in black, dark green or white.

Eleven of the fifteen exterior colors available were new to Camaro for 1970. Wide hood and deck stripes were offered for the Z-28 only; no striping of any sort was cataloged for the SS.

Camaro production for the shortened 1970 model year was 124,889. Super Sport equipment found its way to 12,476 of these, while 27,136 SS and other Camaros had RS front ends. Possibly, just possibly, a few COPO 454 Camaros for 1970 were built (there were certainly dealer-installed 454 conversions).

Considering the late start for 1970, Camaro did fairly well. Forces were at work, however, which would see a production decline of increasing severity during 1971.

Camaro production continued into the 1971 model year with just the slightest changes in appearance. The 1971 bucket seats were high-back units with built-in headrests (they used the Vega's sub-assembly); easily visible through the windows, they are a quick tip-off to a 1971 model.

1971 Camaro SS was virtually identical to 1970 version. High seat backs, visible through windshield were quick tip-off to a '71. Optional (RPO NK4) Sport steering wheel for 1971 Camaro SS was very popular, eventually became standard Camaro wheel.

1971 hub cap, wheel covers and Rally Wheel. Camaro SS came with small cap, could be ordered with others. Gray-finish Sport Wheel was specified for Z-28, could be special ordered for SS Camaro.

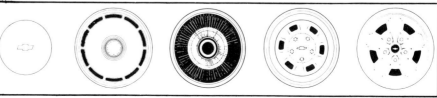

Emissions control and the looming prospect of lead-free fuels brought about a reworking of the SS Camaro's standard 350 V-8. It was now rated at 270 hp (or 210 hp by GM's new net figures). The optional 396/402 (merchandised as a 400) soldiered on into the low-compression regular-fuel era as an SS-only engine (RPO LS-3) developing 300 gross, or 260 net, horsepower; 1,533 were sold. Chrome appearance items on the engines continued from 1970, and the 350 was again equipped with the popular finned aluminum valve covers. Transmission choices were carried over from 1970 as well.

There were two new vinyl roof colors for 1971, dark blue and dark brown. A driver's-side remote-control Sport Mirror was added to the option list and sparos now got a front air-dam valance as well. Available sources conflict as to the continuation of a special black rear panel for 396 cars. SS Camaros could have any wheel or cover offered for the line, except for the Z-28's 15x7 special.

A new four-spoke Sport steering wheel was added for 1971; it would prove so popular that it would eventually become the standard Camaro wheel. Soft mushroom knobs went onto the instrument panel.

The Camaro continued to be a darling of sophisticated American motoring press writers during 1971. *Road & Track*, in one of its "Ten Best . . ." survey articles, entered a 1971 Camaro Super Sport on the list, to their own admitted astonishment: "The fact that the Camaro 350SS [as *Road & Track* called it, giving it a European ring] was nominated by a majority of the staff . . . was something of a surprise to us. Frankly, it's the best car being built in America in 1971 . . . just to make it all clear, no other American car was a serious contender . . ."

While the world's foremost automotive connoisseurs tipped their hats to Bill Mitchell's inspired styling and Chevrolet's fine engineering, they pointed out with no malice intended that, as *Road & Track* phrased it, the SS Camaro tried to "seriously incorporate in it some lessons learned from European GT's."

Sales continued to slip, even with the tremendous publicity given to the Camaro. Production for the model year totaled 114,643. Super Sport equipment was found on 8,377 Camaros for 1971, while 18,404 had the virtually unaltered Rally Sport option trim and frontal group. The best American car was obviously going unappreciated.

1971 Camaro show display featured **SS/RS** front end (left), body and regular Camaro front end with six-cylinder cutaway power plant.

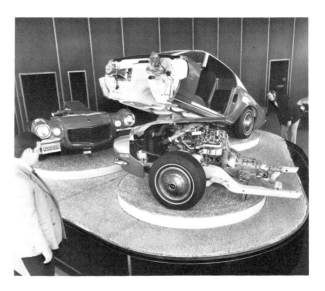

The 1972 model year turned out to be the pits for Camaro, and almost the end. Sagging sales were abetted by a long 174-day strike at the Norwood, Ohio, assembly plant, home of Camaro and Firebird production. Camaros were in short supply from April 1972 until the end of the model year, making for a very limited production run.

The base 1972 Super Sport engine was the 350 V-8 (offered as RPO L48 in other Chevrolets). Further emissions control efforts lowered its net output to 200 hp this year. The 978 big-block 396/402 Camaros built carried the latest LS-3 version, rated at 240 net horses, down 60 from 1971. The LS-3 was not admitted to California in any form. Transmission options were virtually unchanged, but four-speed cars now used the lighter-duty 2.54:1 low box instead of 1971's stronger 2.52:1 unit.

Super Sport option components remained as described for 1970, with the exception of the Sport Mirror added in 1971. 1972's seldom-seen SS 396 Camaros had a black rear panel, and they included the full F41 suspension package.

Grilles had a coarser texture for 1972 for regular Camaros and SS cars with the standard front bumper. The Rally Sport front end remained intact from 1970, except that the RPO Z21 Style Trim group was no longer included without extra charge. This group consisted of plated front-park-

Last Camaro Super Sport was 1972 version. Additional RS equipment continued to feature individual bumperettes, roadlight-type park/turn-signal units.

163

ing-lamp bezels (on regular front ends), hood rear edge molding, roof drip molding, rear pillar moldings, inner taillight bright moldings and body-color door handle accents.

Interior revisions for 1972 were mostly confined to the door panels, which now incorporated map bins and coin holders under the door handle.

By the time Camaro production was able to resume, the 1973 model year was about to dawn. The 1,100 or so Camaros and Firebirds sitting on the Norwood assembly lines were of no further use: they could not be modified to meet the coming 1973 bumper impact laws, so they were junked.

Camaro hit rock bottom on the sales chart for 1972, with just 68,656 units sold. Only 6,562 cars had SS equipment (11,364 carried Rally Sport parts). There was serious debate about the Camaro/Firebird's future.

There was a 1973 Camaro, although the line was kept on short notice. But the Super Sport option was gone, replaced by the new luxo-Camaro Type LT. The Rally Sport made it through 1973, then fell by the wayside too, followed by the Z-28 at the end of 1974.

The Z-28 was revived in mid-1977, to find a new world where the Camaro and Firebird had almost magically established themselves as America's premier GT-type cars. Sales were soaring—in 1978 Camaro set an all-time record of 272,633 cars, still using the original 1970 body style, which continues in production for 1980.

1972 Camaro SS accessory wheel covers included handsome pseudo-wire cover.

CHAPTER TWELVE

Monte Carlo SS 454, The Fascinating Ghost 1970–1971

Chevrolet celebrated the arrival of the seventies by introducing the Monte Carlo, the first Chevrolet spin-off to use a letter other than 'C' to begin its name. Monte Carlo arrived with the full-size Chevrolet, Chevelle and Chevy Nova 1970 models on September 18, 1969. (Camaro and Corvette 1970 editions didn't appear until the following February.) Following introduction, Chevrolet Sales Manager Robert Lund said, "The new Monte Carlo was a prime factor in attracting nearly two million announcement-day visitors to Chevy showrooms."

Monte Carlo appeared only as a coupe. However, a convertible version of the personal luxury car came very close to production. Since the Monte Carlo used the Chevelle's Fisher A-body understructure, it would have been easy to use the 'A' convertible style. The Monte Carlo convertible was pictured in some early literature, and even appeared in some parts books, as style number 13867 (Monte Carlos were internally numbered in the 13000 Chevelle series). But, apparently not one of the handsome cars was built.

The Monte Carlo coupe had the longest hood, at six feet, of any Chevrolet ever. Its 116-inch wheelbase was the same as Chevelle sedans and wagons, but longer than that line's coupes and convertibles by four inches.

Super Sport equipment was offered for Monte Carlo from the beginning. RPO Z20, Monte Carlo SS 454 equipment, obviously had the new

454 Turbo-Jet V-8 for a heart. Rated at 360 hp for Monte Carlo use, the 454 required special suspension components that were included in the package.

Exterior recognition came from SS 454 lettering in the black-accent stripe of the lower body trim line, just behind the front wheelhouse. That was it for emblems, but an astute observer might notice the rectangular chromed exhaust extensions protruding from below the rear bumper, signaling the presence of the 454, which was essentially the same as the 1970 Chevelle LS-5 option.

A Monte Carlo SS 454, with Turbo Hydra-matic and 2.73:1 rear axle was tested by *Car Life* for the February 1970 issue. Top speed was 132 mph, while 0-60 took 7.7 seconds. Quarter-mile times were sluggish, however, as the car took 16.2 seconds to reach the traps at 90.1 mph.

The SS 454 chassis was strengthened with heavy-duty shocks and an automatic level-control feature built into the self-regulating rear air units. Early sales literature didn't say so, but apparently all SS 454's had power front disc brakes. Rally Wheels for the G70x15 wide-profile white-stripe tires came later in the year, apparently. Early SS 454 ads (one in *Ski* magazine, with Jean-Claude Killy and another in *Hot Rod*'s October 1969 issue) showed cars with standard Monte Carlo wheel covers and fender skirts, although power front disc brakes were now listed as standard.

Monte Carlo, designed as a personal luxury Chevrolet, had a very complete option list, of which the SS 454 buyer could freely partake. Most SS 454's as well as numerous standard Monte Carlos, were equipped with optional Strato-bucket seats and a console housing the transmission shifter.

SS 454's were cataloged only with the Turbo Hydra-matic, but four-speed manual specifications were filed with the Automobile Manufacturers' Association (AMA) and cars with both M20 and M21 four-speeds were apparently delivered on special order. (During 1970 it was possible to order virtually any combination of Chevrolet engine and transmission by Central Office Production Order. Perhaps a handful of the 450-hp LS-6 SS 454's were built.)

Despite interference from a strike at an assembly plant, Monte Carlo did very well in the showrooms during 1970. The SS 454, though, was not so well received. Only 3,823 were sold.

Photos of SS 454's are hard to find. Illustration is from 1970 *Showroom Album*. SS 454 signature appeared within lower body trim strip's black band, on front fender. Disc brakes were standard, but apparently the special slotted rims usually supplied with them were not included with the option for 1970 SS 454's.

Monte Carlo entered its second year of production with only minor facelift changes. The Super Sport option, however, was given more identity by stylists. In addition to the SS 454 inserts for the lower front fender moldings, the 1971 cars had special black-accented rear panels in the Super Sport tradition. A small SS emblem was affixed to the right-hand side of the panel, in conjunction with the series script. This year 15x7 Rally Wheels, with trim rings, were included from the beginning, as part of the standard power front disc brakes. At the rear, dual chromed exhaust extensions hinted at the 454's prowess, but the SS 454 still carried no frontal identification. It shared the Monte Carlo's new, finer textured grille and the spring-loaded hood-crest emblem. Front parking lamps were still in the bumper, but became rectangular for 1971, replacing 1970's round units.

'European function symbol' soft knobs were exclusive to the SS 454 on 1971 Monte Carlo instrument panels. The new and handsome four-spoke Sport steering wheel was a popular option, along with the 1971 edition of the Strato-bucket front seats, AM/FM stereo tape units and other comfort/convenience features.

Specification sheets rated the 1971 SS 454's Turbo-Jet V-8 at 365 gross hp, up five from 1970 despite the new regular-fuel 8.5:1 compression ratio. During the year, Chevrolet switched to net horsepower ratings, and the SS 454 was pegged at 285 hp with this method.

Turbo Hydra-matic was listed as a required option again for SS 454 Monte Carlos; but, as in 1970, some special-order four-speed-manual-gearbox cars were delivered. A very few apparently came through with the 425-hp (gross) LS-6 version of the 454 as well. Only a handful of the super-hot 1970–71 Monte Carlos were built; most were finished in black over black, it seems.

Special chassis parts built into the 1971 SS 454 included special front and rear springs, 'heavier duty' shocks with the Automatic Level Control rear air units, a heavier front stabilizer and rear stabilizer. (Interestingly, the 1971 salesman's data album didn't specify four-speed transmissions for Monte Carlo, but an optional heavy-duty clutch *was* listed.)

Chevrolet didn't spend much money promoting the SS 454 Monte Carlo. This 1970 ad ran in *Ski* magazine. SS 454 was totally lacking in frontal identification, looked like any Monte Carlo.

The SS 454 was a fairly macho-looking car in 1971, but it still failed to attract sales. Production declined by almost fifty percent, to 1,919 units for 1971. The poor showing was partly because little publicity was given to the car. No ads or road tests appeared in the widely distributed enthusiast publications. The 1971 *Sales Album* gave the SS 454 due credit, but generally distributed sales brochures almost completely ignored it.

Insurance companies no doubt hurt the SS 454 too, as they applied surcharges to fast-sounding cars in the early 1970's. You could order all the goodies on a regular Monte Carlo, albeit with the 400 V-8 as the top engine choice, and avoid the hassle and high rates.

One wonders if someone at Chevrolet wasn't looking for an excuse to kill off the SS 454 Monte Carlo anyway. The 1972 full-line sales catalog almost gloats over its demise. Under a headline reading "Sorry, no four-on-the-floor," the following copy appears: "You can't get a Monte Carlo with racing stripes. We don't offer a 4-speed box. No special hood scoops or louvers. Monte Carlo isn't that kind of a car." However, careful perusal of the option list could still create a close approximation of "that kind of a car," as bucket seats, Rally Wheels and the current 270 net hp 454 were readily obtainable.

Monte Carlo returned with a sports package for 1973, with the Monte Carlo S, which was fittingly a sort of half-way Super Sport. A rear-ride stabilizer and GR70-15 steel-belted radial ply blackwalls were standard, and white stripes were apparently available. Monte Carlo S was the only 1973 Monte Carlo privileged to wear the contemporary 15x7 Rally Wheels (the Landau's Turbine II wheels could be ordered, too) even as options. Along with the fancy Landau, the 'S' could be ordered with swing-out Strato-buckets, console and other sport goodies including, optionally, the Landau's Sport Mirrors.

The Monte Carlo S survived two seasons, through the end of 1974. Production of 454-equipped Monte Carlos continued into 1975. In 1973 the 454, without complementing SS trim, and rated at 245 net hp, accounted for 12,060 of the 290,695 Monte Carlos built that year.

1971 SS 454 had Rally Wheels for power disc front brakes. Rear end panel with emblem gave a little more recognition to rare Monte Carlo.

CHAPTER THIRTEEN

Monte Carlo SS
The Tradition Returns
1983-1987

*B*uilding a production passenger car to legitimatize a body shape for NASCAR racing purposes was certainly nothing new by 1983. Ford had done it with the Talladega Torino in 1969, as did Dodge and Plymouth with their winged supercars of the same era. But the Monte Carlo SS of 1983, created as a production street version of Chevrolet's NASCAR campaigner, stands uniquely successful in attracting buyers. Now in its fifth year of production as this is being written, the Monte Carlo SS has accounted for more than one quarter of all Monte Carlos built since 1983.

This popular sport coupe grew out of aerodynamic studies prompted by the NASCAR racing success of Ford's 1982 Thunderbird. Chevrolet was locked into Monte Carlo for NASCAR by 1983—there were no other rear-drive, front-engined intermediates in the line-up. Former Chevrolet General Manager Bob Stempel requested a study of possible treatments to make the existing Monte Carlo more aerodynamic by grafting a smoother frontal ensemble onto the production body. Later he would recall, "You know, with many aero experiments you end up with a front that looks like an old Burlington Zephyr streamliner train, but this one looked so good that it just seemed a natural for us to introduce it as an SS package."

It was a smoothly tapered nose with a sloped face bearded by an air dam that looked so good. Drag coefficient was reduced to 0.375, a fifteen-percent reduction over the standard Monte Carlo. Front lift at high speeds was also reduced.

The NASCAR goal achieved, Chevrolet next turned to creating a distinctive and highly visible package for the production version.

Contributing minimally to racing aerodynamics but adding much to the street performance look were air dam extensions for the front fender lowers and a NASCAR-type rear deck spoiler. All the normal Monte Carlo brightwork was either removed or given a black-out treatment. Complimenting multicolor striping encircled the car. Both appearance and handling benefited from the specification for 15x7 special wheels with P215/65R-15 Goodyear Eagle GT white-letter tires.

Sensing a reawakening performance market, Chevrolet decided this would be more than a cosmetic job. Product Promotion Engineering's reknowned former chief, the late Vince Piggins, put together the power-team as one of his final achievements prior to his retirement from a brilliant career at Chevrolet. Piggins based the new engine on a combination of heads and carburetion utilized by West Coast Chevrolet racing engine builder Dick Guilstrand. The displacement was to be 305 cubic inches, the same as the regular Monte Carlo's optional V-8.

By using 9.5:1 heads, Camaro Cross-Fire Fuel Injection, a high-lift and long-duration Corvette camshaft, and a big Quadrajet four-barrel on an aluminum manifold, the engineers were able to milk 175 net horsepower out of the 305, enough to give an eighties car plenty of relative punch. Assisting in power generation while increasing market appeal was an exhaust system that passed through a Corvette-type catalytic converter before branching into a pair of two-inch pipes that produced a street thunder such as had not been heard for more than a decade on a production car.

Selecting a name for this new model couldn't have been easier. The car embodied the traditional qualities of Chevrolet's Super Sport era in many ways. If there could be a Super Sport for this decade, here it was. So, for the first time since 1976, the SS lettering appeared on a Chevrolet passenger car. (El Camino Super Sport appearance packages had been offered right along, however.)

Springing from aerodynamic studies aimed at keeping Monte Carlo competitive in **NASCAR** racing, the 1983 Super Sport was purposeful but attractive in appearance—and had a V-8 worthy of the SS trim it wore.

Devoid of brightwork and available in but two colors, the 1983 Monte Carlo SS was contemporary in design but traditional in concept. Big two-inch dual exhaust pipes made beautiful music.

The automotive public first saw a prototype Monte SS at the South Florida Auto Show in Miami Beach, during November 1982. Spectators gave the white sport coupe high marks. Then, in early February 1983, a group of about seventy Monte Carlo Super Sports paraded at Daytona prior to the 500. These very early production Monte Carlo Super Sports were distributed to Southeastern dealers through a drive-away. Each SS bore a plaque attesting to its use in the Daytona introduction.

Reaching production as RPO Z65, the Monte Carlo SS package was offered only in white or dark blue metallic paint. Either way, the car came with a blue and white cloth/vinyl interior. Special head restraints bore SS lettering. Monte Carlo's optional gauge package, with a 6000 rpm tachometer (redlining at 5000 rpm for this application) was included.

The suspension was modified F41, incorporating both front and rear antisway bars. Power steering, with a 12.7:1 fast ratio, was also included.

Beneath the hood was the Guilstrand/Piggins 305, now assigned RPO number L69. The 175 horses produced maximum power at 4800 rpm and torque peaked at 240 pounds feet at 3200 rpm. Backing this healthy chunk of small-block was a three-speed Hydra-matic featuring a high-stall-

Buried beneath a maze of hoses, wiring and accessory plumbing was the 1983 special Super Sport 305 V-8, pumping out 175 healthy ponies.

Once again, **NASCAR** was the inspiration. This time it was Monte Carlo's rear window area that was altered to achieve a slipperier stocker. Appearing in very limited numbers for 1986, the new Monte Carlo SS Aero Coupe is slated for increased production in 1987.

speed (2025 rpm) lock-up converter. Rear axle ratio was 3.42:1 (no Positraction was cataloged).

The Monte Carlo SS weighed in at just 3,480 pounds and listed for $10,249.

Buff books took an instant liking to this new Monte Carlo model. They were fascinated by the sudden turn of events that made a secretary's boulevard cruiser into a big bad wolf of the streets. Handling won high praise, and the performance was just as impressive.

Typical drive tests put 0-60 figures down as right around eight seconds flat, with quarter-mile runs around sixteen seconds at near 90 mph. Top speed was 120 mph. Rated 1984 horsepower was up to 180 for the Monte Carlo SS HO (high output) engine.

Demand for the Monte Carlo SS built throughout late 1983, but only 4,714 of the sleek coupes were built (out of 96,319 total 1983 Monte Carlos) before 1984 production got underway. By now Chevrolet realized it had an instant winner on its hands, so changes for the first full year of production were minimal.

The 1983 interior, source of some complaints from buyers and critics for its severity, was again standard. But cloth buckets were now an available option as was a floor console. All Monte Carlo SS coupes now had a dual-spoke Sport steering wheel much more in keeping with the car's image than the standard Monte Carlo wheel used in 1983.

Exterior appearance was unchanged, as were the two color choices. By the end of the model year, with orders still flooding in, 24,050 1984 Monte Carlo Super Sports had been built out of the total Monte Carlo run of 136,780 for the year.

New exterior colors were listed for 1985. White was held over, but the dark blue was gone, replaced by black, dark maroon metallic and silver metallic. Interiors were changed to match, now coming in gray or maroon, both available in either bucket or bench seat style.

Stripe graphics were revised for 1985. Chevrolet lettering now appeared at a break in the front facia stripe, on the left. At the rear, the Monte Carlo SS lettering on the deck was changed. The spoiler now had a pin-

Bolder tri-color perimeter stripes and other subtle detailing changes distinguish the 1987 Monte Carlo SS.

stripe, and an outline "bow tie" appeared at its center. SS lettering on the doors was smaller. Stripes were issued in colors contrasting with the new body paint choices.

Big news on the powertrain chart for 1985 was the inclusion of the four-speed automatic overdrive Hydra-matic in the SS package; gas mileage for the 305 HO V-8, still rated at 180 hp, was enhanced. The base price for a Monte Carlo SS rose to $12,466 this year, but weight was down marginally, to 3,384 pounds.

The SS continued to make a strong showing in the sale race, with 35,484 built during the 1985 Monte Carlo production run of 119,057 units.

There was little change for 1986, with colors, powerteams and stripes remaining the same. The cars did have a new look, however, as aluminum wheels similar to those used on the 1981 Z-28 Camaro appeared, shod with the requisite Goodyear Eagle GT tires. Rear axle gearing was now 3.73:1, with 0-60 times remaining in the eight-second range.

Inside the 1986 Monte SS, a cloth-bench front seat in maroon or gray was again standard. Buckets remained an option, but there was a new interior choice this year: a 55/45 split seat.

Final production for 1986 was not released in time for inclusion here, but at one time during the model year it was reported that thirty-eight percent of Monte Carlo production was taken up by the SS.

During mid-1986, Chevrolet unveiled a new Super Sport option for Monte Carlo (coincidentally, it was almost exactly twenty-five years after the first SS package, for the 1961 Impala, had been released). The new package added a bubbled rear window, shortened deck lid and special spoiler to the SS. Chevrolet called this new semi-fastback the Monte Carlo SS Aero Coupe. Once again, NASCAR competition had been the inspiration. The new Aero Coupe had a reduced drag coefficient of 0.365, compared to 0.375 for the notch-backed normal SS.

After unveiling the Aero Coupe at mid-winter auto shows, Chevrolet let production start at a trickle. Only about 200 of the special Super Sports were apparently completed as 1986 models—and these were delivered to dealers in the southeastern United States, where NASCAR fever is at its hottest pitch.

During 1986, the Aero Coupe processing RPO was W62, but for 1987 the unchanged package carries a more familiar RPO—Z16!

Neil Bonnett's Monte Carlo SS NASCAR Aero Coupe for 1986 competition.

The Monte Carlo SS appeared on racetracks almost as soon as it was announced in mid-1983. Darrell Waltrip's Pepsi Challenger was among the top campaigners.

New, bolder tri-color body striping highlights the 1987 Monte Carlo SS. The stripes continue onto the front and rear bumper facias. At the rear, there's a new bumper design and taillamps similar to those released on the mid-1986 Monte Carlo LS. The 1987 notchback SS will share the flat spoiler used by the Aero Coupe.

Colors for 1987 are again white, silver metallic, maroon metallic and black, with complementing interior fabrics. Within the instrument cluster is yet another sign of the renewed automotive spirit in America—for the first time in years, the speedometer reads to 120 mph, instead of 85. A full complement of gauges and a tachometer continue as SS equipment, of course.

For many Chevrolet enthusiasts, the Monte Carlo SS embodies the quintessential American performance car, standing as a just heir to a quarter century of Chevrolet Super Sport tradition. Isn't it great?

El Camino SS

Although the last Super Sport passenger car prior to the 1983 Monte Carlo SS was the 1976 Nova SS, Chevrolet continued to offer an SS package for the El Camino passenger car pickup without interruption into the eighties. However, this amounted to little more than an exterior decor option with special Super Sport stripe treatments appearing for each year.

Forty-five of the sleek, aero-nosed El Camino Super Sports paraded at the Firecracker 400 before being distributed to regional Chevrolet dealers. They were the first of what continues to be the very special, factory-authorized customized El Camino Designer Series.

Choo Choo Customs, in Chatanooga, Tennessee, does the Designer Series conversions. The company had been thinking of doing a special El Camino when the mid-1983 Monte SS appeared. Creating a similar

nose and stripe package for the El Camino was a natural detour.

Although the El Camino Designer Series SS nose appears similar to the Monte's sleek beak, it is a special job that measures 1.75 inches narrower. The bodyside, nose and tail SS decals are similar to the passenger car's. Protective bodyside moldings and Designer Series insert labels for the door handles are additional custom touches.

Beneath the hood, there's only one choice, though: a 305 cid small-block Chevy pumping out 150 bhp and backed by a GM Hydra-matic four-speed automatic with top overdrive. Still, that's enough to boot this 3,500-pound full-dress SS to 60 mph in ten seconds.

Built in limited numbers and with a dramatic street appearance, the Designer Series El Camino SS—the most lavish version of America's last passenger car/pickup—is a sure candidate for future collectibility.

The 1983 Monte Carlo SS had hardly gotten into production before the El Camino version, created by Choo Choo Customs in Tennessee, appeared.

SHOPPER'S GUIDE

The following listings describe Chevrolet Super Sport models and equipment options in their basic forms. Many Super Sports had numerous optional items installed, some of which may replace certain SS parts (wire wheel covers in place of SS full wheel covers, for instance). Camaro Rally Sport equipment is described where applicable, since it was found on many SS Camaros. El Camino SS equipment packages are not described, except for 1968 when the El Camino SS was an actual SS model within the Chevelle line. El Camino SS equipment is approximated by the descriptions for contemporary Chevelle Super Sports.

Engine codes are letters found with the engine number as stamped on Chevrolet blocks in various locations. Those listed here are from internal Chevrolet sources and are believed to be accurate, but may be subject to variation. Replacement blocks may have different codes.

ENGINE CODE ABBREVIATIONS KEY

(3S)	Three-speed manual transmission
(4S)	Four-speed manual transmission
(3-4S)	Three- or four-speed manual transmission
(AC)	Factory air conditioning
(AR)	Air injection reactor
(HDC)	Heavy-duty chassis
(n/a)	Information not available
(OD)	Overdrive transmission (only when special code for OD engine listed)
(PG)	Powerglide automatic transmission
(PO)	Police equipment
(PV)	Positive crankcase ventilation
(TI)	Transistor ignition
(TH)	Turbo Hydra-matic automatic transmission
(US)	Universal service replacement block
?	Displacement or horsepower rating unknown

1961 Impala Super Sport
119-inch wheelbase

Optional Super Sport equipment kit available for Impala Sport Coupe Model 1837; Impala Convertible Model 1867; Impala Hardtop Sedan Model 1839; Impala two-door Sedan Model 1811; Impala Sedan Model 1869.

Exterior features: SS emblems on each rear fender and in center of deck lid; special wheel covers with tri-blade spinners; 8.00x14 narrow-band whitewall tires.

Interior features and appointments: grab bar with SS emblem on right-hand side of instrument panel; instrument-panel pad; floor-shift trim plate (cars with four-speed only); 7000-rpm tachometer in chrome case on steering column.

Performance and handling: heavy-duty springs and shocks; sintered metallic brake linings; power brakes and steering.

Engine Availability

RPO #	Type	CID	Rated HP	Torque	Comp.	Carb.
572	V-8	348	305@5200	355@3400	9.5	4-bbl
590	V-8	348	340@5800	326@3600	11.25	4-bbl
573B	V-8	348	350@6000	364@3600	11.25	3x2-bbl
580	V-8	409	360@5800	409@3600	11.25	4-bbl

Engine codes and insignia
305/348: FL (4S), GE (PG). 340/348: FJ (4S). 350/348: FH (4S). 360/409: Q, QA (4S). Insignia: 348 and 409, crossed flags on deck and grille vee ornaments.

1962 Impala Super Sport
119-inch wheelbase

Super Sport Equipment option (RPO 240) available for Impala Sport Coupe Model 1747 (six-cylinder) and Model 1847 (V-8); Impala Convertible Model 1767 (six-cylinder) and Model 1867 (V-8).

Exterior features: circled SS Impala emblems on rear fenders; Impala SS signature bar on deck lid, right side; full-length body side moldings and rear cove panel with swirl-pattern silver inserts; SS full wheel covers with tri-blade spinners.

Interior features and appointments: individual front bucket seats, all-vinyl upholstery; locking console compartment; passenger assist bar with emblem; floor-shift trim plate (cars with floor-shift manual transmission only).

Engine Availability

RPO #	Type	CID	Rated HP	Torque	Comp.	Carb.
STD.	I-6	235	135@4000	217@2000	8.25	1-bbl
STD.	V-8	283	170@4200	275@2200	8.5	2-bbl
300	V-8	327	250@4400	350@2800	10.5	4-bbl
397	V-8	327	300@5000	360@3200	10.5	4-bbl
580	V-8	409	380@5800	420@3200	11	4-bbl
587	V-8	409	409@6000	420@4000	11	2x4-bbl

Engine codes and insignia
135/235: A, AE, AK, AM (3S); AF, AG, AJ, AZ (3S/AC); B, BE (PG); BG, BH (PG/AC). 170/283: C (3S); CL (3S/AC); CD (OD); D (PG); DK (PG/AC). 250/327: R (3-4S); RA (3-4S/AC); S (PG); SA (PG/AC). 300/327: RB (3-4S); SB (PG). 380/409: QA (4S). 409/409: QB (4S). Insignia (on front fenders): 235, none. 283, chrome vee. 327, chrome vee with crossed flags. 409, chrome vee with crossed flags and numerals.

1963 Impala Super Sport
119-inch wheelbase

Super Sport Equipment option (RPO Z03) available for Impala Sport Coupe Model 1767 (six-cylinder) and Model 1867 (V-8); Impala Convertible Model 1747 (six-cylinder) and Model 1847 (V-8).

Exterior features: circled SS rear fender emblems; body side moldings and rear cove panel with swirl-pattern silver inserts; Super Sport wheel covers with stylized tri-bar spinner.

Interior features and appointments: individual front bucket seats, all-vinyl upholstery; locking console compartment and shift plate (four-speed or Powerglide only); SS steering wheel emblem; swirl-pattern silver instrument-panel inserts.

Engine Availability

RPO #	Type	CID	Rated HP	Torque	Comp.	Carb.
STD.	I-6	230	140@4400	220@1600	8.5	1-bbl
STD.	V-8	283	195@4800	285@2400	9.5	2-bbl
L30	V-8	327	250@4400	350@2800	10.5	4-bbl
L74	V-8	327	300@5000	360@3200	10.5	4-bbl
L33	V-8	409	340@5000	420@3200	10	4-bbl
L31	V-8	409	400@5800	425@3600	11	4-bbl
L80	V-8	409	425@6000	425@4200	11	2x4-bbl
Z11	V-8	427	430@6000	n/a	13.5	2x4-bbl

Engine codes and insignia
140/230: A, AE (3S); B (PG). 195/283: C (3S); CB (PO); CD (OD); CL (3S/AC); D (PG); DK (PG/AC). 250/327: R (3-4S); RA (3-4S/AC); RK (3-4S/AC); S (PG); SA (PG/AC); XE (US). 300/327: RB (3-4S); SB (PG); SG (PG/AC). 340/409: QC (4S); QG (PG). 400/409: QA (4S). 425/409: QB (4S). 430/427: QM. Insignia (on front fenders): 230, badge. 283, chrome vee. 327, chrome vee with crossed flags. 409, chrome vee with crossed flags and numerals. 427, none.

1963 Chevy II Nova 400 Super Sport
110-inch wheelbase

Super Sport Equipment option (RPO Z03) available for Nova 400 Sport Coupe Model 437; Nova 400 Convertible Model 467.

Exterior features: Nova SS emblems on rear fenders, deck; full-length body side moldings with silver-color inserts; body peak moldings; silver-color rear cove insert; Super Sport full wheel covers on required optional 14-inch wheels.

Interior features and appointments: individual front bucket seats, all-vinyl upholstery; Super Sport steering wheel emblem; bright peak molding on instrument panel; electric clock; special instrument cluster with oil, amp, temp gauges; SS emblem on glovebox door; range-selector trim plate (with optional Powerglide floor-mounted shifter only).

Engine Availability

RPO #	Type	CID	Rated HP	Torque	Comp.	Carb.
STD.	I-6	194	120@4400	177@2400	8.5	1-bbl

Engine codes and insignia
194: H, HB (3S); HF (PG). Insignia (on front fenders): 194, badge.

1964 Impala Super Sport
119-inch wheelbase

Impala Super Sport Coupe Model 1347 (six-cylinder) and 1447 (V-8); Impala Super Sport Convertible Model 1367 (six-cylinder) and 1467 (V-8).

Exterior features: circled SS rear fender emblems; right-hand rear deck emblem; body side moldings with swirl-

pattern silver accents; swirl-pattern rear cove panel with bright outline; Super Sport tri-bar full wheel covers.

Interior features and appointments: individual front bucket seats, leather-grain all-vinyl upholstery; SS emblems on door panels; swirl-pattern silver instrument-panel inserts; locking console compartment and shift-lever trim plate unit (with optional four-speed or Powerglide only).

Engine Availability

RPO #	Type	CID	Rated HP	Torque	Comp.	Carb.
STD.	I-6	230	140@4400	220@1600	8.5	1-bbl
STD.	V-8	283	195@4800	285@2400	9.25	2-bbl
L30	V-8	327	250@4400	350@2800	10.5	4-bbl
L74	V-8	327	300@5000	360@3200	10.5	4-bbl
L33	V-8	409	340@5000	420@3200	10	4-bbl
L31	V-8	409	400@3600	425@3600	11	4-bbl
L80	V-8	409	425@6000	425@3600	11	2x4-bbl

Engine codes and insignia
140/230: A, AE (3S); AF, AG (3S/AC); B (PG); BQ (PG/AC). 195/283: C (3S); CB (PO); D (PG). 250/327: R (3-4S); S (PG). 300/327: RB (3-4S); SB (PG); XE (US). 340/409: QC (3-4S); QQ (3-4S/TI); QR (PG). 400/409: QA (4S); QN (4S/TI). 425/409: QB (4S); QP (4S/TI). Insignia (on front fenders): 230, none. 283, narrow chrome vee. 327, narrow chrome vee with flags. 409, narrow chrome vee with flags and numerals.

1964 Chevelle Malibu Super Sport
115-inch wheelbase

Malibu Super Sport Coupe Model 5737 (six-cylinder) and Model 5837 (V-8); Malibu Super Sport Convertible Model 5767 (six-cylinder) and Model 5867 (V-8).

Exterior features: Malibu SS emblems on rear fenders; circled SS emblem, right side of deck lid; body sill moldings; rear fender lower moldings; full-length body peak moldings; front and rear wheelhouse moldings.

Interior features and appointments: individual front bucket seats, leather-grain all-vinyl upholstery; SS emblem on glovebox door; floor-mounted gear-selector trim plate and console (with optional four-speed or Powerglide only); oil-amp-temp gauge cluster replacing warning lamps.

Engine Availability

RPO #	Type	CID	Rated HP	Torque	Comp.	Carb.
STD.	I-6	194	120@4400	177@2400	8.5	1-bbl
L61	I-6	230	155@4400	215@2000	8.5	1-bbl
STD.	V-8	283	195@4800	285@2400	9.25	2-bbl
L77	V-8	283	220@4800	295@3200	9.25	4-bbl
L30*	V-8	327	250@4400	350@2800	10.5	4-bbl
L74*	V-8	327	300@5000	360@3200	10.5	4-bbl

*mid-year
Engine codes and insignia
120/194: G, GB (3S); GF, GG (3S/PV); GK, GL, GN (3S/AC); GM (3S/AC/PV); GH, GJ, KC, KD (TX); K (PG); KB (PG/PV); KH (PG/AC); KJ (PG/AC/PV). 155/230: LM (3S); LL (3S/AC); LN (3S/AC/PV); BL (PG); BN (PG/PV); BM (PG/AC); BP (PG/AC/PV). 195/283: J (3S); JA (4S); JD (PG). 220/283: JH (3-4S); JG (PG). 250/327: JQ (3-4S); JT (3-4S/TI); SR (PG). 300/327: JR (3-4S); SS (PG). ?/327 (Special High Performance); JS (4S). Insignia (on front fenders): 194 and 230, badge. 283, narrow chrome vee. 327, narrow chrome vee with flags.

1964 Chevy II Nova Super Sport Coupe
110-inch wheelbase

Nova Super Sport Coupe Model 0447 (six-cylinder and V-8).

Exterior features: Nova SS emblems high on front fenders; SS emblem, right side of deck lid; silver cove insert; special body peak moldings; Nova Super Sport full wheel covers on 14-inch rims.

Interior features and appointments: individual front bucket seats, all-vinyl upholstery; console (with four-speed or Powerglide only); Nova SS emblem on glovebox door.

Engine Availability

RPO #	Type	CID	Rated HP	Torque	Comp.	Carb.
STD.	I-6	194	120@4400	177@2400	8.5	1-bbl
L61	I-6	230	155@4400	215@2000	8.5	1-bbl
L32	V-8	283	195@4800	285@2400	9.25	2-bbl

Engine codes and insignia
120/194: H, HB (3S); HF (PG). 155/230: LP (3S); LR (3S/PV); BT (PG); BU (PG/PV). 195/283: CH (3S); CJ (3S/AC); CF

(4S); CG (4S/AC); DE (PG); DF (PG/AC). Insignia (on front fenders): 194, badge. 230, badge with numerals. 283, narrow chrome vee.

1965 Impala Super Sport
119-inch wheelbase

Impala Super Sport Coupe Model 16537 (six-cylinder) and Model 16637 (V-8); Impala Super Sport Convertible Model 16567 (six-cylinder) and Model 16667 (V-8).

Exterior features: Super Sport script on front fenders; Impala SS signature bars on grille and within black strip at rear; Super Sport full wheel covers; no wheelhouse moldings.

Interior features and appointments: individual front bucket seats, all-vinyl upholstery; brushed aluminum lower-instrument-panel facing; oil-amp-temp gauge cluster; vacuum gauge (except four-speed and/or 300-, 340-, 400-hp models which have standard tachometer); console and shift trim plate (four-speed or automatic only); SS emblems on doors.

Engine Availability

RPO #	Type	CID	Rated HP	Torque	Comp.	Carb.
STD.	I-6	230	140@4400	220@1600	8.5	1-bbl
L22*	I-6	250	150@4200	n/a	9.5	1-bbl
STD.	V-8	283	195@4800	285@2400	9.25	2-bbl
L77*	V-8	283	220@4800	295@3200	9.25	4-bbl
L30	V-8	327	250@4400	350@2800	9.25	4-bbl
L74	V-8	327	300@5000	360@3200	10.5	4-bbl
L35*	V-8	396	325@4800	410@3200	10.25	4-bbl
L78*	V-8	396	425@6400	415@4000	11	4-bbl
L33	V-8	409	340@5000	420@3200	10	4-bbl
L31	V-8	409	400@5800	425@3600	11	4-bbl

* introduced February 15, 1965.

Engine codes and insignia
140/230: FA, FE (3S); FL, FF (3S/AC); FM (PG); FR (PG/AC). 150/250: n/a. 195/283: GA (3S); GC (PO); GF (PG). 220/283: GK (3-4S); GL (PG). 250/327: HA (3-4S); HC (PG). 300/327: HB (3-4S); HD (PG). 325/396: IA, LF (3-4S); IC (3-4S/TI); IG, LB (PG); II (PG/TI); IV, LC (TH); IW (TH/TI). 425/396: IE (3-4S). 340/409: JB (3-4S); JC (3-4S/TI); JE (PG); JF (PG/TI). 400/409: JA (3-4S); JD (3-4S/TI). Insignia (on front fenders): 230 and 250, none. 283, chrome vee with flags and numerals. 327, chrome vee with flags and numerals. 396, large chrome vee with 396 Turbo-Jet bars. 409, chrome vee with flags and numerals.

1965 Chevelle Malibu Super Sport
115-inch wheelbase

Malibu Super Sport Coupe Model 13737 (six-cylinder) and Model 13837 (V-8); Malibu Super Sport Convertible Model 13767 (six-cylinder) and Model 13867 (V-8).

Exterior features: Malibu SS rear fender emblems; circled SS emblem on right-hand side of deck lid; black-accented grille; wide lower body moldings; black-accented cove area (except black cars which have silver coves); Malibu Super Sport full wheel covers.

Interior features and appointments: individual front bucket seats, all-vinyl upholstery; SS emblem on glovebox door; oil-amp-temp gauge cluster; floor console and shift trim plate (four-speed or Powerglide only).

Engine Availability

RPO #	Type	CID	Rated HP	Torque	Comp.	Carb.
STD.	I-6	194	120@4400	177@2400	8.5	1-bbl
L26	I-6	230	140@4400	220@1600	8.5	1-bbl
STD.	V-8	283	195@4800	285@2400	9.25	2-bbl
L77	V-8	283	220@4800	295@3200	9.25	4-bbl
L30	V-8	327	250@4400	350@2800	10	4-bbl
L74	V-8	327	300@5000	360@3200	10	4-bbl
L79	V-8	327	350@5800	360@3600	11	4-bbl

Engine codes and insignia
120/194: AA, AC (3S); AG, AH (3S/AC); AL (PG); AR (PG/AC). 140/230: CA (3S); CB (3S/AC); CC (PG); CD (PG/AC). 195/283: DA (3S); DB (4S); DE (PG). 220/283: DG (3S); DH (PG). 350/327: EC (4S). Insignia (on front fenders): 194, none. 230, rectangular badge. 283, chrome vee with flags and numerals. 327, chrome vee with flags and numerals.

1965 Chevelle SS 396
115-inch wheelbase

Special equipment option (RPO Z16) available for Malibu Sport Coupe Model 13837.

Exterior features: Malibu SS emblems on front fenders behind wheel opening; 396 Turbo-Jet insignia on front fenders ahead of wheel opening; special half-black rear cove panel, ribbed lower section; Malibu SS 396 bar on right side of deck lid; simulated 14-inch mag wheel covers on 14-inch rims with 7.75x14 Firestone gold-stripe tires.

Interior features and appointments (in addition to normal SS equipment): 160-mph speedometer; 6000-rpm tachometer; Custom Accessory clock; SS 396 emblem mounted in right-hand side of instrument panel; AM-FM Multiplex stereo system.

Engine Availability

RPO #	Type	CID	Rated HP	Torque	Comp.	Carb.
STD.	V-8	396	375@5600	420@3600	11	4-bbl

Engine codes and insignia
375/396: IX (4S). Insignia: large chrome vee with 396 Turbo-Jet bars.

1965 Chevy II Nova Super Sport
110-inch wheelbase

Nova Super Sport Coupe Model 11737 (six-cylinder) and Model 11837 (V-8).

Exterior features: Nova SS rear fender emblems; Nova SS deck emblem; rear cove bright outline and silver-painted insert; ribbed cove divider panel with nameplate and emblem; color-accented body side and rear quarter moldings; hood windsplit molding; Super Sport wheel covers on 14-inch rims.

Interior features and appointments: individual front bucket seats, all-vinyl upholstery; Nova SS emblem on right-hand side of instrument panel; console and shift plate (with four-speed or Powerglide); oil-amp-temp gauge cluster.

Engine Availability

RPO #	Type	CID	Rated HP	Torque	Comp.	Carb.
STD.	I-6	194	120@4400	177@2400	8.5	1-bbl
L26	I-6	230	140@4400	220@1600	8.5	1-bbl
STD.	V-8	283	195@4800	285@2400	9.25	2-bbl
L77	V-8	283	220@4800	295@3200	9.25	4-bbl
L30	V-8	327	250@4400	350@2800	10	4-bbl
L74	V-8	327	300@5000	360@3200	10	4-bbl

Engine codes and insignia
120/194: OK, OM (3S); OR (PG). 140/230: PV (3S); PX (PG). 195/283: PD (3S); PL (4S); PM (4S/AC); PF (3S/AC); PN (PG); PP (PG/AC). 220/283: PE (3-4S); PG (3-4S/AC); PK (PG); PB (PG/AC). 250/327: ZA (3-4S); ZE (3-4S/AC); ZK (PG); ZM (PG/AC). 300/327: ZB (3-4S); ZF (3-4S/AC); ZL (PG); ZN (PG/AC). Insignia (on front fenders): 194, none. 230, badge with numerals. 283, chrome vee with flags and numerals, 327, chrome vee with flags and numerals.

1966 Impala Super Sport
119-inch wheelbase

Impala Super Sport Coupe Model 16737 (six-cylinder) and Model 16837 (V-8); Impala Super Sport Convertible Model 16767 (six-cylinder) and Model 16867 (V-8).

Exterior features: Super Sport nameplates on front fenders; Impala SS emblems on grille and at rear right side of deck lid; Super Sport full wheel covers.

Interior features and appointments: individual Strato-bucket front seats, all-vinyl upholstery; SS emblem on glovebox door, center floor console.

Engine Availability

RPO #	Type	CID	Rated HP	Torque	Comp.	Carb.
STD.	I-6	250	155@4200	235@1600	8.5	1-bbl
STD.	V-8	283	195@4800	285@2400	9.25	2-bbl
L77	V-8	283	220@4800	295@3200	9.25	4-bbl
L30	V-8	327	275@4800	355@3200	10.25	4-bbl
L35	V-8	396	325@4800	410@3200	10.25	4-bbl
L36	V-8	427	390@5200	460@3600	10.25	4-bbl
L72	V-8	427	425@5600	460@4000	11	4-bbl

Engine codes and insignia
155/250: FA, FE (3S); FV (3S/AR); FL (3S/AC); FY (3S/AR/AC); GP (PG/AR); GQ (PG/AR/AC); FR (PG/AC). 195/283: GA (3S); GC (4S); GK (3S/AR); GS (4S/AR); GF (PG); GT (PG/AR). 220/283: GW (3-4S); GX (3-4S/AR); GL (PG); GZ (PG/AR). 275/327: HA (3-4S); HB (3-4S/AR); HC (PG); HF (PG/AR). 325/396: IA (3-4S); IB (3-4S/AR); IG (PG); IC (PG/AR); IV (TH); IN (TH/AR). 390/427: IH (3-4S); IJ (TH); II (3-4S/AR). 425/427: ID (3-4S); IO (TH/AR). Insignia (on front fend-

ers): 250, none. 283, chrome vee with wings. 327, chrome vee with wings and numerals. 396, large chrome vee with Turbo-Jet 396 bars. 427, large chrome vee with Turbo-Jet 427 bars (red-filled).

1966 Chevelle Malibu Super Sport 396

115-inch wheelbase

Super Sport 396 Coupe Model 13817; Super Sport Convertible Model 13867.

Exterior features: SS 396 grille emblem; black-accented grille; twin simulated hood air scoops; ribbed color-accented body sill moldings; SS 396 rear emblem; Chevelle nameplate, set in rear cove; color accent on cove; Super Sport name on rear fenders; 7.75x14 tires on 14-inch rims.

Interior features and appointments: all-vinyl upholstery; padded dash; SS identification.

Engine Availability

RPO #	Type	CID	Rated HP	Torque	Comp.	Carb.
STD.	V-8	396	325@4800	410@3200	10.25	4-bbl
L34	V-8	396	360@5200	420@3600	10.25	4-bbl
L78	V-8	396	375@5600	415@3600	11	4-bbl

Engine codes and insignia

325/396: ED (3-4S); EH (3-4S/AR); EK (PG); EM (PG/AR). 360/396: EF (3-4S); EJ (3-4S/AR); EL (PG); EN (PG/AR). 375/396: EG (4S). Insignia (on front fenders): large chrome vee with Turbo-Jet 396 bars.

1966 Chevy II Nova Super Sport

110-inch wheelbase

Nova Super Sport Coupe Model 11737 (six-cylinder) and Model 11837 (V-8).

Exterior features: SS emblem on grille; Nova SS rear fender script; silver-accented rear deck moldings with Chevy II nameplate and SS insignia; color-accented wide body-sill moldings; wheel opening moldings; front and rear lower fender moldings; Super Sport full wheel covers on 14-inch rims.

Interior features and appointments: Strato-bucket individual front seats, all-vinyl upholstery; SS emblem on glovebox door; floor console and shift plate (four-speed or Powerglide only).

Engine Availability

RPO #	Type	CID	Rated HP	Torque	Comp.	Carb.
STD.	I-6	194	120@4400	177@2400	8.5	1-bbl
L26	I-6	230	140@4400	220@1600	8.5	1-bbl
STD.	V-8	283	195@4800	285@2400	9.25	2-bbl
L77	V-8	283	220@4800	295@3200	9.25	4-bbl
L30	V-8	327	275@4800	355@3200	10.25	4-bbl
L79	V-8	327	350@5800	360@3600	11	4-bbl

Engine codes and insignia

120/194: OK, OM (3S); ZY (3S/AR); OR (PG); ZX (PG/AR). 140/230: PV (3S); PC (3S/AR); PX (PG); PI (PG/AR). 195/283: PD (3S); PF (3S/AC); PE (3S/AR); PG (3S/AR/AC); PL (4S); PM (4S/AC); PS (4S/AR/AC); PN (PG); PP (PG/AC); PU (PG/AR); PO (PG/AR/AC). 220/283: QA (3-4S); QB (3-4S/AC); QC (3-4S/AR); QF (3-4S/AR/AC); PK (PG); PP (PG/AC); QD (PG/AR); QE (PG/AC/AR). 275/327: ZA (3-4S); ZE (3-4S/AC); ZB (3-4S/AR) ZC (3-4S/AR/AC); ZK (PG); ZD (PG/AR); ZF (PG/AR/AC). 350/327: ZI (4S); ZJ (4S/AC); ZG (4S/AR); ZH (4S/AR/AC). Insignia: 194, none. 230, badge with numerals. 283, chrome vee with wings. 327, chrome vee with wings and numerals.

1967 Impala Super Sport and Impala SS 427

119-inch wheelbase

Impala Super Sport Coupe Model 16537 (six-cylinder) and Model 16637 (V-8); Impala Super Sport Convertible Model 16567 (six-cylinder) and Model 16667 (V-8). SS 427 Equipment option (RPO Z24/L36) available.

Exterior features: Impala SS identification on grille, deck lid, front fenders; black-accented grille with bright horizontal bars; black-accented body sill and lower rear fender moldings; black-accented rear deck panel; Impala SS wheel covers.

SS 427 exterior features in addition to or replacing Impala SS equipment: domed hood with simulated bright air scoops; SS 427 grille and deck emblems; special 427 vee-flagged engine insignia on front fenders; 14x6 red-stripe Nylon tires on six-inch rims (narrow-line whitewalls offered as a substitution).

Interior features and appointments: individual Strato-bucket front seats with console or Strato-back front bench seat with center armrest, all-vinyl upholstery; SS emblem on glovebox door, bright interior garnish moldings on Sport Coupe.

Engine Availability

RPO #	Type	CID	Rated HP	Torque	Comp.	Carb.
STD.	I-6	250	155@4200	235@1600	8.5	1-bbl
STD.	V-8	283	195@4600	285@2400	9.25	2-bbl
L30	V-8	327	275@4800	355@3200	10	4-bbl
L35	V-8	396	325@4800	410@3200	10.25	4-bbl
L36*	V-8	427	385@5200	460@3400	10.25	4-bbl

*included with SS 427 equipment, available other Chevrolets.

Engine codes and insignia

155/250: FA, FE (3S); FF, FL (3S/AC); FV (3S/AR); FM (PG); FR (PG/AC); FY (3S/AR/AC); GP (PG/AR); GQ (PG/AR/AC). 195/283: GA, GU (3S); GC (4S/HDC); GK (3S/AR); GS (4S/AR); GF (PG); GO, GT (PG/AR). 275/327: HA (3S); HB (3S/AR); HC (PG); HF (PG/AR); KE (4S); KL (TH); KM (TH/AR). 325/396: IA (3-4S); IB (3-4S/AR); IG (PG); IC (PG/AR); IV (TH); IN (TH/AR). 385/427: IE, IH (3-4S); IJ, IS (TH); II, IX (3-4S/AR); IF, IO (TH/AR). ?/427 (Special High Performance): ID (4S); IK (4S/AR). Insignia: 250, none. 283, chrome vee with flags. 327, chrome vee with flags and numerals. 396, large chrome vee with Turbo-Jet 396 bars. 427 (except SS 427), large chrome vee with Turbo-Jet 427 bars, red-filled. SS 427, large chrome vee with flags and large numerals.

1967 Chevelle Malibu Super Sport 396

115-inch wheelbase

Malibu Super Sport 396 Coupe Model 13817; Malibu Super Sport 396 Convertible Model 13867.

Exterior features: SS 396 emblem on grille and cove panel; Super Sport rear fender scripts; black-accented grille; front and rear wheel opening moldings; ribbed gray-accented body sill moldings; color-keyed side accent stripes; simulated air intakes on hood; black-accented rear cove panel; red-stripe F70x14 wide-profile tires.

Interior features and appointments: black-accented upper instrument panel with SS 396 insignia; SS horn button on steering wheel.

Engine Availability

RPO #	Type	CID	Rated HP	Torque	Comp.	Carb.
STD.	V-8	396	325@4800	410@3200	10.25	4-bbl
L34	V-8	396	350@5200	415@3200	10.25*	4-bbl
L78	V-8	396	375@5600	415@3600	11	4-bbl

Engine codes and insignia

325/396: ED (3-4S/PG); EH (3-4S/AR); EK (PG); EM (PG/AR); ET (TH); EV (TH/AR). 350/396: EF (3-4S); EJ (3-4S/AR); EL (PG); EN (PG/AR); EU (TH); EW (TH/AR). 375/396: EG (4S); EX (4S/AR). Insignia: (all) large chrome vee with Turbo-Jet 396 bars.

1967 Chevy II Nova Super Sport

110-inch wheelbase

Nova Super Sport Coupe Model 11737 (six-cylinder) and Model 11837 (V-8).

Exterior features: Nova SS grille and deck nameplates; black-accented grille; lower body moldings above black-painted sill area; body side accent stripes; front and rear wheel opening moldings, Super Sport rear fender scripts; full-width deck lid trim plate with color accent; Nova SS wheel covers.

Interior features and appointments: individual Strato-bucket front seats, all-vinyl upholstery; embossed vinyl headliner in special pattern; floor console and shift trim plate (with four-speed or Powerglide); SS emblem below glovebox; SS insignia on steering wheel center; bright trim on wheel spokes.

Engine Availability

RPO #	Type	CID	Rated HP	Torque	Comp.	Carb.
STD.	I-6	194	120@4400	177@2400	8.5	1-bbl
L22	I-6	250	155@4200	235@1600	8.5	1-bbl
STD.	V-8	283	195@4600	285@2400	9.25	2-bbl
L30	V-8	327	275@4800	355@3200	10	4-bbl
L79	V-8	327	350@5200	360@3600	11	4-bbl

Engine codes and insignia

120/194: OK, OM (3S); ZY (3S/AR); OR (PG); ZX (PG/AR); 155/250: PV (3S); PC (3S/AR); PX (PG); PI (PG/AR). 195/283: PD (3S); PF (3S/AC); PM (4S/AC); PE (3S/AR); PQ (4S/

AR); PL (4S); PN (PG); PP (PG/AC); PU (PG/AR). 275/327: ZA (3-4S); ZB (3-4S/AR); ZD (PG/AR); ZE (3-4S/AC); ZK (PG); ZM (PG/AC). 350/327: ZG (4S/AR/AC); ZI (4S); ZJ (4S/AC). Insignia: 194, none. 250, badge with numerals. 283, chrome vee with flags. 327, chrome vee with flags and numerals.

1967 Camaro SS 350 and SS 396
108-inch wheelbase

Super Sport Equipment option (RPO Z27) with standard 350 V-8 or optional 396 V-8 (RPO L35) available for Camaro Sport Coupe Model 12437; Camaro Convertible Model 12467.

Exterior features: SS grille emblem; circled SS fuel filler cap identification; SS insignia on front fenders; raised-center hood with simulated air intakes; grille surround stripes; D70x14 red-stripe wide-profile tires on six-inch rims.

Rally Sport exterior features (RPO Z22): full-width black-accented grille with hidden headlamps; parking lamps in lower valance panel; twinline body pinstriping; wide anodized aluminum rocker moldings; all-red taillamps; bright metal wheel opening moldings; chrome drip moldings, coupe only.

Interior features and appointments: circled SS emblem on steering wheel hub.

Engine Availability

RPO #	Type	CID	Rated HP	Torque	Comp.	Carb.
STD.	V-8	350	295@4800	380@3200	10.25	4-bbl
L35	V-8	396	325@4800	410@3200	10.25	4-bbl
L34	V-8	396	350@5200	415@3200	10.25	4-bbl
L78	V-8	396	375@5600	415@3600	11	4-bbl

Engine codes and insignia
295/350: MS (3-4S); MT (3-4S/AR); MU (PG); MV (PG/AR). 325/396: MW (3-4S/TH); MX (3-4S/AR); MY (TH); MZ (TH/AR). 350/396: EI (3-4S); EQ (TH); EY (3-4S/AR). 375/396: MQ (4S); MR (4S/AR). Insignia: 350, SS 350 emblems on grille and gas filler. 396, large chrome vee with Turbo-Jet 396 bars on front fenders.

1968 Impala Super Sport and SS 427
119-inch wheelbase

Super Sport equipment option (RPO Z03) available for Impala Sport Coupe Model 16837 and Model 16487 (V-8); Impala Custom Coupe Model 16447 (V-8); Impala Convertible Model 16367 (six-cylinder) and Model 16467 (V-8). SS 427 equipment option (RPO Z24) available for same models.

Exterior features: Impala Super Sport name bars on front fenders, grille and deck lid; full wheel covers.

SS 427 exterior features in addition to or replacing Impala SS equipment: black-accented grille; special domed hood with simulated air intakes; SS 427 emblems on grille and at rear right side of deck lid; three vertical louvers on each front fender; Firestone Wide Oval red-stripe tires (narrow white band optional at no cost) on 15-inch rims.

Interior features: individual Strato-bucket front seats; center console; floor shift plate (with four-speed or Powerglide, Turbo Hydra-matic).

Engine Availability

RPO #	Type	CID	Rated HP	Torque	Comp.	Carb.
STD.	I-6	250	155@4200	235@1600	8.5	1-bbl
STD.	V-8	307	200@4600	300@2400	9	2-bbl
L73	V-8	327	250@4800	335@3200	8.75	4-bbl
L30	V-8	327	275@4800	355@3200	10	4-bbl
L35	V-8	396	325@4800	410@3200	10.25	4-bbl
L36*	V-8	427	385@5200	460@3400	10.25	4-bbl

* included with SS 427 equipment.

Engine codes and insignia
155/250: CA, CJ, CM (3S); CC, CK, CN (3S/AC); CQ (PG); CR (PG/AC). 200/307: DQ, DO (3S); DP (4S); DS (TH); DH, DR (PG); DK (TH); DP (4S). 250/327: HA, HB (3-4S); HC, HG, HH (PG); HF (TH). 275/327: HI, HL (3-4S); HJ (PG); HM (TH). 325/396: IA (3-4S); IG (PG); IV (TH). 385/427: IE, IH (3-4S); IJ, IS (TH). ID (Special High Performance). Insignia: (all) displacement numerals in front side-marker bezels.

1968 Chevelle SS 396
112-inch wheelbase

Chevelle SS 396 Sport Coupe Model 13837; Chevelle SS 396 Convertible Model 13867; El Camino SS Model 13880.

Exterior features: black-accented grille with SS 396 badge; domed hood; F70x14 red-stripe wide-profile tires (narrow white bands optional at no extra cost); no Malibu fender nameplates; black-finish rear panel with bright outline; rear fender lower moldings; black lower-body finish (except dark colors); optional SS 396 full wheel covers.

Interior features: bright finish plate with SS 396 badge above glovebox.

Engine Availability

RPO #	Type	CID	Rated HP	Torque	Comp.	Carb.
STD.	V-8	396	325@4800	350@3200	10.25	4-bbl
L34	V-8	396	350@5200	415@3400	10.25	4-bbl
L78	V-8	396	375@5600	415@3600	11	4-bbl

Engine codes and insignia
325/396: ED (3-4S); EK (PG); ET (TH). 350/396: EF (3-4S); EL (PG); EU (TH). 375/396: EG (4S). Insignia: (all) displacement numerals in front side-marker bezels.

1968 Chevy II Nova Super Sport
111-inch wheelbase

Super Sport equipment option (RPO L48) available for Nova Sport Coupe Model 11427 (V-8).

Exterior features: black-accented grille with SS badge; twin simulated air intakes on hood; Super Sport lettering on front fenders, red-stripe wide-profile tires on 14x6 wide rims (narrow-band whitewalls optional); black-accented deck lid panel with SS emblem.

Interior features: deluxe steering wheel with horn tabs and SS emblem.

Engine Availability

RPO #	Type	CID	Rated HP	Torque	Comp.	Carb.
STD.	V-8	350	295@4800	380@3200	10.25	4-bbl
L34	V-8	396	350@5200	415@3400	10.25	4-bbl
L78	V-8	396	375@5600	415@3600	11	4-bbl

Engine codes and insignia
295/350: MS (3-4S); MU (PG). 350/396: MX (3-4S). 375/396: MQ (4S); MR (TH).* Insignia: displacement numerals in front side-marker bezels.

* MR listed as 350/396 in some references.

1968 Camaro Super Sport
108-inch wheelbase

Super Sport equipment option (RPO L48 with 350 V-8, RPO L35 with 396 V-8) available for Camaro Sport Coupe Model 12437; Camaro Convertible Model 12467.

Exterior features: SS insignia on front fender leading edge, grille, fuel filler cap; special hood with simulated air intakes (396 uses eight grid bright inserts); color-keyed front accent band; wide-profile red-stripe 14-inch tires on 14x6 rims; black-accented rear panel, 396 only.

Rally Sport exterior features (RPO Z22): full-width black-accented grille with hidden headlamps; parking lamps in lower valance; lower body molding with black-painted rocker areas; special all-red segmented taillamp lenses; bright metal wheel opening moldings; chrome drip moldings, coupe only.

Interior features: none.

Engine Availability

RPO #	Type	CID	Rated HP	Torque	Comp.	Carb.
STD.	V-8	350	295@4800	380@3200	10.25	4-bbl
L35	V-8	396	325@4800	410@3200	10.25	4-bbl
L34	V-8	396	350@5200	415@3400	10.25	4-bbl
L78	V-8	396	375@5600	415@3600	11	4-bbl
L89*	V-8	396	375@5600	415@3600	11	4-bbl

*aluminum heads

Engine codes and insignia
295/350: MS (3-4S); MU (PG). 325/396: MW (3-4S/TH); MY (TH). 350/396: MX (4S); MR (TH). 375/396: MQ (4S). L89 375/396: MT (4S). Insignia: (all) large displacement numerals on front fenders ahead of wheelhouse.

1969 Impala SS 427
119-inch wheelbase

SS 427 equipment option (RPO Z24) available for Impala Sport Coupe Model 16437; Impala Custom Coupe Model 16447; Impala Convertible Model 16467.

Exterior features: black-accented grille with SS badge; Impala SS emblems on front fenders; SS 427 deck emblem; G70 wide-profile red-stripe tires on wide-base 15-inch wheels.

Interior features: SS insignia on steering wheel; head restraints on front seats.

Engine Availability

RPO #	Type	CID	Rated HP	Torque	Comp.	Carb.
L36*	V-8	427	390@5400	460@3600	10.25	4-bbl

* included with SS 427 equipment.

Engine codes and insignia

390/427: LA, LH (3-4S); LC, LI (TH). Insignia: displacement numerals above front side-marker lamps.

1969 Chevelle SS 396

112-inch wheelbase

SS 396 equipment option (RPO Z25) available for Malibu Sport Coupe Model 13637; Malibu Convertible Model 13667; 300 Deluxe Sport Coupe Model 13437; 300 Deluxe Coupe Model 13427.

Exterior features: black-accented grille with SS badge; twin-domed hood; black-finish rear panel with SS 396 emblem; F70x14 red-stripe tires on chromed Sport Wheels with SS center caps; front and rear wheel opening moldings.

Interior features: SS 396 badges on steering wheel and instrument panel.

Engine Availability

RPO #	Type	CID	Rated HP	Torque	Comp.	Carb.
L35*	V-8	396	325@4800	410@3200	10.25	4-bbl
L34	V-8	396	350@5200	415@3400	10.25	4-bbl
L78	V-8	396	375@5600	415@3600	11	4-bbl

* included with SS option.

Engine codes and insignia

325/396: KI, KG, JA, JV (3-4S); KH, JK (TH). 350/396: KB, JC (3-4S); JE (TH). 375/396: KD, JD (4S); KF (TH). Insignia: SS 396 emblems.

1969 Nova SS

111-inch wheelbase

Super Sport equipment option (RPO Z26) available for Nova Coupe Model 11427.

Exterior features: SS badges centered in grille and at rear; black-accented grille; black-accented rear panel; simulated hood air intakes; red-stripe wide-profile tires on 14x6 rims.

Interior features: black steering column, SS emblem on wheel; standard interior upholstery in black, blue or green cloth-and-vinyl combination; all manual-transmission shifters on floor.

Engine Availability

RPO #	Type	CID	Rated HP	Torque	Comp.	Carb.
L48*	V-8	350	300@4800	380@3200	10.25	4-bbl
L34	V-8	396	350@5200	415@3400	10.25	4-bbl
L78	V-8	396	375@5600	415@3600	11	4-bbl

* included with SS equipment.

Engine codes and insignia

325/396: HA (3-4S); HE (PG); HB (YH). 350/396: JF, KE (3-4S); JU (PG); JM (TH). 375/396: JH, KA, KC (4S); JL (TH). Insignia: (all) displacement numerals in front side-marker bezels.

1969 Camaro Super Sport

108-inch wheelbase

Super Sport equipment option (RPO Z27 with 350 V-8, RPO L35 with 396 V-8) available for Camaro Sport Coupe Model 12437; Camaro Convertible Model 12467.

Exterior features: simulated hood air intakes; tapered body-side paint stripes; simulated rear brake cooling ducts with bright outlines; black rear panel; Goodyear Wide Tread white-letter tires on 14x7 rims.

Rally Sport exterior features (RPO Z22): hidden headlamps with louvered doors; headlamp washers; single-unit taillamps with backup units below bumper; wheelhouse moldings, black-accented rocker panels (except dark body colors).

Interior features: special steering wheel with SS emblem.

Engine Availability

RPO #	Type	CID	Rated HP	Torque	Comp.	Carb.
L48*	V-8	350	300@4800	380@3200	10.25	4-bbl
L34	V-8	396	350@5200	415@3400	10.25	4-bbl
L78	V-8	396	375@5600	415@3600	11	4-bbl
ZL1	V-8	427	425@5600	460@4000	11	3x2-bbl

* std. with SS equipment.

Engine codes and insignia

300/350: HA (3-4S); HE (PG); HB (TH). 325/396: JU (4S); JG (TH). 350/396: JF (4S); JL (TH). 375/396: JG, KA, KC (4S); JL (TH). L89-375/396: JJ, KE (4S); JM (TH). Insignia: displacement numerals on front fenders ahead of side-marker lamps.

1970 Monte Carlos SS 454

116-inch wheelbase

SS 454 equipment option (RPO Z20) available for Monte Carlo Coupe Model 13857.

Exterior features: SS 454 nameplate on front fender lower moldings; bright twin tailpipe extensions.

Interior features: none.

Engine Availability

RPO #	Type	CID	Rated HP	Torque	Comp.	Carb.
STD.	V-8	454	360@4400	500@3200	10.25	4-bbl

Engine codes and insignia

360/454: CGW, CGT. Insignia: 454 numerals, front fender lower moldings.

1970 Chevelle SS 396 and SS 454

112-inch wheelbase

SS 396 equipment option (RPO Z25) and SS 454 equipment option (RPO Z15) available for Malibu Sport Coupe Model 13637; Malibu Convertible Model 13667.

Exterior features: black-accented grille with SS badge; domed hood; Sport Stripe and Cowl Induction available; SS 396 or SS 454 emblems on front fenders; 14x7 JK Sport Wheels with SS center caps; F70x14 white-letter Firestone bias belted tires; wheelhouse moldings; white lenses over parking/directional lamps; black plastic rear bumper panel with SS emblem; bright twin tailpipe extensions.

Interior features: black steering wheel and column with SS emblem; black-finish instrument panel with round gauges.

Engine Availability

RPO #	Type	CID	Rated HP	Torque	Comp.	Carb.
L34*	V-8	402**	350@5200	415@3400	10.25	4-bbl
L78	V-8	402**	375@5600	415@3600	11	4-bbl
LS5*	V-8	454	360@5400	500@3200	10.25	4-bbl
LS6	V-8	454	450@5600	500@3600	11.25	4-bbl

* L34 included with RPO Z25; LS5 included with RPO Z15.
** marketed as Turbo-Jet 396.

Engine codes and insignia

350/402: CTX, CTW, CTZ. 375/402: CKO, CTY, CKQ. 360/454: GGU, CGT. 450/454: CRV. LS-6 (with aluminum heads) 450/454: CRS. Insignia: numerals with SS emblems on front fenders.

1970 Chevy Nova SS

111-inch wheelbase

Super Sport equipment option (RPO Z26) available for Nova Coupe Model 11427.

Exterior features: black-accented grille with SS badge; simulated air intakes on hood; black rear panel with SS emblem (or black-ribbed rear panel trim plate if also equipped with RPO ZJ2 Custom Exterior group); E70x14 white-stripe Wide Oval tires on seven-inch rims.

Interior features: black steering wheel and column with SS hub emblem.

Engine Availability

RPO #	Type	CID	Rated HP	Torque	Comp.	Carb.
L48*	V-8	350	300@4800	380@3200	10.25	4-bbl
L34	V-8	402**	350@5200	415@3400	10.25	4-bbl
L78	V-8	402**	375@5600	415@3600	11	4-bbl

* included with RPO Z26 equipment.
** marketed as Turbo-Jet 396.

Engine codes and insignia

300/350: CNJ, CNK, CRE. 350/402: CTX, CTW, CTZ. 375/402: CKO, CTY, CKQ. L89-375/396: CKP, CKT, CKU. Insignia: numerals above front fender marker lamps.

1970 Camaro Super Sport

108-inch wheelbase

Super Sport equipment option (RPO Z27) available for Camaro Sport Coupe Model 12487.

Exterior features: black grille with bright outline, license plate holder between bumper guards; SS emblem on grille; partial bright window moldings; black rear panel (396 only);

F70x14 bias belted Firestone Wide Oval white-letter tires on 14x7 rims; bright dual-exhaust outlets.

Rally Sport additional or substituted exterior features: black and silver grille; resilient grille frame and vertical center bar; license plate holder at the right; Roadlight-style parking lamps; bright accent taillamps and backup lamps.

Interior features: none.

Engine Availability

RPO #	Type	CID	Rated HP	Torque	Comp.	Carb.
L48*	V-8	350	300@4800	380@3200	10.25	4-bbl
L34	V-8	402**	350@5200	415@3400	10.25	4-bbl
L78	V-8	402**	375@5600	415@3600	11	4-bbl

* included with RPO Z27 equipment.
** marketed as Turbo-Jet 396.

Engine codes and insignia

300/350: CNJ, CNK, CRE. 350/402: CJF, CJI. 375/402: CJL, CJH. Insignia: (all) displacement numerals below SS emblem on fenders.

1971 Monte Carlo SS 454

116-inch wheelbase

SS 454 equipment option (RPO Z20) available for Monte Carlo Coupe Model 13857.

Exterior features: SS 454 lettering incorporated into lower front fender moldings; Monte Carlo SS badge on rear deck within black-accented rear panel; G70x15 Goodyear Polyglas tires on 15x7 Rally Wheels; bright dual-exhaust extensions.

Interior features: European-style function symbol soft black control knobs on instrument panel.

Engine Availability

RPO #	Type	CID	Rated HP	Torque	Comp.	Carb.
LS5*	V-8	454	365@4800	465@3200	8.5	4-bbl
LS6	V-8	454	425@5600	475@4000	9	4-bbl

* included with RPO Z20 equipment.

Engine codes and insignia

365/454: CPD. 425/454: CPW, CPX. Insignia: SS 454 identification.

1971 Chevelle SS and SS 454

112-inch wheelbase

SS and SS 454 equipment option (RPO Z15) available with Malibu Sport Coupe Model 13637; Malibu Convertible Model 13667.

Exterior features: black-accented grille with SS badge; domed hood with chrome lock pins; SS emblem on rear bumper; F60x15 Goodyear wide-profile white-letter tires; bright twin tailpipe extensions (SS 454 only).

Interior features: black steering wheel and column with SS hub emblem; black-finish instrument panel with round faces; European-style function symbol soft black control knobs on instrument panel.

Engine Availability

RPO #	Type	CID	Rated HP	Torque	Comp.	Carb.
L65	V-8	350	245@4800	350@2800	8.5	2-bbl
L48	V-8	350	270@4800	360@3200	8.5	4-bbl
LS5*	V-8	454	365@4800	465@3200	8.5	4-bbl
LS6	V-8	454	425@5600	475@4000	9	4-bbl

* included with RPO Z15 SS 454 equipment.

Engine codes and insignia

245/350: CGA, CGC. 270/350: CJJ, CJD. 365/454: CPA, CPD. 425/454: CPZ.

1971 Chevy Nova SS

111-inch wheelbase

Super Sport equipment option (RPO Z26) available for Nova Coupe Model 11427.

Exterior features: black-accented grille with SS badge; simulated air intakes on hood; black-ribbed rear panel with SS emblem; E70x14 white-stripe wide-profile tires on 14x7 rims.

Interior features: black steering wheel with SS hub; ten-inch-wide day/night rearview mirror.

Engine Availability

RPO #	Type	CID	Rated HP	Torque	Comp.	Carb.
L48*	V-8	350	270@4800	360@3200	8.5	4-bbl

* included with RPO Z26 equipment.

Engine codes and insignia

270/350: CJG, CJD. Insignia: 350 numerals above front marker lamps.

1971 Camaro SS

108-inch wheelbase

Super Sport equipment option (RPO Z27) available for Camaro Sport Coupe Model 12487.

Exterior features: black grille with bright outline, SS badge on grille; license plate between front bumper guards; SS emblems with engine numerals on front fenders; F70x14 bias belted white-letter tires on 14x7 rims; twin bright exhaust-outlet extensions; black rear panel on 396-equipped SS only.

Rally Sport additional or substituted exterior features: black and silver grille with resilient vertical center bar; resilient grille frame; license plate below right bumperette; Roadlight-style parking lamps; full side-window moldings; color-accented door handles; bright-accented taillight bezels; SS emblem on grille deleted.

Interior features: none.

Engine Availability

RPO #	Type	CID	Rated HP	Torque	Comp.	Carb.
L48*	V-8	350	270@4800	360@3200	8.5	4-bbl
LS3	V-8	402**	300@4800	400@3200	8.5	4-bbl

* included with RPO Z27 equipment.
** marketed as Turbo-Jet 396.

Engine codes and insignia

270/350: CJG, CJD. 300/402: CLA, CLB. Insignia: (all) displacement numerals below SS emblems on front fenders.

1972 Chevelle SS

112-inch wheelbase

Super Sport equipment option (RPO Z15) available for Malibu Sport Coupe Model 13637; Malibu Convertible Model 13667.

Exterior features: black grille with bright outline and SS badge in center; domed hood with chrome lock pins; SS emblems on front fenders; left-hand remote-control Sport Mirror; SS emblem on rear bumper; F60x15 white-letter tires on 15x7 Sport Wheels.

Interior features: power-disc-brakes pedal; black-finish instrument-panel face with round gauges.

Engine Availability

RPO #	Type	CID	Net Rated HP	Torque	Comp.	Carb.
STD.	V-8	307	130@4000	230@2400	8.5	2-bbl
L65	V-8	350	165@4000	280@2400	8.5	2-bbl
L48	V-8	350	175@4000	280@2400	8.5	4-bbl
LS3	V-8*	402	240@4400	345@3200	8.5	4-bbl.
LS5	V-8	454	270@4000	390@3200	8.5	4-bbl

* marketed as Turbo-Jet 400.

Engine codes and insignia

130/307: F. 165/350: H. 175/350: J. 240/402: U. 270/454: W. Insignia: 307 and 350, none. 402 and 454, beneath SS emblems on front fenders.

1972 Nova SS

111-inch wheelbase

Super Sport equipment option (RPO Z26) available for Nova Coupe Model 11427.

Exterior features: black-accented grille with SS badge; simulated air intakes on hood; black-accented rear panel with SS emblem; E70x14 bias belted ply white-letter tires on 14x7 rims.

Interior features: none.

Engine Availability

RPO #	Type	CID	Net Rated HP	Torque	Comp.	Carb.
L48*	V-8	350	200@4400	300@2800	8.5	4-bbl

* included with RPO Z26 equipment.

Engine codes and insignia

200/350: K. Insignia: displacement numerals above front marker lamps.

1972 Camaro SS

108-inch wheelbase

Super Sport equipment option (RPO Z27) available for Camaro Sport Coupe Model 12487.

Exterior features: black grille with SS badge and bright outline; concealed windshield wipers; left-hand remote-control Sport Mirror; SS front fender emblems; F70x14 bias belted ply tires on 14x7 rims; black-accented rear panel, 396 Turbo-Jet only.

Rally Sport additional or substituted exterior features: silver-accented black grille with resilient vertical center bars and frame; front bumperettes with license plate below right unit; Roadlight-style parking lamps.

Interior features: none.

Engine Availability

RPO #	Type	CID	Net Rated HP	Torque	Comp.	Carb.
L48*	V-8	350	200@4400	300@2800	8.5	4-bbl
LS3	V-8	402**	240@4400	345@3200	8.5	4-bbl

* included with RPO Z27 equipment.
** marketed as Turbo-Jet 396

Engine codes and insignia
200/350: K. 240/402: U. Insignia: (all) numerals below SS emblems on front fenders.

1973 Chevelle SS

112-inch wheelbase coupe and 116-inch wheelbase wagon

Super Sport equipment option (RPO Z15) available for Malibu Colonade Hardtop Coupe Model 1AD37; Malibu Wagon Models 1AD35 and 1AD35/AQ4 (three-seat).

Exterior features: black-finish grille with SS badge; left-hand remote-control and right-hand manual Sport Mirrors; SS emblems on front fenders and rear bumper (tailgate on wagon); lower body-side and wheel-opening striping (keyed to body color); black-accented taillight bezels (except wagon); G70x14 white-letter tires on 14x7 Rally rims with special centers and trim rings.

Interior features: SS emblems on door trim, steering wheel; black instrument bezels with special instrument cluster.

Engine Availability

RPO #	Type	CID	Net Rated HP	Torque	Comp.	Carb.
L65	V-8	350	145@4000	255@2400	8.5	2-bbl
L48	V-8	350	175@4000	260@2800	8.5	4-bbl
LS4	V-8	454	245@4000	375@2800	8.25	4-bbl

Engine codes and insignia
145/350: H. 175/350: J. 245/454: Y. Insignia: 350, none. 454, displacement numerals below SS emblem on fenders.

1973 Nova SS

111-inch wheelbase

Super Sport equipment option (RPO Z26/YF8, black striping; RPO Z26/ZR8, white striping) available for Nova and Nova Custom Coupe Model 1XX27 and Model 1XY27; Nova and Nova Custom Hatchback Coupe Model 1XX17 and Model 1XY17.

Exterior features: black-accented grille; bright windshield and roof drip moldings; tapered black or white body-side and rear-panel stripes; SS emblems on grille, fenders, deck lid; left-hand remote-control and right-hand manual Sport Mirrors; rectangular dual-unit taillights with black-accented rear panel; 14x6 Rally Wheels with special center caps and bright lugs.

Interior features: SS emblem on steering wheel.

Engine Availability

RPO #	Type	CID	Net Rated HP	Torque	Comp.	Carb.
STD.	I-6	250	100@3600	175@1600	8.5	1-bbl
L14	V-8	307	115@3600	205@2000	8.5	2-bbl
L65	V-8	350	145@4000	255@2400	8.5	2-bbl
L48	V-8	350	175@4000	260@2800	8.5	4-bbl

Engine codes and insignia
100/250: D. 115/307: F. 145/350: H. 175/350: J. Insignia: 250 and 307, none. 350, displacement numerals above front side-marker lamps.

1974 Nova SS

111-inch wheelbase

Super Sport equipment option (RPO Z26/19A, black hood and deck striping outlined in gold; RPO Z26/52A, gold hood and deck striping outlined in red) available for Nova Coupe Model 1XX27; Nova Hatchback Model 1XX17.

Exterior features: black grille with SS badge; SS decals on fenders, deck; black-finish left-hand remote-control and right-hand manual Sport Mirrors; black accents around side windows; 14x6 Rally Wheels with SS center caps, trim rings, bright lugs.

Interior features: SS emblem on steering wheel; cut-pile carpeting (including load floor on Hatchback).

Engine Availability

RPO #	Type	CID	Net Rated HP	Torque	Comp.	Carb.
STD.	I-6	250	100@3600	175@1800	8.25	1-bbl
STD.	V-8	350	145@3800	250@2200	8.5	2-bbl
LM1	V-8	350	160@3800	250@2400	8.5	4-bbl
L48	V-8	350	185@4000	270@2600	8.5	4-bbl

Engine codes and insignia
100/250: D. 145/350: H. 160/350: L. 185/350: K. Insignia: 250, none. 350, displacement numerals above front side-marker lamps.

1975 Nova SS

111-inch wheelbase

Super Sport equipment option (RPO Z26/11A, white lower-body dual stripes; RPO Z26/13A, silver lower-body dual stripes; RPO Z26/75A, red lower-body dual stripes) available for Nova Coupe Model 1XX27; Nova Hatchback Coupe Model 1XY17.

Exterior features: black grille with bright accents, SS badge; black-finish headlight bezels with bright accents; black-accented side windows; SS decals on front fenders and rear panel; lower body dual-accent stripes; left-hand remote-control and right-hand manual black Sport Mirrors; 14x6 Rally-type wheels with SS center caps and trim rings.

Interior features: SS emblem on four-spoke Sport steering wheel; cut-pile carpeting (including cargo floor on Hatchback Coupe).

Engine Availability

RPO #	Type	CID	Net Rated HP	Torque	Comp.	Carb.
STD.	I-6	250	105@3800	185@1200	8.25	1-bbl
STD.	V-8	262*	110@3600	200@2000	8.5	2-bbl
L65	V-8	350	145@3800	250@2200	8.5	2-bbl
LM1	V-8	350	155@3800	250@2400	8.5	4-bbl

* 262 V-8 marketed as 4.3-liter V-8.

Engine codes and insignia
105/250: D. 110/262: G. 145/350: H, L. 155/350: J, T. Insignia: none.

1976 Nova SS

111-inch wheelbase

Super Sport equipment option (RPO Z26) available for Nova Coupe Model 1XX27; Nova Hatchback Coupe Model 1XY17.

Exterior features: black mesh grille; black-accented side windows; SS decals on front fenders and deck lid; lower body striping; left-hand and right-hand black Sport Mirrors; 14x6 Rally-type wheels with SS center caps and trim rings.

Interior features: SS emblem on four-spoke Sport steering wheel.

Engine Availability

RPO #	Type	CID	Net Rated HP	Torque	Comp.	Carb.
STD.	I-6	250	105@3800	185@1200	8.25	1-bbl
STD.	V-8	305	140@3800	245@2000	8.5	2-bbl
LM1	V-8	350	165@3800	260@2400	8.5	4-bbl

Engine codes and insignia
105/250: D. 140/305: n/a. 165/350: H. Insignia: none.